RICHARD V. SANDLER

WITNESS TO A PROSECUTION

WITNESS
TO A
PROSECUTION

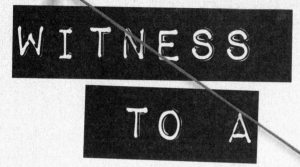

WITNESS
TO A
PROSECUTION

THE
MYTH of
MICHAEL
MILKEN

RICHARD V. SANDLER

Forbes | Books

Published by Forbes Books, Charleston, South Carolina.
Member of Advantage Media.

Forbes Books is a registered trademark, and the Forbes Books colophon is a trademark of Forbes Media, LLC.

Printed in the United States of America.

10 9 8 7 6 5 4 3 2 1

ISBN: 979-8-88750-133-8 (Hardcover)
ISBN: 979-8-88750-134-5 (eBook)

Library of Congress Control Number: 2023903188

Cover design by Matthew Morse.
Layout design by Lance Buckley.

Since 1917, Forbes has remained steadfast in its mission to serve as the defining voice of entrepreneurial capitalism. Forbes Books, launched in 2016 through a partnership with Advantage Media, furthers that aim by helping business and thought leaders bring their stories, passion, and knowledge to the forefront in custom books. Opinions expressed by Forbes Books authors are their own. To be considered for publication, please visit **books.Forbes.com.**

To my wife, Ellen, and children, Scott, Tracy, and Nicholas.

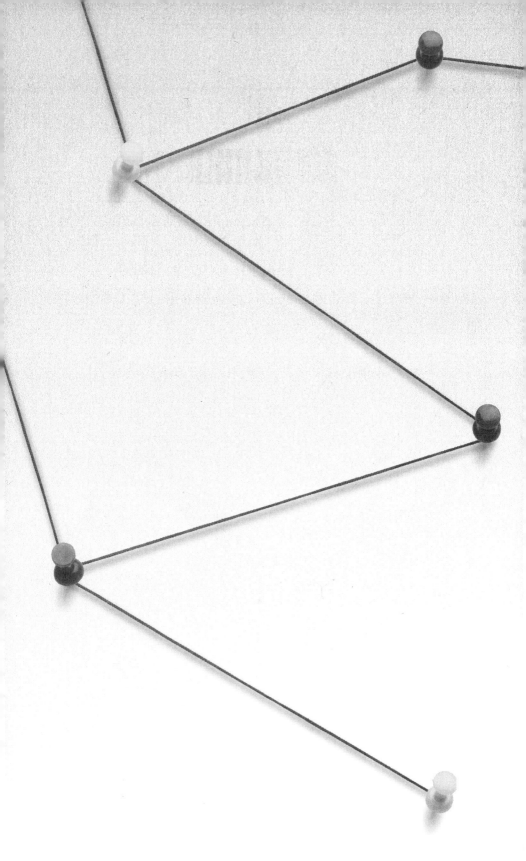

CONTENTS

INTRODUCTION

I have been thinking about writing this book for over twenty years. You see, Michael Milken is a childhood friend. I met him when I was six years old. His younger brother, Lowell—who is my age and two years younger than Michael—and I have been close friends since the first grade. Though Michael was the "older brother," we were in high school together in the San Fernando Valley of Los Angeles, were in college together at Berkeley, and lived together in the same fraternity. Our wives met as sorority sisters at Berkeley and remain very close friends. Our children are friends. In 1983, we began working together, and we still work together to this day. In short, we know each other very well.

In 1986, the Securities and Exchange Commission (SEC) and the US Attorney's Office for the Southern District of New York began an investigation of Michael and Drexel Burnham Lambert and its High Yield and Convertible Bond Department, a department Michael created and headed. Michael was the most successful and innovative financier of his time, and Drexel, due to Michael, was the most successful securities firm on Wall Street.

Before this time, if I read there was a government investigation of an individual or a firm, I would assume the government had good reason to investigate and would act fairly. I would also assume press stories were accurate. But in this case, I knew the individual and the firm very well, and we had been working together for over three and a half years. My prior assumptions about the government and the media proved incorrect. I could not understand why the government would even think it had a good reason to investigate Michael. The press stories were not accurate. I quickly learned the problem. Every institution, whether the government or the media, is made up of people. People are complicated and have different motivations. Reporters want to make headlines and be recognized for their investigative skills. They depend on sources who will cooperate with them. Prosecutors want to win convictions, especially in high-profile cases. That is how they receive recognition and enhance their careers. And they wield enormous power. They rely on cooperating witnesses, and cooperating witnesses have their own issues and reasons for cooperating.

From the moment the investigation started, I became Mike's personal lawyer, responsible for working with the lawyers we hired and overseeing the defense. As such, I witnessed exactly what happened, how it happened, and why it happened.

Michael Milken and this prosecution have been described in books and articles by others who had no firsthand knowledge of the events and were motivated to describe what happened in a certain way. I, too, am motivated to describe what happened, but I am motivated because I want the true story told, and I do have firsthand knowledge. I lived this matter day in and day out for over ten years. Michael was a public figure then and is still a public figure in financial and philanthropic circles. It is important for history to reflect what happened and how it happened.

As the first step to writing this book, I taught a class on the subject at Stanford Law School in both 2012 and 2020. These classes allowed me to gather all the information that only I had access to and to tell the story to students who knew little about Michael but cared about how the system worked. The prosecutor in charge of the case and the head of enforcement at the SEC at the time were guest lecturers, and they explained how they viewed this case both at the time and years later.

Whether you are (1) one of the thousands of people who attend Milken Institute events because of Michael Milken's presence and ideas, (2) one of the thousands of people who grew up in the financial services business in the 1980s and know of Michael Milken as the most important financier of his time, (3) someone who has gone to business school, has worked in the financial services industry, has heard of Michael Milken, and is interested in knowing who he really was and what really happened to him, or (4) someone who is interested in understanding the criminal investigative process, especially in white-collar cases, and the incredible power the government wields in that process, this story is one that I believe will interest you.

Almost thirty-six years later, it is finally time for me to set the record straight. Everything in this book is based upon court documents, transcripts from the classes I taught at Stanford Law School, and my experience as one intimately involved in the workings of the High Yield Department at Drexel and in the details of the investigation and the defense. Thank you for your interest in this important story.

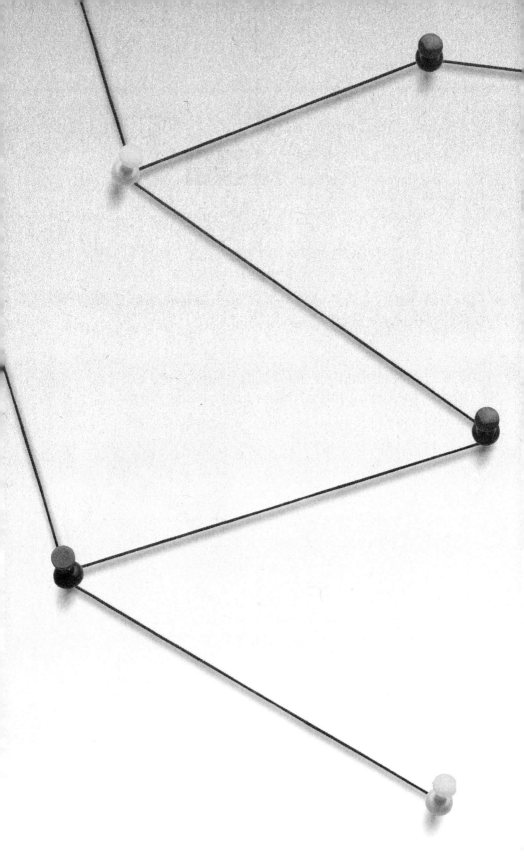

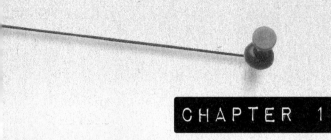

CHAPTER 1

September 1966 / November 14, 1986

It was Friday, November 14, 1986. I was sitting at my desk in my office at 9560 Wilshire Boulevard in Beverly Hills, planning to leave a little early since it was my son Nicholas's sixth birthday. A few minutes after one o'clock, Lorraine Spurge, who worked in the Drexel Burnham Lambert High Yield and Convertible Bond Department two floors above my office, walked in and asked if I had seen the news that had just come over the tape—that Ivan Boesky had agreed to plead guilty to securities violations and to pay $100 million in a settlement with the United States Attorney's Office for the Southern District of New York and the SEC. Ivan Boesky was the most famous arbitrageur of that time and had relationships with most firms on Wall Street. Drexel had completed a financing for the Boesky organization the previous March, and I was an investor in that financing. This was earthshaking news for the financial markets, especially for the many Wall Street firms that dealt with Ivan Boesky.

I had left the practice of law three and a half years earlier to help form a consulting group that would work closely with the members of the Drexel High Yield Department, helping to structure and oversee investments made by the members of the department. Many of the investments were in companies that Drexel financed, such as the Boesky entity. My position put me at the pulse point of the department.

When Drexel raised money for the Boesky organization in March 1986, some of my partners had done work on the transaction, and partnerships that we were responsible for had invested. Within a few minutes, I learned that federal marshals were serving grand jury subpoenas and SEC subpoenas on Michael Milken, Lowell Milken, and entities I had invested in. Suddenly, at thirty-eight years old, my life dramatically changed. I never imagined that I would be part of a criminal investigation.

Several years before I left the practice of law, I began representing members of Drexel's High Yield Department. I learned much about the business and the members of the department. That experience allowed for a smooth transition as I went from being a practicing attorney to a business consultant, and a client, as I interacted with lawyers advising on the transactions I was working on. I witnessed firsthand the vision Michael brought to the financial services industry and his personal commitment to excellence and creating value in everything he did. I learned firsthand about the inner workings of what was the most innovative and entrepreneurial investment banking firm at the time.

My responsibilities prior to 1:00 p.m. on November 14, 1986, had me working closely with members of Drexel's High Yield Department, members of the Corporate Finance Department, and Drexel lawyers. But on November 14, 1986, my responsibilities changed. Suddenly I was a lawyer again, a white-collar criminal defense attorney, and I did not know what they did. I learned quickly over the ensuing months.

I could not have anticipated on that day that this process would dominate my life for the next twelve years. I was still a licensed attorney of law but had no experience with a criminal investigation, and certainly nothing approaching this magnitude. My normal reaction that day would have been to meet with Lowell Milken to strategize as to who we needed to contact and what we needed to do. Lowell had been ill and was not in the office. I spoke with Kevin Madigan, who was the in-house counsel and compliance officer for Drexel in the High Yield Department. We had no idea what Michael Milken or Drexel was being investigated for. We knew that Ivan Boesky was involved in insider trading, and the grand jury subpoena referenced something called the Racketeer Influenced and Corrupt Organizations Act.

> I could not have anticipated on that day that this process would dominate my life for the next twelve years.

I did understand that this was serious and that we needed the assistance of attorneys who were experienced in such matters. Lowell came into the office later that afternoon. We met in his office and began to discuss how to proceed. Lowell and Michael also were in contact with Drexel's management in New York, which had also received subpoenas, and Fred Joseph, Drexel's CEO, and Leon Black, the head of Drexel's Corporate Finance Department, arranged to fly to Los Angeles two days later, on Sunday. We started compiling a list of defense counsel. I kept asking myself throughout that weekend, *How can this be happening to people I know so well?*

Almost exactly twenty years earlier, in September 1966, a friend picked me up at my home in Encino, California, and we drove to Berkeley as I began my college career as an eighteen-year-old freshman. I was naturally apprehensive but also excited as I left for college. I had decided to attend the University of California at Berkeley and to room together with Lowell Milken, my closest friend since the first grade, as freshmen in the university dormitory. We chose Berkeley in part because it was an outstanding university and in part because Lowell's brother Michael was a student there and highly recommended it. Orientation for freshmen took place a few days before they would officially move into the dorms and prepare for their first year in college. Lowell was going to miss orientation, as he had recently undergone eye surgery for a detached retina, but would be joining me the following week as we moved into Norton Hall. I spent my first night at college at Michael's apartment.

Though Michael Milken was barely two years older than me, at that time of life two years was a generation. I had known Michael since I was six years old, but mainly as Lowell's older brother. When we were at Birmingham High School together in Van Nuys, California, Mike was a varsity basketball player, head cheerleader, prom king, and generally a big man on campus. As head cheerleader, he was always out in front of the crowd and seemed very comfortable being there.

On my first night in Berkeley, Michael gave me a tour of the campus and went over my class schedule. He was a member of the Sigma Alpha Mu fraternity, which Lowell and I both pledged as freshmen. Michael was president of the fraternity. Who could have known then that twenty years later, just as I looked to Michael for guidance and support when I was a college freshman, Michael would look to me for guidance and support as he became the target of a criminal investigation?

After graduating from the University of California at Berkeley in 1970, I attended UCLA School of Law and upon graduation joined my father's law firm at Sandler & Rosen. Our practice focused on the civil side of the law with an emphasis on business transactions and real estate. My father, Raymond Sandler, was a very successful attorney.

We worked together for ten years, during which time he instilled in me, as he had through my entire life, the importance of hard work, loyalty, and integrity. A number of his clients had become his close friends, and I observed his devotion to them as well as their devotion to him. My father had also taught me the importance of one's word and one's reputation. I am sure that background had a significant effect on how I conducted myself throughout this investigation, and it definitely influences my motivation for writing this book: to tell the true story of Michael Milken and his prosecution.

As Arthur Liman, the brilliant lawyer who led the defense team for Michael, stated in his memoirs, *Lawyer: A Life of Cases, Counsel, and Controversy*,

> Throughout my career, I've known and represented some powerful figures in the financial industries, but none like him. None so modest in how they lived, or for whom money meant so little. None as committed as he was to his own visions and aspirations. An enigmatic figure to me, even now. But I think I can say this about him. He was the most imaginative financier of his generation. He was also the least understood—and, surely, the most demonized.

Michael is still a public figure, and what happened in this investigation is still misunderstood.

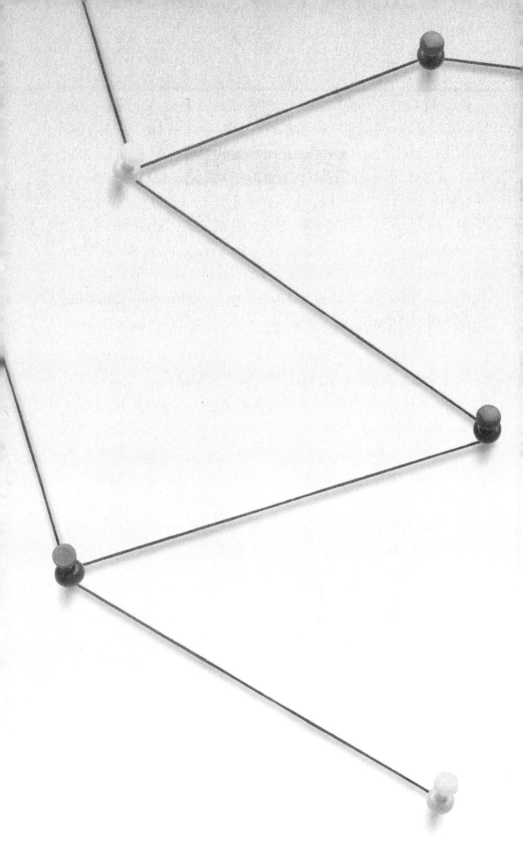

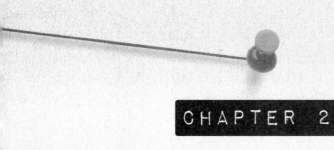

CHAPTER 2

Why Michael Milken?

In the late 1960s, fraternities and sororities began to decline in popularity on the Berkeley campus. There was a focus on the Civil Rights Movement, the anti–Vietnam War activities, and the women's liberation movement, and fraternities were identified with the "establishment." Sigma Alpha Mu was one of the strongest houses on campus at the time, and our members were very engaged in these issues and everything *but* establishment. I have always considered myself fortunate to have been at Berkeley during this period. I believe I received not only a first-class education in the classroom but also an equivalent education about people and society outside the classroom. The most important figures in the country would speak at Berkeley, and many classes focused on the issues of the time.

While Michael was president of the fraternity, we had an incident where the pledge class pulled a prank that caused considerable damage to the house. It was traditional that each pledge class would take a "sneak," where they would invite the president of the house to go away with them for the weekend and they would leave in the middle of the night and usually create a mess for the members left behind to clean up. In this case the "mess" was unusually extensive, and the members decided they would blame Michael and not clean up until he returned. When he did return, he faced an angry group, who many of us felt had overreacted. Michael's reaction was to try to calm the situation. Instead of confronting those who were angry, he rolled up his sleeves and began to clean the place up.

As I look back over the many years I have known Michael, this was the first time that I recall his extraordinarily nonconfrontational nature and his desire to fix any problem and resolve any conflict as calmly as possible. When the year ended, Michael was presented a plaque as a thank-you for his service as president.

On the plaque was inscribed the poem "If," by Rudyard Kipling:

If you can keep your head when all about you
Are losing theirs and blaming it on you,
If you can trust yourself when all men doubt you,
But make allowance for their doubting too;
If you can wait and not be tired by waiting,
Or being lied about, don't deal in lies,
Or being hated, don't give way to hating,
And yet don't look too good, nor talk too wise:
If you can dream—and not make dreams your master;
If you can think—and not make thoughts your aim;
If you can meet with Triumph and Disaster
And treat those two impostors just the same;
If you can bear to hear the truth you've spoken
Twisted by knaves to make a trap for fools,
Or watch the things you gave your life to, broken,
And stoop and build 'em up with worn-out tools:
If you can make one heap of all your winnings
And risk it on one turn of pitch-and-toss,
And lose, and start again at your beginnings

And never breathe a word about your loss;
If you can force your heart and nerve and sinew
To serve your turn long after they are gone,
And so hold on when there is nothing in you
Except the Will which says to them: "Hold on!"
If you can talk with crowds and keep your virtue,
Or walk with Kings—nor lose the common touch,
If neither foes nor loving friends can hurt you,
If all men count with you, but none too much;
If you can fill the unforgiving minute
With sixty seconds' worth of distance run,
Yours is the Earth and everything that's in it,
And—which is more—you'll be a Man, my son!

I found great meaning in these words back then, and I find even greater meaning in this poem today.

Michael was home from college in the summer of 1965 after the Watts riots, one of many civil rights protests for racial equality and civil rights that exploded in major cities in the 1960s. He visited South Central Los Angeles in the aftermath of these protests and saw buildings where people worked burned down, to the detriment of the residents of the area as well as the owners of the businesses who did not live in the area. Michael speaks often of his reaction to people burning down the buildings where they worked. He decided then and there that going into the financial services business and providing capital to people who could build businesses and create jobs was the best way for him to have a positive effect on society.

As Arthur Liman said in his memoirs, Michael Milken was the most innovative and successful financier of the 1970s and 1980s. He may be the most influential financier of the last century. He revolutionized the world of finance by his use of high yield securities to finance companies. He disrupted and disintermediated the traditional way that businesses were financed on Wall Street by making capital available to companies that traditional banks and Wall Street firms previously did not finance. He created and headed the High Yield and Convertible Bond Department at the Wall Street firm of Drexel Burnham Lambert. Prior to Michael Milken, issuance of securities and financing of businesses were principally done through traditional banks or large established financial firms on Wall Street. The clients of these firms were the largest and most successful companies in the country. Small and medium-size businesses were not able to access the public markets to get capital to grow their businesses. Michael Milken and Drexel changed that. They democratized access to capital for the 99 percent of companies previously unable to access the public market. They started a financial revolution and fueled unprecedented economic growth from the late 1970s that continues to this day.

Michael showed a particular interest in business, finance, and accounting as an undergraduate at the University of California.

> **Michael Milken and Drexel democratized access to capital for the 99 percent of companies previously unable to access the public market. They started a financial revolution and fueled unprecedented economic growth from the late 1970s that continues to this day.**

After graduating Berkeley, Michael wanted to continue his business education and was accepted at the Wharton School at the University of Pennsylvania. In 1969, while still a student at Wharton, he began working at Drexel Burnham Lambert. His studies included financial history, credit analysis, and corporate capital structure. Mike concluded from his studies that investing in what was known as high yield securities (referred to by many investors as "junk bonds") with a focus on proper research and analysis would provide extraordinary returns.

As I have heard Mike explain a number of times, there is a big difference between investing in stocks and investing in bonds. The stock market is emotional. One could research a company and be right about a company, but if the market did not agree that it was a good company, the stock would likely decline or not increase in value.

Bonds are different. Bonds are a contract. If the company has the ability to pay interest and then principal when due, the bondholder will receive what the contract provided for. If the market did not like the bond, the bond will trade at a discount, and the investor who does like that bond will make outstanding returns.

Michael began studying this subject while at Berkeley, where he discovered the work of W. Braddock Hickman entitled *Corporate Bond Quality and Investor Experience* (1958). This research concluded that the lower ratings on many bonds were misplaced, because the market considered them to be riskier than they actually were. The key to investing in these bonds was research and evaluating the companies rigorously.

Michael went to Drexel, not because it was one of the prestigious firms on Wall Street (it wasn't) but because it emphasized research as the foundation for investing. Michael became head of research while in his twenties; he convinced his boss his theory was valid. Drexel gave him capital to invest. He combined his theories with an extraordinary encyclopedic mind and an enormous drive and work ethic as well as a very engaging personality. He quickly doubled the value of the capital the firm allotted him.

Michael initially worked at Drexel's Philadelphia office. He and his wife, Lori, were living in Cherry Hill, New Jersey, across the river from Philadelphia. When he was transferred to the Wall Street office, he continued to live in Cherry Hill with Lori and their infant son, Gregory, and would commute by bus every day. He would use the commute time to study prospectuses and do his research.

Michael was researching companies that had issued debt as he bought and sold securities in the debt markets. There are different types of debt: US government debt, municipal bond debt, mortgage debt, consumer debt (such as credit cards and auto loans), and corporate debt. Corporate debt is in the form of bonds issued by corporations to investors. Corporate debt was rated principally by Moody's Investors Service and Standard & Poor's. For better or worse, these two firms were the standard in rating corporate bonds in the 1970s and 1980s when Michael Milken was building the business. Higher-rated or investment-grade bonds have ratings such as AAA, AA, A, or BBB. Anything rated below BBB is called high yield or, pejoratively, "junk bonds." Still today, there are fewer than five hundred companies in the United States that are rated investment grade. Over 99 percent of all companies that might be eligible to issue debt in the marketplace are rated below investment grade.

When Michael Milken first started investing in the high yield bond market, there were basically two types of high yield bonds: "fallen angels" and "conglomerates." Fallen angels were bonds originally rated as investment grade and later downgraded when the issuing corporations had financial difficulties. Conglomerates were companies that were making many acquisitions in often unrelated industries and would issue bonds to help make those acquisitions. Those bonds did not receive investment-grade ratings and were purchased principally by institutional investors such as insurance companies and pension funds. Michael would carefully research the companies issuing these high yield bonds and would identify bonds that he believed provided yields in excess of any risk the company might default on its payments. The rating agencies gave a rating based on the past. Michael did research to understand the future, where a particular company was going and where its industry was heading. This research often included meeting the management of the company, since Michael believed the most valuable asset was human capital, and that was not on the balance sheet. Michael, as long as I have known him, has been focused on people—human capital.

The high yield bond market grew rapidly from the early 1970s when Michael Milken became involved through the time he left the market in 1989. Toward the end of the 1970s, the size of the market was about $70 billion. Ten years later it was approximately $700 billion. The market in 2022 is over $2.2 trillion. Michael Milken created an industry that fundamentally changed opportunities for new businesses, investors, and entrepreneurs.

Through the 1970s Mike spoke to scores of investors and companies about his theory regarding high yield debt. He developed and grew the High Yield Department at Drexel as his "theories" proved correct. Drexel's returns on the funds allocated to him were outstanding. Drexel and Michael then decided there was an opportunity to create value for businesses and society by financing smaller, growing companies that needed capital and allowing them to access the debt market to issue debt.

Drexel began providing financing to companies that otherwise could not access the markets. This decision by Drexel fulfilled one of Michael's goals in going to Wall Street: to provide capital to sound businesses and their founders who otherwise could not secure capital to grow, and to provide jobs. The number of investors in high yield securities grew, including mutual funds, investment funds, insurance companies, savings and loans, and other investors. High yield securities were recognized as a legitimate asset class with a good risk/reward ratio. That is why today almost every firm on Wall Street has a high yield department.

This decision to finance non-investment-grade companies changed the corporate landscape in America and created millions of jobs. A small sample of such companies includes the following: (1) Warner Communications, now Time Warner; (2) McCaw Cellular, the largest cell phone operator in the country at one time, later acquired by AT&T; (3) Turner Broadcasting and CNN, where Ted Turner's vision revolutionized television and news; (4) Wynn Resorts, then known as the Golden Nugget, where Steve Wynn's vision revolutionized the hospitality industry in Las Vegas and elsewhere; (5) US Homes and Pulte Home Builders; (6) TCI (Liberty Media), where John Malone's vision changed television viewing; (7) Viacom, Cablevision, Telemundo, and Metromedia, also in the cable/entertainment industries; (8) Toys "R" Us, Mattel, and Hasbro in the toy industry; and (9) MCI Communications, which was the first company to challenge American Telephone and Telegraph's monopoly on long-distance telephone service.

Michael Milken and Drexel also provided, for the first time, access to capital to companies owned by minorities and women, who had never been able to access public markets. Michael received hate mail for financing Reginald Lewis, an African American entrepreneur who bought Beatrice International Foods in 1987. Beatrice reported revenue of $1.8 billion in 1987. Drexel was financing entrepreneurs building businesses and entire industries.

As Drexel grew, financing businesses and expanding the market for high yield securities, it became a major force in the financial services/investment banking industry. Michael Milken and Drexel received attention as a result of the amount of business they were doing that traditional Wall Street firms were not participating in. Because Michael was focused on financing companies and on a trading operation that grew to several billions of dollars in securities, and because he was a very private individual, he did not talk to the media. He was also an intense competitor who was not interested in educating other financial firms about his business. Drexel continued to grow. In retrospect, this failure to develop relationships with competitors on Wall Street or with the media contributed to his being an attractive target for regulators, prosecutors, and the media in 1986.

As Drexel and Michael received more and more attention, the attacks from competitors on the asset class of "high yield securities" began in earnest, especially after Drexel decided to finance individuals and leverage buyout firms who were interested in trying to take over undervalued public companies. In the early 1980s, many companies were undervalued, and the management of many of these companies did not have significant ownership. Drexel had been financing entrepreneurial and visionary managers who also had ownership stakes in the companies they were building. It was only natural for Drexel to then finance individuals and firms who wished to acquire undervalued companies whose owners, the shareholders, had no voice in management. The interests of the owners and the management were not aligned. These buyers were willing to pay a premium over the stock's existing price because they realized these companies were undervalued.

One of the first transactions that I worked on when I initially left the practice of law was Mattel Inc. The company had suffered significant losses due to an electronics product called Intellivision. An investor group, which included Drexel, saw tremendous value in the company, especially its Barbie doll franchise. The company's investment bankers were not able to obtain any financing for the company, which needed capital to pay down debt and grow the profitable parts of its business. The investor group then worked with Drexel to restructure the company and provide significant capital for the benefit of its shareholders and the new investor group.

Drexel had built great credibility in the market by putting its reputation and capital on the line and issuing to its clients what was known as a "highly confident letter" indicating Drexel was highly confident it would be able to provide financing. These entrepreneurs were then able to start the process of trying to acquire large corporations. Sometimes these acquisitions were "friendly"; the target company negotiated and reached an agreement with the acquirer (such as Mattel). Sometimes these acquisitions were "hostile"; the target rejected the overtures from the potential buyer, and the buyer acquired stock and made a tender offer anyway. The Wall Street establishment was not happy when this firm of young financiers led by this wunderkind in his early thirties from California was earning large fees for financing attempted hostile takeovers of their clients' large companies. Union Oil Company of California, Walt Disney Company, and Phillips Petroleum Company were some of the companies that became the objects of these takeover attempts financed by Drexel. The boards and management of these companies as well as the investment bankers that represented them were outraged that they could be challenged by potential buyers who ten years earlier would not have had the capital to do this. These companies lobbied regulators as well as lawmakers to stop this financial revolution pioneered by this firm, Drexel with its "junk bonds," and its most important employee. There was even a bill introduced in Congress to restrict the purchase of debt issued by non-investment-grade companies.

When Congress was considering such action in the latter half of the 1980s, arrangements were made for Michael Milken, Howard Marks—who had headed high yield securities investing at Citibank and later became cofounder of Oaktree Capital, and Ralph Ingersoll Jr., a newspaper publisher and high yield securities issuer, to visit with key members of Congress. The goal of the visits was for these three individuals who were most knowledgeable about high yield securities to explain high yield securities and the companies that issued them. There was a large gap between the perception and the reality of high yield securities and their value. The mantra of critics was that high yield securities were being used to take over established companies and burden them with debt, and as a result, workers were being laid off. In fact, the opposite was true.

L. Gordon Crovitz, who later became the editor of the editorial page of the *Wall Street Journal*, wrote an article in October 1990, published in the *National Review*, called "Milken and His Enemies":

> It is a telling irony that Michael Milken, although wildly successful, remained almost anonymous until he became involved in the hostile takeover battle. Ironic because less than 10% of the junk bonds went to finance these takeovers. Mr. Milken built his career on a simple observation. When he was a student at Wharton, he realized that people commonly made the mistake of assuming that what happened in the past is necessarily a good indication of the future; if this were true, the railroad stocks would still make up the bulk of big board listings. From this insight, Mr. Milken came up with the hypothesis that the credit rating agencies, which

investment bankers had long relied upon to assess the creditworthiness of firms, might systematically err in favor of firms with long histories and high reported earnings. He would in time conclude that what really counted was future cash flow and the quality of a firm's management team. Mr. Milken helped raise funds for more than one thousand small firms, many of which have become household names such as MCI Communications, KinderCare, and the Turner Broadcasting System. The debate over whether takeovers were on the whole good or bad should have been settled when hundreds of billions of dollars flowed directly into the pockets of shareholders—pension plans and mom-and-pop investors as well as the big players. Between 1970 and 1989, the total number of private sector jobs went from fifty-nine million to more than ninety-one million. During that time the Fortune 500 companies—most of them, of course, of investment grade—accounted for a loss of more than two million jobs. Yet, because of small and medium-size firms' net jobs increase, it was still more than thirty-two million …"

The purpose of the visits to members of Congress by Michael, Howard Marks, and Ralph Ingersoll Jr. was to explain that the issuers of high yield securities accounted for all the job growth in the country at the time and allowed entrepreneurs to have access to capital to create industries, make existing companies more efficient, and add value to shareholders. Michael and Howard discussed this meeting at the 2022 Milken Institute Global Conference where Howard referred to the reception they received as ranging from "ineffective to unpleasant." Pete Domenici, then senator from New Mexico, showed no interest in what

Howard was trying to explain, as the senator accused Howard of just trying to "feather his own nest" when in fact he was just trying to do the right thing. Michael recalls that when they met with the congressman from North Dakota, a state with only one representative to the House of Representatives, Michael had a chart by state of the investment-grade companies (companies rated investment grade by Moody's and Standard & Poor's) in each state. There was not one investment-grade company located in the state of North Dakota. When Michael explained that legislation to restrict access to capital would adversely affect every company located in the state, the congressman responded that the citizens of North Dakota would sacrifice to stop the scourge of high yield bonds.

The lack of understanding and knowledge about high yield bonds at the time was demonstrated most clearly when Michael and I had the opportunity to meet with Paul Volcker, then chair of the US Federal Reserve in 1987. Mr. Volcker was very polite and seemed interested in learning more about these high yield or junk bonds. Michael gave him a list of one hundred well-known companies at the time and asked the chair to identify which companies he believed were not investment grade, or high yield. Mr. Volcker reviewed the list for several minutes and gave it back to Michael with about four companies checked. When Michael

> The lack of understanding and knowledge about high yield bonds at the time was demonstrated most clearly when Michael and I had the opportunity to meet with Paul Volcker, then chair of the US Federal Reserve in 1987.

explained that all one hundred companies on the list were high yield, the chairman was surprised. The reason Michael Milken was so successful is that he understood an asset class that so few bothered to research. The reason Michael was such an attractive target for so many was that he understood this asset class so much better than his competitors, the regulators, and the investment-grade issuers. Writers, bankers, and economists who have studied Michael's business at the time of the investigation have since confirmed the importance of the business he developed and the value created by it.

Despite this extraordinary success, or possibly because of it, Drexel went out of business at the end of 1989, one year after Michael Milken was forced out of Drexel, as will be discussed in chapter 5. Drexel was blamed for every financial crisis at the time. There was a crisis in the savings and loan industry in the late 1980s. When many of these institutions made unwise loans against real estate, they lost money and their depositors started withdrawing funds, which resulted in bankruptcies. The General Accounting Office of Congress found that high yield bonds were the second-best investment by these institutions. (The best investment was credit cards.) Savings and loan institutions' assets were more than $1 trillion in the 1980s, of which only $10 billion, or 1 percent, was invested in high yield bonds. Since the government had insured the deposits, it had to pay out the deposits that the savings and loans were unable to satisfy. Though Congress passed the laws allowing deposits to be insured, it required these institutions to divest all of their high yield bond holdings over a five-year period. This caused the prices of these bonds to fall precipitously and artificially forced savings and loans to sell at the worst possible time, exacerbating the problem.

Mr. Crovitz also discusses in his article a second Milken enemy: the media. Michael Milken became more and more vilified in the press as the government continued its investigation of him. A number of articles accused him of causing damage to the economy, and he became the scapegoat for any financial woes the financial media could conjure up.

An article by William D. Cohen in *Institutional Investor* on May 1, 2017, entitled "The Michael Milken Project—How Did a 70-Year-Old Ex-con Barred for Life from Wall Street Become One of the Most Respected Men?" provides a glimpse of how Michael Milken was viewed in the late 1980s compared to how he is now viewed—at least by those who understand financial markets:

> "The only worthwhile recent innovation in finance is the ATM machine," quipped Paul Volcker in 2009 … it was a clever and memorable line. … It was also totally wrong. The greatest innovation in the recent history of finance was not the ATM, whatever the benefits of skipping the teller's line. It was the junk bond.
>
> To this day, high yield bonds remain a brilliant innovation because they elegantly solve a simple yet ubiquitous problem: they give companies with less-than-stellar credit ratings access to capital.
>
> These bonds created and grew entire industries, such as wireless communications and cable television, just as they created and grew immense pools of wealth. Their invention has done nothing less than bring about the democratization of finance.

The man behind this industry was Mike Milken, who

> "Revolutionized the way companies—in particular companies involved in corporate transactions—were financed," says David Boies, super litigator and cofounder

of the law firm Boies, Schiller, Flexner. "He changed that fundamental. If you look at the way companies were financed, there is before Michael Milken and after Michael Milken."

It is ironic to note that this quotation comes from David Boies, who was a litigator in a lawsuit attacking Michael Milken in the 1980s:

> Milken's innovation was to realize, in the 1970s, that investors could make more money on a risk-adjusted basis from buying bonds issued by companies with lower credit ratings than they could by investing in the bonds of triple A rated companies …

The article then quotes David Solomon, who worked with Milken at Drexel and is now chairman and CEO of Goldman Sachs Group:

> "The markets continue to grow," says David Solomon. "Generally, the conventional wisdom was that nobody would want a bond unless it was investment grade, and he [Milken] basically said, 'You should be able to price that risk.' He basically turned a bunch of academic theory into a practical business." … Milken went on to finance Rupert Murdoch as he transformed News Corp into an international powerhouse and Craig McCaw as he built a national cellular communications company with two million subscribers before selling it in 1994 to AT&T for $11.5 billion. Milken helped billionaire entrepreneur John Malone grow his cable television empire. Milken got Ted Turner the $1.4 billion he needed to buy MGM and start his cable TV empire. … "What Milken did was to pierce the wall of the estab-

lishment," says (Michael) Thomas, a former longtime partner of Lehman Brothers Holdings. "In a way, he disrupted the financial structure in the industry, but in a way you might also say he disrupted the social structure of American finance."

David Solomon also spoke of his experience working for Michael Milken:

> Milken remained influential because he was, and is, nothing less than extraordinary. He's got an incredible ability to digest information and synthesize it and communicate around it. There are some people that are incredible salesmen; there are some people that are incredible traders. Mike is top decile in a whole range of skills.

Michael's ability to digest, retain, and synthesize information in situations when no one else would think of utilizing that information is part of the genius that has allowed him to succeed to such an extraordinary extent as a financier and a philanthropist.

Harlan Platt at Northeastern University published in the *Journal of Applied Corporate Finance* 5, no. 4 (Winter 1993) the article "Underwriter Effects and the Riskiness of Original-Issue High Yield Bonds," in which he discusses "the myths at the time versus the realities of Michael Milken's business":

> Countless criticisms have been levied against Michael Milken and Drexel Burnham Lambert for both the rise and the fall of the high yield bond market.
>
> Edward Altman's most recent updating of junk bond returns reveals that, over the period 1977–1992,

investors' net returns on high yield bonds exceeded the returns on treasuries of comparable maturities by an average of 176 basis points per year. Moreover, my recently completed study of 557 high yield bond issues floated between 1977 and 1988 finds ... that Drexel-underwritten junk bonds had a lower default rate (as well as lower expected default risk at the time of issue) than the bonds issued by most other underwriters.

Stephen Moore, former senior economist for the Congressional Joint Economic Committee, wrote the following in the June 2005 *American Spectator*:

For all the vilification of Michael Milken, his firm Drexel Burnham easily created more wealth for American shareholders singlehandedly than all the trustbusters in American history combined.

Norman Barry, a professor of social and political theory at the University of Buckingham, wrote the following in a September 2006 *Financial Times* article:

In retrospect, most American economic observers say that Mr. Milken was good for the economy; his actions led to the breakup of conglomerates and the necessary reorganization of American business. His prosecution was more of a persecution.

Alvin Toffler, the futurist and author of *Future Shock*, stated in his book *Powershift* that

[Milken] made bitter enemies of two extremely powerful groups. One consisted of the old-line Wall Street firms who previously had had a stranglehold on the flow of capital to American corporations; the other consisted of the top managers of many of the largest firms. Both had every reason to destroy him if they could. Both also had powerful allies in Government and the media.

All these quotes and comments present a clear picture of why Michael Milken was an attractive target for a prosecutor, especially a politically ambitious one. Drexel Burnham Lambert created a new market that it dominated and was financing individuals who would threaten the traditional clients of traditional firms. Michael Milken was a disruptor. Like many innovators and disruptors throughout history, he was bound to come under criticism at the time. Galileo was jailed for coming up with new scientific theories. John D. Rockefeller, Andrew Carnegie, Henry Ford, and Cornelius Vanderbilt are often referred to as "robber barons" though they revolutionized their industries and created valuable businesses and philanthropic institutions that exist to this day. Innovators of today such as Bill Gates, Mark Zuckerberg, Jeff Bezos, Jack Dorsey, and Elon Musk are under constant scrutiny by the government and the media.

> Michael Milken was a disruptor. Like many innovators and disruptors throughout history, he was bound to come under criticism at the time.

Once the investigation began and the media frenzy started, it did not matter what Milken had done or had not done. All that mattered was that he was successful, disrupted traditional finance on Wall Street, and was under investigation because he did business with Ivan Boesky. Though most firms on Wall Street also did business with Mr. Boesky, it turned out that he had committed crimes. When Ivan Boesky decided to cooperate with the government and plead to criminal conduct on November 14, 1986, he made a good "bargain" by agreeing to incriminate others, including the successful young financier who regulators and prosecutors considered the biggest prize of all. As Michael himself said in an interview with *Forbes* magazine in 1992, "It was obviously a terrible mistake ever doing a single trade with him [Boesky]. But people forget that in the 1980s Boesky was celebrated by the media. Just about every investment house on Wall Street dealt with him, and those that didn't mostly wanted to. Everyone thought he was a great arbitrageur and wanted his business. But he was only a tiny part of Drexel's business."

And Michael Milken was the most successful financier on Wall Street in 1986, though only forty years old. Defense lawyer Aubrey Harwell said to me at the beginning of the investigation, "When the government wants to get you, they will get you." Aubrey worked in the Justice Department for the attorney general Robert Kennedy investigating Jimmy Hoffa. Had Hoffa not disappeared, Aubrey said the government would have indicted and convicted him of something. "Richard, I am not comparing Michael Milken to Jimmy Hoffa, but for reasons I cannot explain, I have never seen a case where the government wanted to get someone this badly since Hoffa."

The facts about Michael Milken in 2022 are not that complicated. He created a completely new way of financing companies that has continued and grown from the time he started over forty years ago. When he was forced out of the business by the government in 1989, every major firm on Wall Street entered that business. His effect on the industry is evident even today, as he is called upon as a keynote speaker by major financial institutions such as Citibank, JPMorgan, and Goldman Sachs to explain his views of the financial markets, human capital, and society in general—and how they all relate to one another. He was in the business for less than twenty years and has been out of the business for over thirty years. Almost every customer, client, competitor, or coworker of Michael Milken still speaks of him with respect for who he is, what he created, and how much he has contributed to the financial system of the United States. They are among the five thousand people who attend the Milken Institute Global Conference each year to continue to be exposed to Michael Milken and his ideas.

Michael Milken was a maverick who created a market outside the confines of Wall Street's traditional boundaries. The view of Michael Milken today is either that he was a visionary and brilliant financial innovator who helped create new industries, grow companies, and create jobs or someone who went to prison because he operated in violation of the law, although he created a marketplace where investors and companies could benefit. As Michael observed in an interview with *Forbes* magazine almost thirty years ago, "We were matching capital to entrepreneurs who could use it effectively. We were creating investments that money managers needed in volatile markets."

Let's take a closer look at how Michael Milken became the subject of probably the most intensive securities law investigation ever and ended up pleading guilty to violations of the securities laws and going to prison.

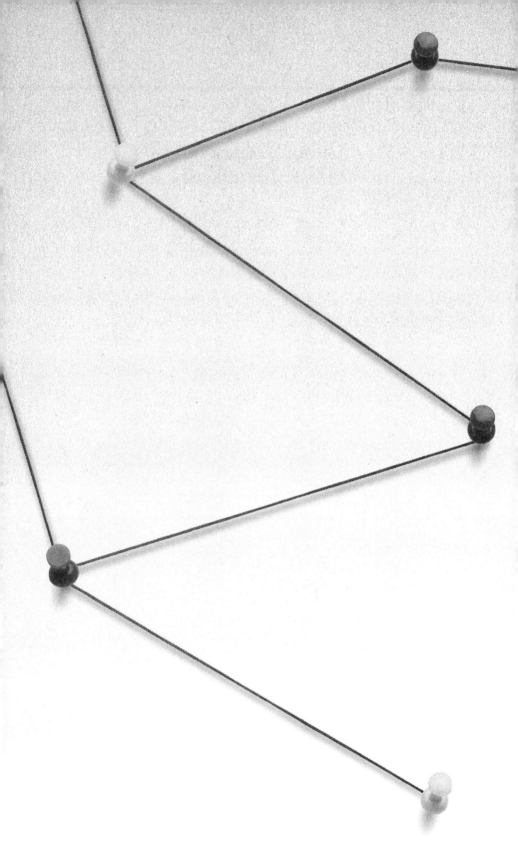

CHAPTER 3

The Investigation Begins,
and a $5.3 Million Fee

The High Yield and Convertible Bond Department at Drexel Burnham was relocated to Los Angeles from New York in 1978. Michael and Lori Milken had always planned to move back to Los Angeles. Both of their families lived in Los Angeles, and that is where they grew up. Since Michael had been so successful at Drexel and since technology was at a point where information could be shared between the East Coast and the West Coast seamlessly and economically, Drexel was willing to grant its star employee's request to move the department to California. At the time, Mike and Lori had two children, Gregory and Lance, both under five years old, and Michael's father, Bernard Milken, was being treated for advanced melanoma cancer. Mike also wanted his father to spend as much time as possible with Mike and Lori's children.

Late on that Friday afternoon in November 1986, Michael, Lowell, Kevin Madigan, and I gathered in Lowell's office. Mike did not use an office. He conducted all of his business from his desk on the trading floor. Every conversation he engaged in could be overheard by numerous individuals who sat around him. Lowell had been out ill that day but came into the office when he learned of the subpoenas.

WITNESS TO A PROSECUTION

None of us in that room had ever dealt with anything remotely similar to what we were now facing. We had no idea what exactly this was all about but did understand it was serious and had to do with Ivan Boesky. One of the most important lessons in life is to know what you don't know and to find someone who does know it. We knew we needed to get advice from those who had experience with what we were dealing with—top white-collar criminal defense lawyers in New York and/or Washington, DC. The subpoenas were from the Southern District of New York and the Securities and Exchange Commission in Washington, DC.

> ## None of us in that room had ever dealt with anything remotely similar to what we were now facing.

Michael had met Edward Bennett Williams, who was considered at that time by many as the best criminal defense lawyer in the country. He and his law firm, Williams & Connolly in Washington, DC, were well respected. Mike and I were able to get Ed Williams on the phone that evening, and he agreed he would meet with me the following week in Washington, DC. He made an interesting, if not prophetic, statement to us on that phone call. The grand jury subpoenas referenced the Racketeer Influenced and Corrupt Organization Act, or RICO, a statute originally meant to apply to organized crime. Ed said he knew about RICO. It was never intended for an investigation like this, but he was not surprised that the US Attorney for the Southern District of New York, Rudolph Giuliani, would try to use that statute in this investigation to increase pressure. Ed referred to Giuliani as "the biggest piece of political meat I have seen since Thomas Dewey." Thomas Dewey was a prior US Attorney for the Southern District of New York who later became governor of New York and ran for president of the United States. Ed said that Giuliani was as politically ambitious as Dewey and would look at this investigation from the perspective of furthering his political career. Mr. Giuliani did leverage his reputation as a tough prosecutor to become mayor of New York City and then pursue presidential ambitions. He has continued to bring attention to himself ever since.

My home in the San Fernando Valley of Los Angeles was located a block from Michael's home. After celebrating my son Nicholas's sixth birthday that evening, I visited with Michael. Mike always believed one reduces risk by having as much information about a subject as possible. He devoted a great deal of time and effort researching markets, companies, and people before investing in them. And now he was in the biggest fight of his life with no frame of reference whatsoever and facing previously unimaginable risks. I made it clear to Michael that I would be there for him as we decided how we were going to navigate these uncharted waters. Michael was clearly concerned. Boesky was an insider trader. Michael had more access to material nonpublic information in the 1980s than probably anyone. He knew he'd never shared confidential nonpublic information with Ivan Boesky or anyone else. He also knew he had spoken to Mr. Boesky on several occasions where Boesky was seeking information. He did not know what Boesky was saying to the investigators. He did know that powerful forces existed that would like to see his demise. And he did know that the government had given Mr. Boesky a very favorable plea bargain based on what he was saying. Boesky was an insider trader who was permitted to plead in court to a single count of violating a securities regulation with respect to a transaction that the government claimed Michael Milken was a party to.

Over the next several days in November, Mike and I gathered all trading records of transactions between the High Yield Department and the Boesky organization and all information about a $5.3 million fee paid by Boesky to Drexel that previous March that was referenced in some of the subpoenas. The subpoenas were very broad and asked for many documents but did not indicate why. They did refer to the financing Drexel did for the Boesky organization the previous March.

The SEC/US Attorney insider trading investigation really began in June 1986. Dennis Levine was indicted for insider trading violations and pleaded guilty in June 1986. Dennis Levine was a managing director at Drexel Burnham Lambert, where he had worked since 1985. Prior to that time Levine was a specialist in mergers and acquisitions at Lehman Brothers. Mr. Levine had sold nonpublic inside information for cash to Ivan Boesky and had also personally traded on such information when he was at Lehman Brothers. Levine tried to hide his activity by opening secret bank accounts in the Bahamas and trading for his own account through several brokers to hide what was happening. A brokerage firm he had accounts with was affiliated with Merrill Lynch. Someone at a Merrill Lynch office detected suspicious activity, which led to a discovery of Levine's activities. Levine would sell inside information to Ivan Boesky and receive payment in bags of cash, which he would deposit into a Bahamian bank. Levine pleaded guilty on June 5, 1986, to securities fraud, tax evasion, and perjury charges and agreed to pay $11.5 million, which at the time was considered a very large payment.[1]

Levine cooperated with the prosecutors and implicated others who were involved with him in those illegal activities—one of whom was Ivan Boesky. Boesky at first fought the investigation but quickly made a "deal" and implicated Martin Siegel, another employee involved in mergers and acquisitions at Drexel Burnham; Boyd

---

1   Dennis B. Levine, "The Inside Story of an Inside Trader," *Fortune* magazine, May 21, 1990.

Jefferies, who had started the securities firm of Jefferies & Company; and others, including Michael Milken. Jefferies, Levine, Siegel, and Boesky all quickly decided not to contest charges and agreed to plead guilty to various offenses and cooperate with the government. They all violated the law and received relatively light sentences (i.e., less than a year—except for Ivan Boesky, who received a three-year sentence, and Dennis Levine, who received a two-year sentence).

Boesky violated the most basic securities laws by paying for and trading on inside information, and he was allowed to plead to a single count of violating the securities laws, paid $100 million, and served two years in prison. The government advocated for him since he agreed to implicate others in his wrongdoing, including the most successful financier of the time, Michael Milken.

In this particular situation, Ivan Boesky was violating the law in his dealings with others away from Drexel. He told the prosecutors he could help them find wrongdoing by other high-profile members of the financial services industry. The prosecutors were therefore incentivized to accommodate their source and to pursue the investigation. As I came to painfully learn, their success is measured by convictions obtained. Michael conducted his business differently, and despite what the prosecutor and the SEC believed (or wanted to believe), Michael was in no position to admit such charges or implicate others.

This $5.3 million fee became a major focus of the government's investigation. The government alleged that Michael Milken and Ivan Boesky entered into a series of illegal transactions ranging from insider trading to stock parking. "Stock parking" became a familiar phrase in all the government investigations at the time. It refers to transactions where one investor has an interest in securities held on another investor's books and records or where in effect one investor "parks" its interest with the other. The theory was that Drexel and Boesky would keep track of transactions to determine who owed what to whom and that this all resulted in the Boesky organization's paying the $5.3 million fee in March 1986. Charles Thurnher, who worked in the High Yield Department, and Setrag Mooradian, who did book-keeping work for the Boesky organization, kept records of various transactions that the Boesky organization was involved in, though they could never agree on the significance of the records nor could they ever reconcile their respective records.

This recordkeeping became a major focus of the investigation, but why these records were kept or what information was in them was never proven. In retrospect, it is entirely possible that this investigation either would never have taken place or would never have been as intense without this recordkeeping, since without it there was no support for the allegations of inappropriate transactions. Ivan Boesky was a very difficult client of Drexel's. An arbitrageur's job is to get as much information as legally available to make decisions on buying and selling securities.

Michael's experience with Mr. Boesky involved Mr. Boesky seeking as much information as possible. As an example, in one instance Mr. Boesky, as an arbitrageur, wanted to acquire stock of a company that a Drexel client had announced he was interested in acquiring. He asked Michael Milken what he thought. Michael told Mr. Boesky that the client had publicly indicated he was interested in the company in question, but Michael knew nothing more than that. He certainly did not discourage Mr. Bocsky from buying the stock. When many months went by and the acquisition didn't take place, Mr. Boesky would complain to Michael that Mr. Boesky had lost money on the investment and was holding Michael responsible. This is where Michael's nonconfrontational nature came to haunt him. In hindsight, Michael should have stopped talking to Mr. Boesky.

Of course, that would be confrontational. Instead, Michael would say something to the effect of "Okay, if you really lost money on this transaction, I will make it up to you." Michael did not intend to write Mr. Boesky a check. He just assumed that over time they would discuss enough investment ideas that there would be situations where Mr. Boesky would make money if Mr. Boesky really lost money, though Michael never believed he was responsible for any loss. It was a customer accommodation that would affect no one but Michael Milken, and there was never evidence that Michael ever actually "made up" any such claimed loss.

When Michael learned that Boesky was keeping track of situations where he claimed Drexel owed him money, Michael asked Charles Thurnher to also keep records and find out what Mr. Mooradian was keeping records of for Boesky. He also asked Mr. Thurnher to keep track of situations where Michael believed Boesky had made a profit. What our legal team learned as we went through this investigation was that no records existed that ever matched or showed who might have owed what to whom. When Messrs. Thurnher and Mooradian would meet and discuss the records, they could never reconcile them. Both Mr. Thurnher and Mr. Mooradian ended up being immunized government witnesses, meaning the government agreed not to prosecute either of them as long as they cooperated with the government. Neither of them could ever produce records that were of any benefit to the government or that reflected any improper transactions. It was unfortunate that Michael continued to do business with Boesky.

Michael Milken was not the only one at Drexel whom Mr. Boesky called seeking information. Boesky sought advice from numerous people at Drexel over the years. He never paid for the advice given nor did he do much business with Drexel. In March of 1986 Drexel raised the money to finance Boesky's business through a new entity.

As part of this transaction, Boesky was liquidating his companies and transferring all his future operations to the new company. When that financing was about to close, Michael believed he had the leverage to insist that the old company pay a fee to Drexel for all the research and other work performed over the years regarding investments, acquisition candidates, and other advice. Though the new company would be paying a fee to Drexel for the financing, Michael and Boesky agreed that the old company would pay Drexel an additional fee of $5.3 million for all the work that different departments of Drexel had done over the years for the old Boesky company.

Two documents were created on March 21, 1986, that referenced this $5.3 million fee. One was a handwritten memo that Charles Thurnher prepared at Michael's direction stating that the fee should be allocated among the High Yield Bond Department, the Drexel Equity Research Department in New York, and the Drexel Corporate Finance Department.

The second document relating to the $5.3 million fee was a letter signed by Lowell Milken. Michael flew to New York at the close of business on March 21, 1986. Before he left, as was his usual practice, he reviewed with Lowell any outstanding matters that might arise while he was gone. One of those matters was this $5.3 million fee. Michael mentioned that Boesky had agreed the old Boesky company would pay this fee for past services provided by Drexel. This was all Lowell knew about the fee. Later that afternoon, while Michael was in the air, Boesky's accountants, Oppenheim, Appel, Dixon & Co., requested backup for the $5.3 million fee because they were closing the books on the old Boesky organization. Boesky and the accountants called Drexel and eventually spoke with Lowell. Lowell did not like dealing with Ivan Boesky and tried to minimize his contact. After various discussions, Lowell and Donald Balser, an officer of Drexel who worked in the High Yield Bond Department, signed a letter sent by Oppenheim, Appel, Dixon & Co. and reviewed by an attorney on behalf of Drexel and on behalf of Lowell. It read as follows:

> RE: Consulting Services Fee Due Drexel Burnham Lambert Incorporated—$5,300,000.00
>
> Gentlemen:
>
> There was an oral understanding with Ivan F. Boesky of the Ivan F. Boesky Corporation that Drexel Burnham Lambert Incorporated would provide consulting services. There were no formal records maintained for the time devoted to such consulting services. There were no prior agreements as to the specific value of such consulting services to be performed. There was no prior determination of the specific value for such consulting services until March 21, 1986, which amounted to $5,300,000.00 due to Drexel Burnham Lambert Incorporated. Such amount was mutually agreed upon.
>
> If you agree with the above, kindly sign where indicated.
>
> Very truly yours,
>
> OPPENHEIM, APPEL, DIXON & CO.
>
> By: David Beach, Partner
>
> I have examined the above, and found it to be correct.
>
> By: Donald Balser—for Drexel Burnham Lambert Incorporated
>
> By: Lowell J. Milken

The letter was accurate. Lowell knew nothing more about the subject than was in the letter; neither did Donald Balser. Mr. Balser was the appropriate person to sign the letter, and the accountants also insisted that Lowell sign the letter.

The information sought in the subpoenas and the ensuing months and years made it clear that Ivan Boesky told the prosecutors and SEC staff that he had engaged in wrongdoing with Michael Milken and that the $5.3 million fee was proof of such wrongdoing. Charles Thurnher was the first Drexel employee to receive immunity. The process the US Attorney normally uses in deciding whether to grant immunity is first to meet with the attorney for the witness. The attorney then makes what is known as a "proffer" to the US Attorney, summarizing generally what their client might say if granted immunity. Based upon the proffer, the US Attorney makes a decision whether to grant immunity to that witness. Once immunity is granted, the witness has an obligation to meet with the US Attorney upon request and answer any and all questions truthfully. Seth Mooradian, who did the recordkeeping for Boesky, was also an immunized and cooperating government witness. Neither Charles Thurnher nor Seth Mooradian produced any such records. The only document I ever saw produced by Thurnher that related to the $5.3 million fee was the allocation among Drexel departments referred to previously.

To understand the $5.3 million fee, one has to understand that business on Wall Street is not that much different than any other business. Individuals who are in the same industry and who regularly engage with one another are always exchanging ideas or information. In order to be most effective in transacting business, individuals want as much information about the subject matter they are dealing with as they can get. Reasonable exchanges of such information are perfectly legitimate. In the securities industry, it is of course improper to disclose material nonpublic information. Michael Milken was adamant throughout the investigation that he never disclosed material nonpublic information in violation of any law or duty. The investigation never found otherwise. In the financial services industry, the value of services is measured by fees or profits earned, usually when transactions are completed.

Until the Drexel/Milken investigation, each high-profile individual who pleaded guilty in these investigations was guilty of one or more offenses, such as insider trading where money would trade hands, tax evasion, and/or violations of other securities laws. Each of these individuals (such as Boyd Jefferies, Martin Siegel, and Ivan Boesky) quickly pleaded, became a cooperating witness, and received a lesser sentence. Unlike Ivan Boesky, Dennis Levine, and Marty Siegel, Michael did not engage in insider trading. Michael also paid his taxes. He, too, was interested in reducing the risk and ending this ordeal, but he was not going to plead to something he did not do. So he defended himself and would not agree to provide assistance to the government in the investigation as the others had. Over the next three years, I learned, the US Attorney's Office for the Southern District would not, or could not, admit it might be wrong or mistaken in a high-profile case, especially when that US Attorney was Rudolph Giuliani. They had

> Michael Milken was adamant throughout the investigation that he never disclosed material nonpublic information in violation of any law or duty. The investigation never found otherwise.

made a deal with Boesky to get Milken, which made headlines, and that is what they were committed to do.

In 1989 I saw a movie called *True Believer*, featuring James Woods and Robert Downey Jr. This is a courtroom drama where James Woods ends up defending a client imprisoned for a murder he did not commit. The plot of the movie is that the murder was committed as a crime of passion by a drug informant who had helped the district attorney obtain a number of convictions. As a result, the district attorney earned a reputation as a tough prosecutor, which he used to pursue a political career. The DA framed James Woods's client, who resembled the informant. When James Woods uncovered this framing in a dramatic court scene, the DA tried to convince the judge not to allow the questioning to continue because the work the DA was doing was so important and because the fact he may have framed an unknown individual was justified. In other words, the DA was a "true believer." He could not be wrong.

Even though the Michael Milken case was a much different type of case, when I saw the movie *True Believer,* I immediately drew the connection to our case. The young prosecutors who were assigned to our case clearly were true believers in the work they were doing and the importance of convicting Michael Milken. The Southern District of New York office of the US Department of Justice considered itself the crown jewel of the US Attorney offices. They were too important to be wrong. Clearly these prosecutors were not framing anybody, but they were trained to win, and over time it became clear that they had made up their minds that Michael Milken was guilty of something and needed to be convicted to justify the agreement made with Mr. Boesky and all the publicity about the case. Fiction truly did imitate life, which imitated fiction.

One significant difference between the Levine and Boesky cases and the Michael Milken case was that there was no publicity about these other matters until the individuals pleaded guilty. Michael Milken became the subject of intensive newspaper articles, press leaks, rumors, and innuendo for years before he was charged with anything. I am sure Giuliani and his team of prosecutors believed that Mike would succumb to the pressure and quickly settle and cooperate and implicate others. When this did not happen, the prosecutors became more committed to using their immense power to pressure Michael and try to win at all costs.

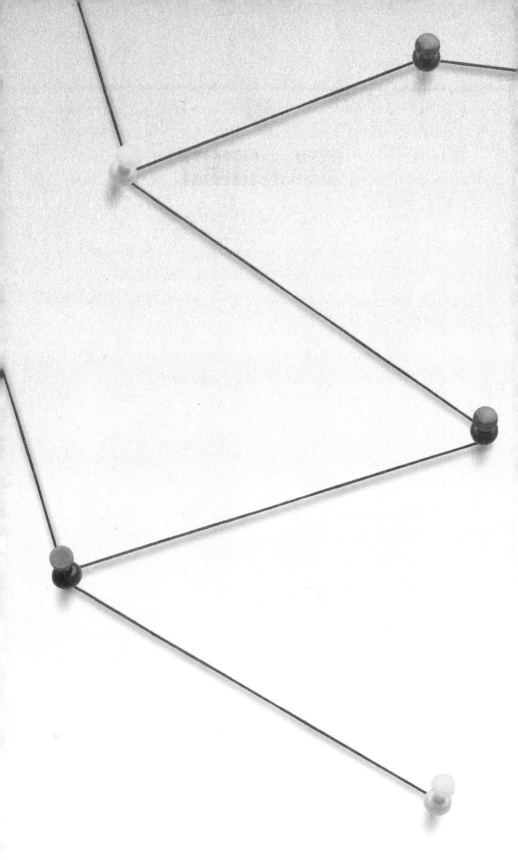

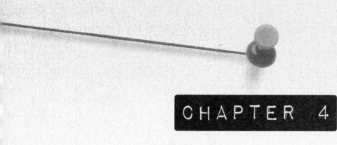

CHAPTER 4

Choosing Lawyers and
Prosecutorial Powers

I n the US Supreme Court case of *Berger v. United States* (295 US 78 [1935]), Associate Justice George Sutherland states,

> The United States Attorney is the representative not of an ordinary party to a controversy, but of a sovereign whose obligation to govern impartially is as compelling as its obligation to govern at all; and whose interest, therefore, in a criminal prosecution is not that it shall win a case, but that justice shall be done. As such, he is in a particular and very definite sense the servant of the law, the twofold aim of which is that guilt shall not escape or innocence suffer … it is as much his duty to refrain from improper methods calculated to produce a wrongful conviction as it is to use every legitimate means to bring about a just one.

The prosecutors we encountered in the Southern District were trained to believe that by winning, justice was done. The federal criminal justice system is set up to create such an environment. The US Attorney works with investigators from the first day. At the end of the investigation, the same prosecutor who did the investigation makes the recommendation whether to indict. At this point, that prosecutor has a vested interest in the case. During the investigative stage, the prosecutor has immense power. It has a grand jury at its disposal to take testimony from individuals whose lawyers are sitting out in the hallway. It can use the grand jury subpoena power to obtain documents. Then the prosecutor can decide whether to send a "target letter" to a witness indicating that the witness is close to being indicted. One can only imagine the effect such a letter can have on the witness. And the prosecutor can offer to give a witness immunity for favorable testimony. The defense lawyers have no rights to compel a potential witness to talk to them nor to subpoena documents from anyone. The criminal justice system differs significantly from the civil system, where plaintiffs and defendants have equal discovery rights and a level playing field.

John Carroll, the lead prosecutor assigned to the Milken case by US Attorney Rudolph Giuliani, addressed this issue at a class I taught at Stanford Law School on April 16, 2012:

> The criminal justice system is basically an exercise in raw power. I probably didn't understand it when I was the prosecutor. I certainly understand it now. ... It is very much an uneven game where the Government has enormous power ... exercised by very young and very inexperienced people ... a good prosecutor has to be energetic, black and white, zealous, ambitious—personally ambitious, because that's what drives the engine.

In 1987, John Carroll was that young and inexperienced prosecutor who was energetic and zealous.

I quickly learned about the criminal justice process and the power of the prosecutors, but I had no understanding of this on November

17, 1986, when Kevin Madigan, in-house counsel for Drexel in the High Yield Department, and I flew to New York to meet with Tom Curnin, a partner at Cahill Gordon, Drexel's corporate counsel at that time, to start developing a strategy and interviewing attorneys. I first met on that Monday with Peter Fleming and his partner Eliot Lauer of the firm Curtis Mullet. Peter was a former Assistant US Attorney in the Southern District of New York. He made it clear within five minutes that he felt he was the right person to represent Michael Milken. Peter immediately impressed me with his demeanor, his toughness, and what appeared even then to be a deep commitment to his clients and to fairness. Still, I was not going to reach any conclusions as to whom I would recommend to Michael or to Lowell until after I met with several other attorneys in New York as well as Edward Bennett Williams the next day in Washington, DC. Michael also had a relationship with Arthur Liman, one of the most respected lawyers in New York who was also a former Assistant US Attorney in the Southern District. Ultimately Michael would decide who would represent him, but he was relying on me to conduct these interviews and then advise him.

Later that day, I met with Michael Armstrong, another former Assistant US Attorney from the Southern District of New York. Michael was one of the most decent and committed individuals I have ever met. I reported this to Lowell, who retained Michael Armstrong after meeting with him in New York. I also met with a half dozen other impressive defense lawyers, most of whom had served together as Assistant US Attorneys in the Southern District of New York when Robert Morgenthau was the US Attorney. They all knew each other well. They all respected each other and worked together on many cases. And they would all tell me over the next several years how nothing in their careers had prepared them for the Drexel/Milken investigation, which they called *sui generis*—translated to mean "of its own kind"—different from any case they had ever been involved in. They had never been involved in a case where the US Attorney was so reluctant to share information, leaked information to the media, and used its powers to scare witnesses. They also had never been involved in a case where they were up against both the SEC and the US Attorney simultaneously and where the US Attorney worked so closely with the SEC. Each division of the government brought its own action against Michael Milken, Lowell Milken, and Drexel.

I left New York the next morning for Washington, DC, believing I had met outstanding lawyers to recommend to various individuals who would probably need representation. In Washington I met with Seymour Glanzer and then later with Edward Bennett Williams. Sy Glanzer was a former Assistant US Attorney in Washington, DC, and had been involved in prosecuting defendants involved in the Watergate break-in at Democratic National Committee headquarters in the 1970s—the case that resulted in President Richard Nixon resigning his presidency. Sy was a very down-to-earth individual who certainly had what I would call an outstanding bedside manner for whomever he represented. He ended up representing Charles Thurnher, who was an honest, decent individual. He was the first Drexel employee to receive immunity and agree to cooperate with the government.

The next day, I met with Edward Bennett Williams and his associate Robert Litt, who had recently worked as an Assistant US Attorney in the Southern District of New York. I was a young thirty-eight-year-old who had never been through this process before but had read for years about Edward Bennett Williams. I was greatly looking forward to the meeting. It was obvious from the first few minutes of our conversation the reason Edward Bennett Williams had such an outstanding reputation. He had a presence. He was easy to talk to and in total command of the room. We discussed what we knew about the case at some length, and he restated his comment about Rudy Giuliani being a "raw piece of political meat." I told Ed that Michael also had a relationship with Arthur Liman of the Paul, Weiss, Rifkind, Wharton & Garrison firm. We discussed the possibility of Ed and Arthur jointly representing Michael Milken, since Arthur was familiar with Drexel and many of its clients. Ed said he had tremendous respect for Arthur and that they had worked together in the past, but he felt very strongly that only one person could be in charge. The analogy he used was that if you were going into surgery and had two excellent surgeons consulting, you would only want one of them holding the scalpel when it came time to cut.

I also nervously asked Ed about his health, since it was rumored he had cancer. He could not have been more forthcoming as he told me he had been diagnosed with cancer, had received treatments over time, and had never missed a day of work because of the disease. He indicated he felt fine.

Ed Williams also instructed me on the criminal process. Ed explained that during the period of time when the rules were written about civil procedure and criminal procedure, most of the respected lawyers were in the civil field and provided safeguards and rules of litigation that were fair to defendants and plaintiffs alike. But when it came to developing the rules for criminal process, all the benefit went to the prosecution with very little consideration given to the rights of defendants, especially since the prevailing concern was putting away the criminal. He explained to me that often young prosecuting attorneys in white-collar cases complained they did not have the resources of the wealthy defendants they were investigating and prosecuting. Ed told me he would be happy in any criminal investigation, including ours, to provide the entire resources of his firm to the prosecutor if the prosecutor would give him grand jury subpoena power and the ability to call witnesses before the grand jury.

Ed asked about the other lawyers we had talked to, and it was clear he, too, respected them, but he had a special respect for Peter Fleming. I later learned that right after I left the Williams & Connolly office, Ed called Peter Fleming to tell him he wanted him to represent the firm of Drexel Burnham. Ed often commented that it was important for Drexel to remain in the case as long as possible, though he believed someday they would make a deal with the government. Ed liked to say that he had more scars in his belly than he did in his back from people who'd disappointed him in serious litigation matters. Still, he felt it was important to keep Drexel as part of the defense as long as possible. I knew that Drexel wanted Peter to represent them, though Peter was interested in representing one of the principal individuals being investigated. It was a sign of the respect Ed commanded that one call from him convinced Peter Fleming of whom he needed to represent. I was prepared to recommend that Edward Bennett Williams and possibly Arthur Liman together represent Michael, though Ed had already begun working.

I returned home to report to Michael and Lowell on our meetings and to recommend whom I thought they should meet.

Mike and I flew late Saturday night to Washington, DC, to meet with Edward Bennett Williams on Sunday morning and then to New York to meet with Arthur Liman on Sunday afternoon. At the end of the trip, we had Mike's legal team in place. Mike knew Arthur, and not surprisingly, he instantly connected with Ed. Mike made it very clear to both Ed and Arthur that Boesky was unimportant to his business. It was true that he had done business with Boesky, as had many others, and that Boesky was very demanding. He was relentless. Mike also made it clear he had no personal relationship with Boesky.

Mike was concerned and wanted both Ed Williams and Arthur Liman to understand two things: (1) Mike did not believe he had ever done anything that justified a criminal investigation, and (2) he would like to find a way to make it all go away in as nonconfrontational a manner as possible. Mike made it clear to both lawyers that he had started with nothing and had built the business and his net worth from scratch; if he had to start over again, he was willing to do that. It was clear that now, ten days from the serving of subpoenas and the beginning of the investigation, he sensed this was serious and was going to continue for some time. I understood the point he was making. Mike did not like confrontation and was risk averse. He knew there was far greater risk in being the target of a criminal investigation, a process he was not familiar with, than rebuilding the business that he'd created and knew better than anyone. He understood credit and the financial markets and had confidence he could build or rebuild wealth through investing if he needed to do so.

It became clear to me over the ensuing months, as I learned more about how the process worked, that had Michael stopped doing business with Ivan Boesky when he first became "demanding," or never engaged in any recordkeeping, or never demanded that Boesky pay Drexel the $5.3 million fee, the investigation would not have proceeded as it did. Both Ed and Arthur made it clear to me that they believed Michael and did not believe he deserved to be criminally prosecuted, but it was still a complicated and serious matter, and the US Attorney had all the power.

Even though we now had our legal team in place, Mike would receive calls from friends who wanted to be supportive and had recommendations for lawyers. I would speak to these individuals. The most interesting comment made to me was that if a lawyer with the stature of Edward Bennett Williams was going to lead the team, people would assume Mike must be guilty of something. I found this fascinating. I was only beginning to understand the gravity of this matter and the pressures we would be subjected to, but I knew we needed the best lawyers possible. It did not matter what anyone else thought; it only mattered what the result would be. There was no question then, and there is no question now, that in Edward Bennett Williams and Arthur Liman we had the best team possible. We also had a team that believed in Michael's innocence and a team Michael believed in.

Arthur designated his partner Martin Flumenbaum to run the case day to day, and Marty designated two young associates, Eric Goldstein and Brad Karp, to work with him. My role was to both manage the legal team and be a direct liaison to Michael. Arthur, Ed, and I agreed that Paul, Weiss would take the lead in gathering documents and complying with subpoenas and that the two firms would work together to do a lot of the research and manage the defense process. It was also clear that Edward Bennett Williams was lead counsel, especially when it came to dealing with prosecutors.

> I was only beginning to understand the gravity of this matter and the pressures we would be subjected to, but I knew we needed the best lawyers possible.

When Martin Flumenbaum came to California to begin the task of complying with both the SEC and the grand jury subpoenas, I told him I felt the subpoenas were too broad. They asked for information that I believed should remain confidential. Marty turned to me as if he was instructing a child and said, "Richard, do you understand the power of the United

States Attorney's Office? If they wanted to, they could back trucks up to your building tomorrow morning and take every file cabinet and piece of paper, and there's nothing you could do about it." And so I began my education in the immense power of the prosecutors.

When this case started, I looked at the prosecutors and SEC investigators as evil and trying to ruin our lives. John Carroll became the lead prosecutor. After this case was over, John Carroll became the head of the fraud unit in the US Attorney's Office for the Southern District. After leaving the US Attorney's Office, he became a defense counsel at the firms of Clifford Chance and Skadden, Arps, Slate, Meagher & Flom. I got to know John during this process and realized that this person I thought I disliked was a bright and ambitious young lawyer trained to do what he was doing. He had also prosecuted drug cases before this where the people he prosecuted did not have the education or the resources of Dennis Levine and Ivan Boesky. John Carroll did not know Michael Milken but was trained to believe Michael was no different and that what he was told by cooperating witnesses was true.

John and I have stayed in contact over the years. I taught a class at Stanford Law School relating to the Milken case in 2012 and again in 2020, and John was a guest lecturer both times. He said the following at those classes:

> I spent my life doing white-collar criminal defense. There have been very few cases as celebrated as this one [i.e., the Michael Milken case]. I started as a prosecutor in 1983. I went to NYU Law School, clerked for a couple of years after that, and went from a clerkship to becoming a pros- ecutor. I worked six months in the private sector before becoming a prosecutor. I had never done any criminal defense work when I was in the private sector. Within

the office, I spent a year in what was called "general crimes." I spent two or three years doing narcotics cases and then organized crime narcotics cases. I came to this case basically as a narcotics prosecutor. I moved over to the securities fraud unit in the beginning of 1987 and was asked to take on this case shortly thereafter. I had taken one securities regulation class.

Very complex cases are assigned to people who have very limited background in the subject matter of those cases. I came to the case with no substantial securities background, no great understanding of markets, probably never heard of what a high yield bond was, had never heard of Boesky before he was arrested, and had never heard of Michael Milken.

Mike was a focus of the investigation from the day when Ivan Boesky talked about transactions and the $5.3 million fee. At that point, Mike became a focus of the investigation—one of several, but in a real sense the top of the mountain.

If you think of the currency with which prosecutors get paid ... I mean, you don't get paid in terms of a lot of money. You get paid in terms of whether you're working on a case that is drawing attention.

Boesky came in, said, "I did bad things with this other person. Here are the bad things I did. I can tell you about it and could corroborate what I'm saying with the document and this payment and you could talk to these witnesses." And so, and with a key witness who was horribly flawed, Boesky set us on a trail and gave us quite a story. ... From the time Boesky said,

"I committed these crimes with this fella, Milken," the Government had an expectation, an investigative interest, in all of those people—wanting to make cases if those cases could be made. We had a credible witness who certainly was not anywhere near proof beyond a reasonable doubt, who gave us a case to investigate. As it turned out, it was a big deal case. I mean, I had a substantial personal investment in making the case. On day one I'm 31 years old. I know I don't know shit about the securities fraud market. I'm learning on the go.

Clearly, unlike the directive of the Berger case, the Assistant US Attorneys in the Southern District of New York were trained to make cases and win cases, especially those that got notoriety. They were not trained to see that justice is done. John Carroll goes on to say the following:

After a certain amount of time, I thought we had a case that could be made. Now, was it venal in the way Boesky's conduct was venal? No. Did that fact get lost? Yeah. Did someone within the Government talk to the press, early and often? You bet. I don't know who talked to the press early and often, but somebody did, and that's horribly unfair. And does it sort of taint the Government? Yeah. When I read that there's this case that's going to be made against Drexel and Mike Milken, my ability to pull back from that is limited. … We got into this sort of three-year contest where every day we went to respective trenches, and over that time we probably gained ground that we needed, an inch at a time. I'm not sure there was another way to do it.

When young lawyers who are trying to make a name for themselves are given this kind of power and are convinced their job is to bring a case, you have a dangerous situation where the target of the investigation has very little chance of being successful, even if the target has the resources of Michael Milken, which most targets do not. If the defense makes mistakes, the defendant suffers; if the prosecutor makes mistakes, usually the defendant suffers. John Carroll explains further:

> No one should have any illusions about the criminal law. The criminal law is violent. It's just an exercise in power. And the soldiers of the criminal law trenches are people who are young people who don't have children, who haven't done much else in their lives, who haven't thought at all about what it is to take a person away from their children, from two years or seven years of their family's growth. Once you have had that life experience, it leads you to understand that the world is made up of shades of gray more than it's made up of black and white. ... There are a lot of excesses in law enforcement that come from that singlemindedness from 28-year-olds who have only worked in law enforcement and only have that perspective that they're avenging angels.

Yet on November 14, 1986, this case was about Ivan Boesky and his relationship with Michael Milken. That relationship was never what Boesky said it was, but Boesky had an incentive to make as good a deal for himself as possible. The government decided to let Boesky plead to one regulatory violation. They arranged for him to be sentenced in front of the most lenient judge in the district so that he got a three-year sentence, of which he would only serve two years.

And possibly most surprising of all, once he agreed to plead and cooperate, the SEC allowed him to unwind his securities positions before his plea was announced.

That is correct. When Boesky came in and made a deal with the government, he was running an investment business engaged in daily transactions in the securities markets. If it were public knowledge that Boesky had violated the securities laws, it would have affected the decision-making of those institutions that otherwise transacted business with the Boesky organization. Nevertheless, the government allowed Boesky to liquidate his positions without disclosing his violations. It is arguable that the SEC was in effect conspiring with the Boesky organization to trade on insider information.

Nowhere was this idea of the criminal justice system being a violent exercise of raw power that can destroy lives better demonstrated than in the government's commitment to investigate and indict Lowell Milken. John Carroll told me a couple of times that, in retrospect, indicting Lowell was a mistake. Professor David Mills, with whom I cotaught the class at Stanford, asked Mr. Carroll whether bringing Lowell into the case with the lack of evidence the prosecutors had at the time made it look more like a pressure tactic to force Michael Milken to settle. Mr. Carroll's comment was "One hundred percent correct." When asked if it was extortion, he said, "Others might describe it as leverage, but look—you know, thirty-five years later, what decisions do I wish I hadn't made?" I believe the person really responsible for bringing this case under the RICO statute and including Lowell as a target was Rudolph Giuliani. The subpoena issued under RICO on November 14, 1986, predated John Carroll's entry into the case.

Edward Bennett Williams had colorfully described his view of Rudy Giuliani's political ambitions. When the subpoenas arrived on

November 14, 1986, there were both grand jury subpoenas issued through the US Attorney's Office for the Southern District of New York and SEC subpoenas issued by the Securities and Exchange Commission out of its DC office.

The head of enforcement at the SEC at the time was Gary Lynch. I spoke to Mr. Lynch in 2019, and he confirmed that these cases began with the Dennis Levine case. He indicated that the investigation of the securities cases that resulted in the investigation of Ivan Boesky and the Michael Milken cases, at least up to the time of the Milken/Drexel investigation, originated with the SEC. The SEC presented the Levine case and then the Boesky case to the US Attorney for the Southern District of New York. Mr. Lynch said Mr. Giuliani had very little interest in these cases until the Boesky plea. The day after the plea was announced, the articles about the plea made front-page headlines in the major newspapers in New York and across the nation. Mr. Giuliani had obtained a conviction in an unrelated, well-publicized New York political corruption case on the same day, which was reported as a secondary story to the Boesky plea.

Giuliani's use of raw power to gain publicity manifested itself in early 1987 when Richard Wigton, a vice president at Kidder Peabody & Co.; Timothy L. Tabor, a former Kidder Peabody arbitrageur; and Robert M. Freeman, the head of the Goldman Sachs & Co. Risk Arbitrage Department, were physically and publicly arrested and taken into custody. Tabor was arrested at his home the evening of February 11, 1987, and spent the evening in jail before being released on bond. Freeman and Wigton were each arrested the next day in their offices in front of their colleagues and employees and taken away in handcuffs and in tears.

This action by Giuliani humiliated these three individuals and damaged their reputations, but none of them were ever tried. Gary

Lynch informed me that he received a call early on the morning of February 11, 1987, from Charles Carberry, who was the lead prosecutor on these cases before he left the office early in 1987 and turned the matter over to John Carroll. Mr. Carberry informed Mr. Lynch that Giuliani had ordered the arrest of Tabor, apparently based on information from Ivan Boesky, since Giuliani believed that Tabor would "fold" under the pressure and plead. He was never tried nor did he ever plead to anything. Mr. Carberry also informed Mr. Lynch they were going to proceed with the arrests of Freeman and Wigton, again believing that they would plead. Mr. Lynch was surprised that these arrests were made. Each of the three individuals claimed their innocence and were released on bond. All three were indicted several months later, and all pleaded not guilty. The Southern District never pursued the cases against Wigton and Tabor and dropped all charges, and Freeman pleaded guilty two and a half years later to one count of mail fraud. Freeman ended up serving four months in a federal prison camp and was suspended by the SEC for three years. He never acknowledged serious wrongdoing nor agreed to cooperate with the prosecutors to make cases.

The only direct contact our legal team had with Mr. Giuliani was a couple of years into the investigation, after Ed Williams passed away. After two years of intensive media scrutiny and investigation that saw the government make deals and grant immunity to numerous individuals, Michael wanted to explore the possibility of ending the investigation. Michael Milken hated confrontation and always tried to minimize risk, and this investigation involved both to the highest degree.

A meeting was arranged between prosecutors John Carroll, Jess Fardella, and Rudy Giuliani on the one hand and Arthur Liman and Marty Flumenbaum, representing Michael, on the other. I was not at the meeting, since Arthur and Marty advised me not to be too visible with the prosecutors because of my closeness to Michael. They advised that it was both in my personal interest and Mike's interest for me to stay behind the scenes. The meeting was clearly a "nonstarter." I was waiting outside the US Attorney's Office in a car with Bob Litt, and both Arthur and Marty looked disgusted and angry when they came out less than an hour after the meeting started. Mr. Giuliani had made it clear the only way he would entertain an agreement with Michael Milken would be if he could deliver a number of other high-profile individuals and help make criminal cases against them. Mr. Giuliani expressly stated that if Michael wanted Lowell out of the case, he would have to make even more cases. Michael was not in a position to make cases against anyone. This meeting confirmed that Lowell was in the case to bring pressure on Michael.

We were stuck in an intense and highly publicized investigation. Almost all the lawyers representing the various Drexel parties entered into a joint defense agreement, allowing them to share information while maintaining the attorney-client privilege. This at least allowed us to discover the direction of the investigation from the various lawyers who had either met with the prosecutors or the SEC or who had clients deposed or who appeared before the grand jury.

Bill McLucas became the head of the enforcement division at the SEC during this investigation. He had replaced Gary Lynch and taken over the oversight of the Milken/Drexel case in 1989. Mr. McLucas was also a guest lecturer at the Stanford Law School class David Mills and I taught in 2020. Here are some of his comments on the case thirty years later:

> Dennis Levine, whose case brought all this into the fore, was an investment banker who had gone down to a bank in the Bahamas, set up a secret bank account, and

was taking payment in connection with insider trading through his Bahamian bank account, which eventually got unmasked by the Government. The intrigue around investigating Wall Street and going after insider trading was something that was a big deal.

When you're on the Government's side and you're a lawyer and you're doing these investigations, your objective is: Did people break the rules, and what are the consequences? I won't say you don't look at the facts. The way you look at them … you look at them to bring a case, and you can be aggressive. And the Government, generally speaking, was probably more aggressive in my view because Drexel and Milken were not as bad as they were perceived to be. They weren't the threats to western civilization and the markets, which if you were reading the newspapers at the time and you were watching the process at the time, you would have thought they were from this process. … People today suggested Michael Milken was guilty of insider trading, and it's just not true.

You don't get rewarded for never bringing a case.

So now I look at the process, the power, and the degree to which somebody who is a prosecutor has over the life of a person. This idea that the system is fair and can be vindicated is only true to a degree. The fact is, your life is ruined the day you are charged.

I will tell you as your hair gets gray, the world is not black and white. Believe me, the degree of it which involves shades of gray gets larger and larger with every year.

> But the thing you need to learn the day you take
> an oath as a prosecutor or as a Government lawyer, or
> anyone with the kind of power you have when you're
> with the Government, is that your job is not to bring
> cases. It's to do the right thing. ... That discipline does
> not get emphasized enough and brought home enough
> to people who are at an early stage in their careers and
> end up being prosecutors.

Mr. McLucas confirmed that there was very little chance the government was not going to bring a case against Drexel and Michael Milken once the Boesky settlement was announced and subpoenas were issued. "Every year the chairman would say to me, 'How many cases this year?' And every year I would say, 'Why does it matter?' And he'd say, 'Because we have to beat last year.'"

The system can fail. Having money and/or fame is no protection. In fact, prosecutors gain notoriety when they use their power to bring down high-profile targets. The comments from the prosecutor, John Carroll, who was in charge of the case, and Bill McLucas, the head of the enforcement at the SEC at the time, reflect what I experienced over thirty years ago. Once the Boesky deal was made, the power of the government was directed at Michael Milken, and justice became a secondary idea, if it was considered at all.

Attorney General of the United States Robert H. Jackson stated it well at a conference of US Attorneys back in 1940 when he talked about the federal prosecutor as follows:

> The Prosecutor has more control over life, liberty, and
> reputation than any person in America. His discretion
> is tremendous. He can have citizens investigated, and
> if he is that kind of person, he could have this done to

the tune of public statements and veiled and unveiled intimidations. The Prosecutor can order arrests, present cases to the Grand Jury in secret session, and on the basis of his one-sided presentation of the facts, can cause a citizen to be indicted and held for trial. If he obtains a conviction, the Prosecutor can still make recommendations as to sentence. While the Prosecutor at his best is one of the most beneficent forces in our society, when he acts from malice or other base motives he is one of the worst.

Your positions are of such independence and importance that while you are being diligent, strict, and vigorous in law enforcement, you can also afford to be just. Although the Government technically loses its case, it has really won if justice has been done.

If the Prosecutor is obliged to choose his cases, it follows that he can choose his defendants. Therein is the most dangerous power of the Prosecutor— that he will pick people that he thinks he should get rather than pick cases that need to be prosecuted. With the law books filled with a great assortment of crimes, a Prosecutor stands a fair chance of finding at least a technical violation of some act on the part of almost anyone.

A sensitiveness to fair play and sportsmanship is perhaps the best protection against the abuse of power. And the citizen's safety lies in the Prosecutor who tempers zeal with human kindness, who seeks truths and not victims, who serves the law and not factional purposes, and who approaches his task with humility.

The comments by the US Supreme Court in *Berger v. United States* in 1935, by Attorney General Robert Jackson in 1940, by John Carroll in 2012 and 2020, and Bill McLucas in 2020, together with my experience from 1986 to 1998 support the thesis that the federal prosecutor has raw and significant power that can easily be used unfairly in a way to affect the outcome of a prosecution. The next several chapters look at how the power manifested itself in this case, what charges were finally brought, and what Michael Milken really did.

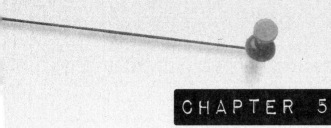

CHAPTER 5

Use of Government Power

In the summer of 1983, a couple of months after I left the practice of law to form a consulting group to oversee investments made by members of the Drexel Burnham Lambert High Yield and Convertible Bond Department, my family and I were invited to a family picnic for the members of the department and their families. It was held at a park, and we played softball; there were horseback rides, food stations, and a number of other activities for children of all ages. Everyone was given a T-shirt with his or her name on it. There was no distinction between anyone—whether salesman, trader, assistant, or support staff. Everyone was welcome and treated exactly the same. Michael and Lori Milken interacted with everyone. When Michael spoke, he emphasized that he considered everyone there part of a large family: "No matter what we accomplish individually or as a group, we can never forget who we are and where we come from." Lori and Michael have never forgotten who they are. Over these many decades I have known them, they have not changed either in how they view themselves or how they treat others.

It was such a peaceful time back in 1983, and it lasted until November 1986 when the investigation began. Two employees present that day would be forever changed by the investigation: Lisa Jones, a young trading assistant in the Drexel Burnham Lambert High Yield and Convertible Bond Department, and her boss, Bruce Newberg, a young trader in the department. Both Lisa Jones and Bruce Newberg were decent, hardworking employees at Drexel who were in the wrong place at the wrong time when they were indicted. They both became victims of the investigation, as they were treated by the government like objects to send a strong message to Drexel and its employees. The same was true of the investment firm of Princeton/Newport Partners, a client of Drexel Burnham that Lisa and Bruce interacted with.

The Racketeer Influenced and Corrupt Organizations statute— commonly known as RICO—was passed in 1970 as part of the Organized Crime Control Act of 1970. If at least two predicate acts take place within a ten-year period that can be indicative of a pattern of racketeering activity, the act is triggered. And if a person or entity is found to have engaged in racketeering activity, they are subject to imprisonment and forfeiture of any and all proceeds, directly or indirectly, resulting from such activity. The act was intended as a broad and effective tool to be used by the government against organized crime syndicates.

Drexel and Princeton/Newport were in the business of buying, selling, and trading securities. If as part of that operation they were found to have been involved in transactions that could be securities fraud, mail fraud, or wire fraud twice in ten years, they could be alleged to have committed predicate acts under RICO. Since two of those acts in a ten-year period could suggest a pattern that would result in a RICO enterprise, the statute could also be used to prosecute any business or its owners or employees far removed from organized crime. Predicate acts under RICO also include activities regularly associated with organized crime, such as murder, arson, and extortion. Mail fraud and wire fraud as predicate acts give prosecutors more tools to claim a RICO violation, and under RICO, the government is able to obtain a pretrial restraining order against the business before ever calling its first witness. Such a restraining order can be devastating to a financial firm, which depends on credibility with creditors, clients, and investors.

This threat of a RICO restraining order was of great concern to the management of Drexel Burnham from the beginning of the investigation, especially after this weapon was used against Princeton/Newport. Princeton/Newport's principals were indicted for alleged violations of tax and securities laws as well as violations of the RICO statute. Those individuals chose to claim their innocence and stand trial rather than settle with the government.

The Princeton/Newport case provided the government with the perfect vehicle to show its power and strength and put fear into the management and employees of Drexel Burnham as well as test its theories and methods in prosecuting a securities firm under RICO. Princeton/Newport traded securities using sophisticated mathematical analysis. It was a highly respected organization that provided outstanding rates of return for its investors over a twenty-year period. Princeton/Newport's clients included major universities among a blue-chip client list. It was a fraction of the size of Drexel Burnham.

Princeton/Newport was founded by Jay Regan and Ed Thorp. Ed Thorp had written a book, *Beat the Dealer*, which provided a mathematical system to give blackjack players an edge over casinos in blackjack. This book caused the casinos in Las Vegas to change the way they dealt cards at blackjack tables. They started using multiple decks to make it more difficult for players to count cards. Ed Thorp had also been using his mathematical expertise to develop arbitrage techniques in the stock market. When Jay Regan approached Ed Thorp about using mathematical models to determine securities that were mispriced in relationship to one another, Princeton/Newport Partners was born. (Jay Regan went to school at Princeton, and Ed Thorp lived in Newport Beach, California.)

In order to maximize after-tax returns, Princeton/Newport wanted to avoid having long-term losses. The goal was to have long-term gains (since the tax rates are more favorable for long-term gains than they are for short-term gains) and to have short-term losses to offset short-term gains. When a loss position held by Princeton/Newport was about to go long term, Princeton/Newport would sell that position to firms such as Drexel Burnham before it went long term and then later buy the security back.

A trader who worked for Princeton/Newport learned that a large investor was legally accumulating shares in a company called Storer Broadcasting in order to facilitate a takeover bid. This trader secretly went out and bought an option in Storer Broadcasting for his own account, violating the insider trading laws. The government was investigating trading activity in Storer Broadcasting stock and subpoenaed this Princeton/Newport trader. The government told this trader that if there was anything he could tell them about the Princeton/Newport firm that would help the government prosecute Princeton/Newport, they would immunize him from prosecution. Otherwise he could be prosecuted. He therefore told the prosecutors there were these "crazy tax trades" going on at Princeton/Newport, some of which were with Drexel Burnham. When he mentioned Drexel Burnham, the prosecutors gave him immunity.

What this trader described as "crazy tax trades" constituted the essence of the business of Princeton/Newport. Princeton/Newport had never had a losing quarter in twenty years and had legal advice that these trades were legitimate.

When the government learned Princeton/Newport was doing these trades with Drexel Burnham, it concluded there must be tax fraud, if not securities fraud, involved. The government was extremely interested in finding illegal activity by Drexel away from Ivan Boesky. In addition, one of Jay Regan's closest friends was Robert Freeman, who was one of the individuals Rudy Giuliani had arrested in his office and taken out in handcuffs but had not yet indicted. Since the US Attorney's Office in the Southern District of New York had been publicly criticized for arresting Robert Freeman, Jay Regan became even more important.

The US Attorney's theory was that Princeton/Newport was merely parking securities with Drexel, that all the transactions must be pre-arranged, and that therefore there was no market risk and there was fraud. The prosecutors issued a search warrant and had postal inspectors show up, unannounced and wearing flak jackets, to Princeton/Newport's offices to conduct a search. In the course of that search, they came across a couple of audio tapes of phone calls. Princeton/Newport taped its phone conversations when it did trades in case issues came up at a later date. After a period of time they would destroy or erase the tapes, but there was a tape in a desk drawer that nobody remembered.

The tape was of a conversation between a trader at Princeton/Newport named Charles Zarzecki and Bruce Newberg, a trader at Drexel Burnham. Drexel was underwriting a convertible security for a company known as COMB. Since a convertible bond can be converted by the holder into the stock of the company, the company would normally pay a lower interest rate on a convertible bond than it would have to pay if it issued a straight bond. The holder of the convertible bond has two ways to profit: (1) hold the bond and be paid interest and principal, or (2) convert the bond into stock at the conversion price and sell the stock, provided the stock price exceeds the conversion price. The conversion price is determined as a premium over the closing price of the common stock of the company on the day the convertible bond is priced and sold to investors. From the company's standpoint, it would like to see the stock price as high as possible, since that would mean that a holder of the convertible security would have to convert at the higher price. From the investor's point of view, they would like to see the stock price as low as possible, since that would mean there would be greater value to the convertible bond if the stock price increases.

In this particular case, COMB stock started increasing in price for no particular reason shortly before the date the new issue was going to be priced. Drexel was suspicious about this unusual activity in the stock that caused the price to go up. The tape found in the desk drawer at Princeton/Newport was a recording of a conversation between Bruce Newberg, a trader of convertible securities at Drexel, and his friend at Princeton/Newport, Charles Zarzecki. Bruce asked Charles to test the market by selling stock in the market. Zarzecki reported back that he sold shares in the market and that doing so had no effect on the price. Mr. Newberg told him not to do anything further and said to Zarzecki something to the effect of "Welcome to the world of being a sleaze."

The financial services business is like any other; people who work together and do business together share information and do each other favors as long as it does not violate any law. Mr. Newberg and Mr. Zarzecki were friends and did business frequently. They were engaging in what they thought was a private conversation and referring to whomever was causing the stock to go up in price as a "sleaze." Though it might have been banter between these two friends, it was on tape and became extremely valuable to the government in its investigation of Princeton/Newport and of Drexel.

The government decided to indict the principals of Princeton/Newport rather than the company itself, including Messrs. Zarzecki and Regan as well as Bruce Newberg. There was this tape of a transaction where a trader at Drexel Burnham asked a trader at Princeton/Newport to do a favor and then talked about "sleaze." There were tax trades the government decided were suspicious. The head of the firm, Jay Regan, had a personal relationship with Bob Freeman, and an employee of Drexel who worked for Michael Milken was on this tape. In the words of Ted Wells, the attorney who represented Jay Regan, "Giuliani was hell-bent on trying to make a case, and he saw Milken as the big prize and Bob Freeman as the second big prize." And the US Attorney's Office made a decision that Jay Regan perhaps could give them both Milken and Freeman and was using its power to bring pressure on Jay Regan and Bruce Newberg to provide testimony against Bob Freeman and/or Michael Milken.

During the investigation, the head of the fraud unit in Giuliani's office, a prosecutor named Bruce Baird, stated to one of the Princeton/Newport lawyers that if the Princeton/Newport defendants did not cooperate, the prosecutors would "destroy" them: "We're going to roll over you to get to Drexel." Ted Wells told me that Baird later denied making such a comment, but the lawyer who Baird made the comment to told Ted Wells that that was exactly what Baird said. From that point forward, the Princeton/Newport lawyers believed they were basically pawns in a much bigger game. In the words of attorney Ted Wells,

> They [the prosecutors] tell us in all candor, they're going to destroy us unless Jay becomes a government witness and says something about Freeman or something about Milken, and they tell us that they're going to bring a case as a RICO case. Though tax violations are not predicates to RICO cases, mail fraud and wire fraud are. Since the tax trades were done over the phone, and since

tax returns are sent through the mail, the government had a hook to bring this as a RICO case, though up to this time there had never been a RICO case against a financial institution. (Comment made to class at Stanford Law School on May 21, 2012.)

Jay Regan was asked by the prosecutors to come in to their office on a Saturday to listen to the tapes in hopes that would convince him to "cooperate." Jay went to the prosecutor's office with his lawyers wearing a hat emblazoned with the slogan "Shit Happens." That gives you some indication of how Jay felt about this. After listening to the tape, Jay still did not believe he had done anything wrong and decided he was not cooperating and would go to trial.

According to Mr. Wells, referring to the tape,

It was that line ("Welcome to the world of being a sleaze") that resulted in the convictions across the board—not just the securities fraud but also the tax claim.

Before a RICO indictment can be filed, the defense has an opportunity to make a case to the Department of Justice in Washington, DC, as to why it should not be a RICO case. As luck would have it, there was actually no attorney general available to review Princeton/Newport's presentation. The attorney general, Edwin Meese, was being investigated by the US Attorney in New York, Rudolph Giuliani, in an unrelated matter. Therefore, there was now an unusual situation where the lawyers for persons being investigated by Mr. Giuliani were trying to make a case to the Justice Department as to why the US Attorney for the Southern District of New York should not be allowed to bring a RICO case, and that same US Attorney was targeting the Justice Department. As a result, it was difficult for the people in the RICO section at the Department of Justice to do anything against Giuliani's wishes.

The Princeton/Newport indictment included securities fraud counts relating to the COMB transaction that was discussed on the tape. That made the tape part of the evidence to be introduced at trial. The remaining charges alleged tax fraud, which were also being charged as mail and wire fraud. Therefore, the government charged the defendants with operating an entity with a pattern of racketeering activity, making it a RICO enterprise and violating the RICO statute separate and apart from claims of tax fraud.

By using the RICO statute, the government was able to seek the pretrial restraining order seeking to restrain all the assets of Princeton/Newport, which is exactly what it did here. Princeton/Newport held over a billion dollars of assets, and the government was trying to pressure Jay Regan. The government was able to obtain a pretrial order against the assets of Princeton/Newport. This freeze put tremendous pressure on Jay Regan to try to save his business.

Not surprisingly, the pretrial restraining order caused concern among the creditors and investors of Princeton/Newport. The nature of Princeton/Newport's arbitrage business resulted in very large lines of credit with numerous financial institutions. These financial institutions became concerned about continuing to do business with Princeton/Newport. No Wall Street entity had ever before been charged with RICO. What was now happening with Princeton/Newport certainly was noticed by Drexel Burnham management.

The investors in Princeton/Newport asked their lawyers whether they would be able to get their money back. There was no case law on this. Though most of the restraining order was not to be publicly distributed in order to avoid any misunderstanding by creditors, the entire restraining order got leaked to the media, and creditors threatened to pull their line of credit.

Princeton/Newport decided to appeal the restraining order to the Second Circuit Court of Appeals to try to calm its creditors and investors. The Second Circuit determined that if defendants were convicted at trial, all that was forfeitable was the defendants' interests in Princeton/Newport and not the investors' money. As a result, the defendants could post a bond equal to the value of their interest in Princeton/Newport (approximately $20 million) and avoid the pretrial restraining order. That would have been a fair result, but now the government said it was going to bring a superseding indictment in October 1988 with new charges that might require an additional bond, which again concerned creditors and investors.

The Princeton/Newport investors had a right to withdraw their money at year-end as long as they gave notice that they were exercising this right by October 31, 1988. When no superseding indictment came in October, Princeton/Newport was able to push back the withdrawal date to December 5. At this point, still with no superseding indictment, the limited partners had run out of patience, and Jay Regan made the decision to shut down the business and distribute the money to the investors of Princeton/Newport. Finally, in mid-December, a superseding indictment was filed that contained nothing new from the original indictment. The trial had not started. No evidence had been presented. And Princeton/Newport, which denied any wrongdoing, was out of business. The government had used its powers to create enough uncertainty to put

> **The government had used its powers to create enough uncertainty to put a respected financial institution out of business.**

a respected financial institution out of business. Drexel management was very concerned about Drexel's future as it watched the RICO indictment unfold.

The Princeton/Newport trial began in June 1989. At the trial, the "world of being a sleaze" tape was played numerous times. The only defendant who agreed to testify was Jay Regan. The decision as to whether a defendant testifies at his or her trial is one of the most important decisions that defense counsel and a defendant make in a criminal trial. Normally, the government has to prove its case "beyond a reasonable doubt" to convict a defendant. If the defendant testifies effectively, that standard really no longer applies. Once a defendant testifies, most juries will acquit or convict based upon that defendant's testimony and if they believe him or her. Since the prosecution is going to bring on numerous witnesses and also have a chance to cross-examine the defendant and attack the defendant's credibility, the defendant is at great risk by testifying.

Nevertheless, in this case, Jay Regan started the business, developed the business, and truly believed that the tax trades were legitimate, the "world of being a sleaze" tape represented everyday banter between traders, and the business was legitimate. I was present in court for Jay's testimony, and he was an excellent witness. I so admired his willingness to take the risk of testifying as well as the way he responded to cross-examination as he explained his business and why he believed he was innocent of the charges. Unfortunately, as Jay Regan attorney Ted Wells had indicated, he could not overcome the tape. At the end of the trial in August, the jury returned a verdict of guilty against Zarzecki and Newberg on the COMB transaction and against all the defendants on the tax trades and RICO charges.

The trial then proceeded to what is known as the "penalty phase" to determine how much money the defendants would have to forfeit.

In this case, the government argued the forfeiture should be $20 million—the amount of the bond the defendants had posted. Yet the same jury that had convicted the defendants under RICO determined the amount forfeited to be $3 million. The court then scheduled sentencing of the defendants for November 1989. In the interim, the Justice Department announced a policy that RICO is not to be used in a prosecution for tax fraud or tax violations. The trial judge, Judge Robert Carter, became aware of this policy before sentencing and sentenced Jay Regan, the lead defendant, to six months in prison and the other defendants to three months. Judge Carter said Jay Regan received three months for giving "false testimony." That is why it is so risky for a defendant to testify. The testimony was only deemed false since the jury found defendants guilty, and Jay was, in effect, punished for defending himself and testifying.

Judge Carter also ruled that under the circumstances of this new Justice Department policy, a forfeiture would violate the Eighth Amendment of the Constitution as cruel and unusual punishment and reduced the forfeiture on the tax charges to zero. Using the draconian RICO statute against an established financial firm for activities that had never before been considered a violation of criminal law destroyed the firm but resulted in minimal sentences and no forfeiture. The defendants appealed the verdict to the Second Circuit, and none of the defendants began serving their sentences pending the appeal. The Second Circuit reversed the convictions and sent the case back for a new trial.

By the time of the Princeton/Newport verdict, Drexel, having seen Princeton/Newport go out of business before the trial started, entered into a settlement agreement with both the SEC and the US Attorney. The terms of the Drexel settlement included an agreement by Drexel to sever its relationship with Michael Milken and Lowell Milken and to cooperate with the government. Neither Michael nor Lowell agreed to settle, and the government proceeded in April 1989 with an indictment against Michael Milken and Lowell Milken, alleging violations of various securities statutes and the RICO statute. The indictment also charged Bruce Newberg a second time under RICO, even though at that time he had already been tried under his first RICO indictment for the exact same conduct. Now that Drexel had settled and Michael Milken had been indicted, the government decided the case was not worth pursuing any further and never proceeded with a new trial. The government had been effective in "rolling over and destroying" Princeton/Newport without retrying the case, and none of the defendants ever served a day in prison. The government also never pursued the second indictment of Bruce Newberg.

There was a second element to the Princeton/Newport story that also demonstrates the use of government power to achieve its objective of "getting" Michael Milken and sending a message to Drexel and its employees. Bruce Newberg's trading assistant, Lisa Jones, was also prosecuted by the US Attorney for the Southern District of New York. Lisa never knew her father and was brought up in an abusive home in New Jersey. She ran away from home when she was fourteen years old and came to California. In order to get a job, she lied about her age and went to work at a bank. She worked hard and had talent, and after a few years she learned there was an opening for an assistant at the Drexel Burnham office in Beverly Hills. She applied for the job, again misrepresenting her age as well as her schooling. Everyone she worked with seemed to have come from a stable family and had a normal education. Therefore, she made up a story suggesting she was not any different. She came to work at Drexel, worked hard, and was good at what she did. Lisa looked at Drexel as the family she'd never had and her boss, Bruce Newberg, as a father figure. Lisa, against all odds, became a productive member of the community.

One evening in December 1987, there was a knock at her door. Government investigators served her with a grand jury subpoena and also asked her numerous questions about her work at Drexel, Bruce Newberg, and Princeton/Newport. She contacted Drexel's attorneys. They began to represent her as they had several other employees. She appeared before the grand jury in January 1988 and, with the advice of counsel, invoked her Fifth Amendment right against self-incrimination. The prosecutors have a powerful tool to compel testimony of someone who otherwise can refuse to answer questions by asserting their Fifth Amendment right: they grant that person immunity from prosecution, which they did with Lisa Jones. That meant she could not be prosecuted as a result of anything she disclosed in her testimony. She could still be prosecuted for perjury if the prosecutors felt she was not being truthful. Arguably, at this time Drexel's lawyers should have recommended that Lisa retain her own counsel. They continued to represent her.

So Lisa gave testimony. The prosecutor told Drexel's lawyers that he thought she was lying, since her testimony was inconsistent with a tape recording the government had from its search of Princeton/Newport, and she could be prosecuted for perjury. The prosecutor would not allow Drexel's lawyers to hear the tape recordings. She then retained separate counsel, and once she heard the tape, Lisa indicated the tapes refreshed her recollection and she was willing to provide testimony based upon her refreshed recollection. That was not enough for Assistant US Attorney Mark Hanson, who was also the lead prosecutor in the Princeton/Newport case. Lisa Jones was indicted for giving false testimony.

The investigation was something none of us were prepared for, and Lisa Jones, like so many others, was totally unprepared, frightened, and vulnerable. It was clear to me at the time that Lisa Jones was indicted by the US Attorney for the Southern District of New York to send a message to Drexel Burnham and its employees. Mark Hanson went after Lisa with a vengeance at her trial. He brought up her entire history, including the fact that she had previously lied about her age to get a job. Lisa was convicted and sentenced to eighteen months in prison.

After her conviction, Lisa retained another separate counsel, Dan Bookin, to appeal her sentence. Lisa Jones contended that the district court erred in allowing her to be cross-examined about making false statements when applying for a job. The Federal Rules of Evidence prohibit evidence being used of prior statements to prove someone acted in conformity with the character of untruthfulness.

> Lisa Jones was indicted to send a message to Drexel Burnham and its employees.

She also contended that Drexel's counsel had a conflict of interest in representing her and as a result she did not have adequate representation before the grand jury.

After trial and her appeal, the court of appeals decided her trial attorney did not have a conflict of interest, and the questioning about her past history was permitted. The Second Circuit did find, however, that whatever evidence Lisa Jones was able to provide was not any different from substantial evidence the government already had on the subject matter. Therefore, the court vacated the sentence as being too long and sent the case back to the trial court for resentencing.

Upon resentencing, the judge reduced Lisa's sentence from eighteen months to ten months, which meant that she would serve five months in prison and five months in a "halfway house" near her home.

Lisa's counsel, Daniel Bookin, allowed her to do a television segment with Connie Chung, a reporter, while the case was still on appeal. Mr. Hanson, the prosecutor, also appeared on the show. When he was confronted by Ms. Chung with the accusation that it appeared he was looking for blood, his response was as follows:

> The fact of the matter is that sometimes in a search for justice blood gets spilled and that's an unfortunate fact of life.

This is quite an unusual comment, as at this point in time the prosecutors were not searching for justice since they already had all the information Lisa Jones could provide to them. They were interested in sending a message to Drexel and its employees. The day Lisa Jones was indicted, a shiver went through the entire Drexel Burnham organization; every employee received the message that they were at risk, and Drexel Burnham's management received the message that every employee was at risk.

Mr. Hanson was removed from the case for appearing on this television segment. Dan Bookin describes Mr. Hanson: "He's a brilliant lawyer, very effective in the courtroom, but he was a zealot, and he was out to get Lisa Jones."

It did not matter that Lisa was distraught and frightened when she was on the witness stand. Not one of the Princeton/Newport defendants served a day in prison. Marty Siegel, the Drexel mergers and acquisition executive who dealt illegally in inside information with Ivan Boesky, received a two-month sentence. Lisa Jones received ten months and served her sentence.

The government went after Lisa Jones with a vengeance, and "blood was spilled." Was this really a "search for justice"? Princeton/ Newport was out of business, and the convictions of its principals were overturned. The government decided it was not worth retrying the case. Bruce Newberg was indicted twice, though the government never pursued the second indictment against him. Lisa Jones did serve a prison sentence. Drexel settled with the government. So now the government could focus on Michael Milken and the indictments against Michael and his brother, Lowell.

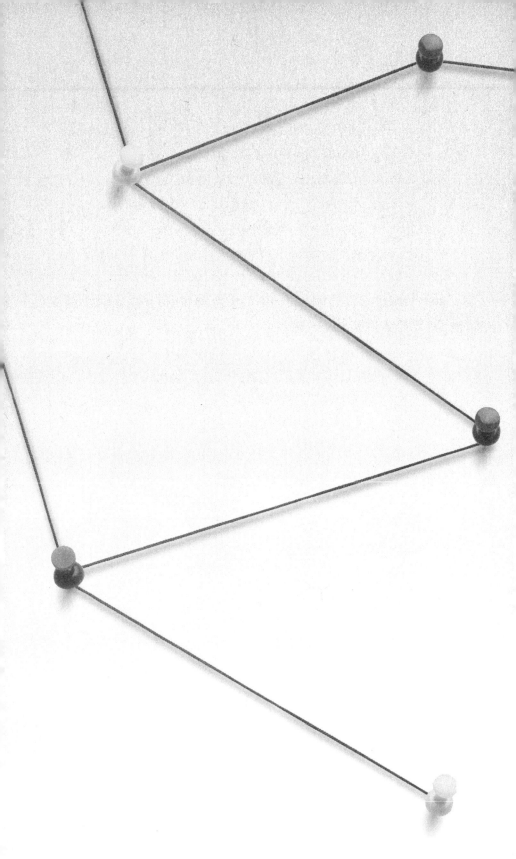

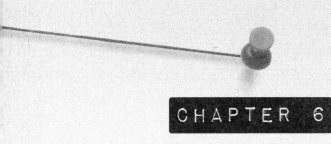

CHAPTER 6

The Loss of Edward Bennett Williams

Michael believed in Edward Bennett Williams and his ability to help Mike navigate those very troubled times. Ed and Mike connected immediately. Ed exuded confidence and sincerity. It was clear he liked Mike and also believed in him. Only a week after Michael and I had first gone to Washington, DC, to meet with Ed, we were meeting in our office in Los Angeles on Thanksgiving morning. The phone rang, and it was Ed Williams. He just wanted to say hello and wish Mike a happy Thanksgiving. He stated he knew how difficult these situations were, especially on a holiday, and he wanted us to know he was thinking about us. Ed saw in Mike a kindred spirit who believed in excellence in everything he did and respected his fellow man regardless of background or station in life. And Mike saw in Ed a kindred spirit devoted to his client and who had the talent to be successful no matter what obstacles were in front of him.

Ed told Michael exactly what he thought on every topic. Michael was not an easy client. As Arthur Liman stated in his memoirs,

> Milken was as difficult a client as I have ever represented. He hovered over us all like a hawk, questioning us constantly, exploring this, then that scenario,

> making up his mind only to change it. It was like having
> a good lawyer for a client. A perfectionist in his own
> business, he tried to be one in ours. (Arthur Liman and
> Peter Israel, *Lawyer: A Life of Counsel and Controversy,*
> PublicAffairs, 1998)

Ed had a different way of stating it. He would tell Mike he has known people in his life who could not see the forest for the trees. "Mike," he would say, "at times you can't see the bark for the moss." Mike would smile, but as Arthur said, Mike was a perfectionist. He would also focus on a minute detail. I recall working with the legal team on a document for the court and sending Mike a draft. When I had not heard from Mike, I called him to see if he had any comments; the document would include numerous exhibits, and we had to put everything in a binder to deliver to the court the next morning. Mike told me he would call me back. A half hour later, he called back and told me that the document was "all wrong." When I asked him to be more specific, it turned out he had a problem with less than 10 percent of this lengthy document, but that 10 percent made it difficult for Mike to see the balance of the document.

Then there was the time Ed told Mike he was acting like he was his own surgeon getting ready to remove his own appendix, in which case he would seriously injure himself. Having a client who is such a perfectionist and who wants to be involved in such minute details is never easy, especially when the client does not understand or cannot accept the process he is in. When that client's world is tumbling down around him, it only exacerbates the situation.

Mike had a habit of taking everything he wanted to read home with him each night or on trips with him when he traveled, no matter how voluminous. These materials filled multiple canvas bags. Once when we were meeting with Ed, Mike was organizing the papers in four or five of these bags. At one point Ed turned to him and said, "Mike, are you listening to anything I'm saying?"

Mike responded, "Ed, I'm listening to everything you're saying" and then repeated almost verbatim what Ed had said.

Ed replied, "Mike, I believe you're listening to me, but I'd feel better if you looked at me when I spoke. Also, I noticed that you bring those bags with you every time we meet. You take all the papers out of the bags and put them in different piles, and then you take the piles and put them back in the bags. I have a suspicion that you don't look at those bags again until the next time we get together, when you go through the same routine all over again." I started laughing, since this was an accurate analysis.

One morning in the first few months of 1987, I received a call from Ed, who asked if I could call him back with Mike. Mike came to my office, and we called Ed. Ed told us that he had not been feeling well and apparently had a blockage from a prior treatment he'd had for cancer that needed to be removed surgically. He anticipated a short recovery and would be back on the case within weeks.

A couple of weeks earlier, Mike and I received a call from Arthur Liman, who told us he had been asked to become the chief counsel to the Senate Select Committee investigating the Iran-Contra matter revolving around President Ronald Reagan's alleged approval of the sale of arms to Iran in exchange for release of American hostages in Lebanon. Later, the Justice Department found evidence that proceeds from the armed sales had been diverted illegally to fund the contra anticommunist guerillas in Nicaragua. The question then became the following: What did President Reagan know, and when did he know it? Though it was never proven that President Reagan knew anything about the covert actions, the Senate led an investigation, and they tapped Arthur Liman as the chief counsel to oversee this investigation into Iran-Contra.

So here we were in the early months of the investigation with one of our lawyers taking a "several week" (which became several months) hiatus to lead the Senate investigation and our other lawyer going into surgery. After our call with Ed, Mike turned to me, shook his head, and said, "Our lawyers are dropping like flies," and he was not being humorous. Mike believed 100 percent in Edward Bennett Williams.

Ed did recover and invited Mike and me to lunch at his home in Maryland. He told us he was ready to go back to work at full strength. Unfortunately, Ed was never 100 percent after that. He did a masterful job representing Mike in an appearance before Congressman John Dingell's Subcommittee on Oversight and Investigations in the US House of Representatives the following year, but Ed's health was deteriorating. On Saturday morning, August 13, 1988, I was working in my office in Beverly Hills. I received a call from Ed's partner, Vince Fuller, to tell me Edward Bennett Williams had died. I called Michael with the sad news and then tried to process it myself. I went outside to get fresh air. I was so sad. I felt I'd lost a dear friend. Michael and I attended the wake and the funeral. It was no wonder we both cried for this man we did not know twenty-one months before. We had lost a friend who was a giant in his profession and a father figure. Mike and Lori believed Ed was uniquely special and would be able to counter all the lies and successfully defend Mike. I shared that belief.

My eighteenth wedding anniversary was August 16, 1988, but I was not home celebrating with my wife, Ellen. I was with Michael at the funeral of Edward Bennett Williams. As we sat together in church to say goodbye to our recent but dear and trusted friend, we listened to the wonderful eulogies, captured by these words from Reverend John E. Brooks, SJ, president of College of the Holy Cross, Ed's alma mater:

What initially attracted me to Ed, what constantly fed and nourished my friendship with him, what led me to an admiration and love of Ed that can best be described today as being limitless, were his relentless pursuit of excellence and his willingness to pay the price, to make the necessary sacrifices that would allow him to achieve his goals. … Edward Bennett Williams was indeed a giant of a man who did right, loved steadfastly, and walked humbly with his God.

We also had deep respect for Arthur Liman, who proceeded to do everything humanly possible to defend Mike. He was certainly as brilliant a lawyer as I have ever known, but there was only one Edward Bennett Williams. The country lost a great lawyer, and Mike and I lost the person we were relying upon.

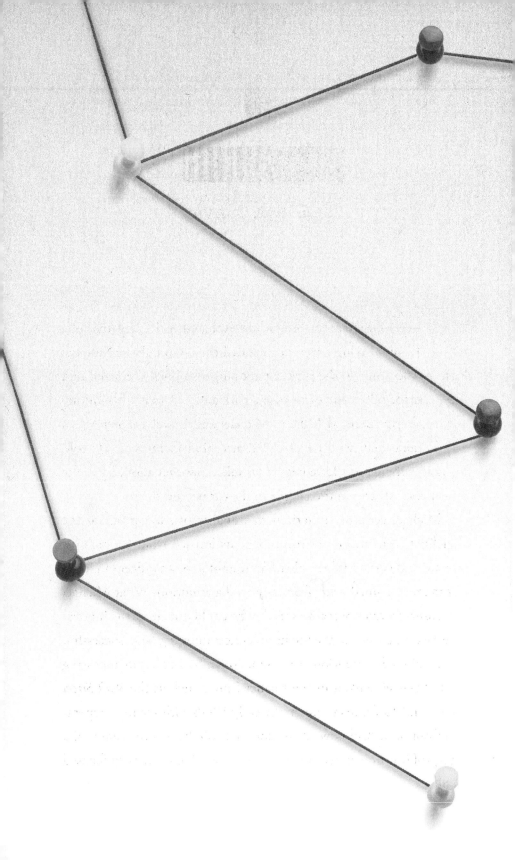

CHAPTER 7

The Blank Canvas

When we were growing up, Lowell shared with me details of a family driving trip that included the Grand Teton National Park. As they entered the park, a park ranger stopped them and said they were the billionth visitor to the park and had won a free dinner and a raft trip. Bernard Milken, Michael and Lowell's father, was a very humble man who never called attention to himself. He told the ranger there must have been a mistake, that they should give the dinner and raft trip to the people in the car behind them.

Michael certainly inherited this quality of staying out of the "limelight." He also never forgot lessons learned from his parents, Bernard and Ferne Milken. He never sought to be an officer of Drexel Burnham and shied away from any media attention. What Michael unfortunately did not realize was that he could not create the innovations he created within the financial services industry, be so successful, and avoid media attention at the same time. Stories began appearing about Michael Milken in the financial press such as the *Wall Street Journal* and *Forbes* magazine in the early 1980s without any cooperation from him. And now, at the end of 1986, he was the center of a high-profile criminal investigation with a spotlight intensely focused on him.

The investigation and prosecution of Michael Milken was about as high profile as possible at that time in the financial world. In the 1980s there was no internet, no social media, no 24-7 news cycle where the public could receive information from any number of outlets instantaneously. Newspapers, magazines, and television news were the most important sources of information and opinion, and they viewed Michael as reclusive and uncooperative.

Michael Milken was indicted in early 1989, but the investigation of him had been making headlines for more than two years prior to the indictment. As Bill McLucas stated at a class at Stanford Law School in 2020,

> Newspaper articles were pretty regular, and details came out that the only people that knew the details were SEC lawyers, people in the United States Attorney's Office, some FBI or postal agents, and the defense bar. So there was a lot of finger pointing about where the leaks came from, but you could pretty much calculate where they came from depending on which way the story went. My view is there were certainly leaks on the government side and I had the view when I was there and I have the view now, it's unforgivable. When you have people who leak information, it's a breach of every obligation you take on when you become a prosecutor or a government lawyer.

Or as John Carroll said, also at Stanford Law School,

> I don't know who talked to the press early and often, but somebody did, and that's horribly unfair.

Michael Milken was being depicted in the media as a criminal—and as a caricature of a person. But, Michael tried to avoid the media and did not cooperate with the media; he may have been well known throughout the financial and business communities, but the picture of who he really was was a blank canvas, and others who did not know him began to paint his portrait the way they wanted it to look.

At this time, I was thirty-eight years old and thought I was sophisticated. I soon realized how little I knew about governmental investigations, the power of the government, and how media paints portraits. I knew we received subpoenas, and I knew what the subpoenas were asking for. But I had no idea what the government knew or thought it knew or what it was looking for. I was aware that as a result of the Dennis Levine and now the Ivan Boesky pleas, the government was interested in insider trading. I had no idea why the government thought Michael Milken would be involved in insider trading.

In a criminal investigation, the government controls the process completely. The people under investigation have no right to get

> **Michael Milken was being depicted in the media as a criminal—and as a caricature of a person.**

any information until they are indicted. It was not until both the US Attorney's Office and the Securities and Exchange Commission started calling witnesses and taking depositions that our legal team became aware at least of the subject matters the government was looking at. Since other than insider trading the securities laws or regulations the government seemed to be investigating had never been the subject of criminal investigations before, even our experienced legal team acknowledged that they were trying to navigate through uncharted waters.

In addition, the media was writing about Michael Milken almost from the moment the investigation started, and the information they relied upon about who Michael Milken was did not come from Michael Milken. And the media kept writing through the time Michael Milken was sentenced in November of 1990, four years later. The prosecutors and the SEC investigators affected the media and they were affected by the media. They clearly spoke to the media. The blank canvas soon became a portrait that the government and the media wanted the public to see.

Michael Milken could not have been in a worse position. It was several months into the investigation when we finally decided to hire a media consultant to devote full attention to our case. We retained the firm of Robinson, Lake, Lerer & Montgomery. Kenneth Lerer was the partner in that firm who was devoted full time to our case. At Stanford Law School on April 30, 2012, he told me the following:

> I think part of the issue was that Michael Milken never gave interviews, never defined who he was. He was a mystery man with a blank canvas. The government and the media were able to paint whatever picture they wanted to paint.

As Michael became more and more of a force on Wall Street with no interest in giving interviews, he looked reclusive and was a mystery. The press did not know him and had no sympathy for him. As Kenneth Lerer explained,

> In almost every visible criminal or civil case, it is typical for one of the major media outlets to try to own the story. Once one of those outlets is able to start zeroing in on the story and getting sources from the government, they tend to double down on the story because if they are looked at as owning the story, they want to beat their competitors at every turn. So just as the *Washington*

Post owned the Watergate story when Richard Nixon was President, the *Wall Street Journal* came to own the Milken story primarily through its writer James Stewart, who had won a Pulitzer Prize for his reporting on the Dennis Levine case. His job would be to develop sources inside the SEC and the US Attorney's Office as well as an internal team of reporters working with him.

So there we were—with a client who was being vilified in the press and fighting for his life. The public perception of Michael Milken was being painted primarily by people who wanted to portray Michael in the worst possible way, and they painted a portrait quite different from the real person. Ken Lerer believes to this day that if Michael Milken had had a press strategy in place before the investigation ever started, he could have defined who he was and avoided indictment. Michael had no political base from which to defend himself. His competitors on Wall Street and powerful corporations concerned about Drexel's clients certainly were on the side of the government.

When I suggested to our legal team that we retain the Robinson, Lake, Lerer & Montgomery team to handle the intense media, Arthur Liman immediately understood and agreed. Ed Williams felt the only place we needed to focus on was the courtroom. He did not want to be distracted by a media strategy. His view was that he would go to court, try the case, and that's all that mattered. If we did not like what was being written in the press, we should just stop reading it. I remember Ed telling me once that as owner of the Baltimore Orioles, he would tell his players not to read about themselves in the press. As he put it, "When you read about yourself in the media, even if it is a good story, you will not like it. The subject of the article feels like everyone in the country is reading the article and focusing on the most negative parts of it." Arthur convinced Ed we should do something about the media.

I met in Ed's office in Washington, DC, in early 1987 with Ed, Linda Robinson, and Kenneth Lerer. Linda advocated for a press strategy where she was engaged every day in all decisions. Ed listened politely and then stated that a trial was like a prize fight. Every day was like a round of the fight. At the end of every round, you determine how you are doing on points and develop your strategy for the next round. Ed would be worrying about his trial strategy every day and did not want to be distracted. Therefore, he was willing to have Linda Robinson and Ken Lerer work on the case as long as they understood there was a bright line. On one side of the line was the press strategy. On the other side of the line was the legal strategy. As long as Ken and Linda stayed on their side of the line, they would get along great with Ed. Though Linda wanted to be more involved, both she and Ken Lerer understood and respected what Ed had said. It was great to have them both involved as Ken took the lead in representing us in media strategy. Ken was quite skilled in understanding personalities and how to work with everybody, and he turned out to be a great partner for me, as I interacted with Michael every time there was an article or media request.

Ken Lerer did not know who Michael Milken was when they first met. He quickly came to believe in our case and was totally committed to working with us. His firm was retained by the Paul, Weiss firm to maintain the attorney-client privilege. Unfortunately, by the time Ken was retained, there had been dozens of stories written about Michael Milken, and a portrait was already being painted. The canvas was no longer blank.

Our strategy was to contact and try to establish relationships with reporters who were covering the case on a day-to-day basis. To the extent we were successful doing that, we would have a chance to influence some stories. As Ken Lerer put it, his job was to put himself in the reporter's brain, figure out what they would write, and then figure out if we wanted to help shape the story. These decisions were made on a story-by-story basis. At the same time, the press could write whatever they wanted to write, especially when writing about a high-profile public figure. Michael was a high-profile target, and high-profile targets have little chance of avoiding indictment—or severe consequences if they go to trial and lose.

The challenge was that the *Wall Street Journal* owned the story and had the best sources in the government. Every time the *Wall Street Journal* would put out a story, other publications would call Ken Lerer for a comment and write a follow-up story. Ken tried to establish relationships with many of these writers. Michael even met with certain reporters for off-the-record conversations. These meetings had some effect, but we were still swimming against a tidal wave. A few stories were written about the respected companies that would not have existed if it were not for Michael Milken and about the work Michael did in the community as a philanthropist. These successes at least created some balance in the minds of some reporters and their readers about who Michael Milken really was and what he really did.

It was very difficult to witness the effect all this was having on Michael. Before Ivan Boesky made his deal with the government, Mike was somebody who created something very valuable and very special. Chief executive officers, entrepreneurs, and investors from all over the world wanted to come and talk to him about their companies and their ideas and get his thoughts on what they were doing and how they should be financed. He would spend his time trying to understand these companies in addition to managing a multibillion-dollar portfolio of high yield securities. If Drexel issued a high yield security, the High Yield Department would make a market in that security. If a company Michael/Drexel financed got in trouble, Mike would sit with management and try to figure out the best strategy to allow the company to continue to strive and get through the tough period it was experiencing. He felt an obligation to the company and to the holders of its bonds. He was working an incredible number of hours a day focused on his business.

All of a sudden, he needed to focus on himself. The government was trying to cut his knees out from under him. He was frustrated. He was scared. And he took each and every story personally. If he did not see the story, inevitably someone would tell him about it or send it to him. As Ken Lerer said, "The government used the press in this case as much as I've ever seen the government use the press for their benefit." Ken Lerer was a cofounder of the *Huffington Post* and had seen numerous situations where the government worked with the press.

The only time Michael was not consumed by the news stories was when he interacted with Ed Williams. Ed's passing changed all that.

There is an old adage: "You are never going to successfully chase lies with the truth." As Winston Churchill said, "A lie gets halfway around the world before the truth has a chance to get its pants on."

> As much as we tried to stay on top of every single story at every single moment and allow our strategy to shift as the circumstances required, the media battle was always an uphill one.

So, as much as we tried to stay on top of every single story at every single moment and allow our strategy to shift as the circumstances required, the media battle was always an uphill one. And there's no question the media affects the environment in which you are living. It affects your family; it affects your friends; it affects everyone. And it very much affects the person being written about.

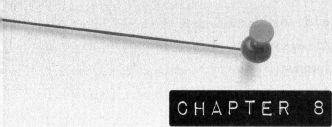

CHAPTER 8

Indictment and SEC Complaint

As if the pressures of the investigation were not enough, after one of my many weeks in New York, I was returning to Los Angeles with Michael and Lori. We were flying back together from Teterboro Airport. It was a cold, snowy evening. On the way to Teterboro, the windshield of the car kept fogging up, and Lori asked the driver if he could see. The driver indicated he could. As we drove closer to the airport on a very dark street, Lori yelled that she heard a whistle blow or a whistle sound. The driver stopped abruptly as a train sped by about ten feet in front of us. Lori and I looked at each other and commented that as difficult as this process was getting, being hit by a train was not the story we would want in the newspaper.

The first action by the government was a complaint filed by the SEC against Drexel Burnham Lambert Incorporated, Michael Milken, Lowell Milken, and others in September of 1988. The complaint was 184 pages long and was signed by fifteen separate attorneys at the SEC. The complaint alleged wrongdoing by Drexel and Michael Milken in fifteen separate transactions, thirteen involving Ivan Boesky or the Boesky organization, and the other two alleging insider trading by Drexel and Michael Milken. At that point, it was a Boesky case.

Joseph Grundfest, former commissioner at the Securities and Exchange Commission, who was a commissioner at this time, later told me that at the time the SEC staff made a presentation to the SEC commissioners to bring the Drexel/Milken case, Giuliani personally appeared before the SEC to encourage it to bring the case. Mr. Grundfest indicated that in all his years as a commissioner, he had never seen or heard of a situation where a US Attorney personally appeared before the SEC to advocate for its taking a particular action. No matter what Milken had done or not done, this case had taken on a life of its own.

Bill McLucas, former head of enforcement at the SEC, acknowledged that Boesky was a very unreliable witness and that the SEC was concerned about bringing an action that relied solely on Ivan Boesky. When addressing my Stanford class on February 24, 2020, McLucas also acknowledged that Michael Milken never traded on inside information. Michael denied each of the SEC's claims.

In March 1989, six months after the SEC complaint was filed and after almost two and a half years of rumors, innuendo, and leaks to the media defining Michael Milken and the evolving government charges, a ninety-eight-count indictment came down from the grand jury charging Michael Milken, Lowell Milken, and Bruce Newberg with offenses including violations of the RICO statute. Lead prosecutor John Carroll acknowledged some years later that he regretted including Lowell Milken and Bruce Newberg in this indictment—Lowell because he really had no direct involvement in the transactions being investigated, and Bruce since he was now being indicted a second time under RICO.

Nevertheless, the lives of Lowell and Bruce were forever changed.

As the government continued to attack on the two fronts, our legal team at Paul, Weiss and Williams & Connolly worked feverishly to review all dealings between Drexel or Michael Milken and Ivan

Boesky and all other matters we believed were being investigated by the SEC and the US Attorney.

Between the September 1988 SEC complaint and the March 1989 indictment, the most significant event affecting the Milken case was the settlement by Drexel Burnham Lambert. After being charged as a defendant in the SEC complaint, Drexel's leadership decided its relationship with its creditors and other financial institutions—and its survival—required it to settle with the SEC and the US Attorney. The Princeton/Newport trial was about to begin, and Princeton/Newport was out of business. Drexel was also concerned about its ten thousand employees. Lisa Jones had been indicted. So Drexel began negotiations with both the US Attorney's Office and the SEC about settlement. Peter Fleming, one of the lead lawyers for Drexel, kept me generally informed about the negotiations. I let him know it would be detrimental to Michael if Drexel settled. Of course, he knew that better than I did.

Peter called me one day and indicated he was trying to figure out a way for Drexel to settle without hurting Michael's case. He asked me if I thought Mike would be amenable to being moved off the trading floor but remaining employed by Drexel with his own office and a small portfolio to manage. I explained to Peter that Mike came to the office between four and five in the morning every day (Los Angeles time). He returned home close to six thirty to have dinner with his family. In addition, he often held meetings at the office very early on Saturday and/or Sunday mornings so the employees could get home in time to be with their families. He managed a portfolio of several billion dollars, and the heads of major corporations throughout the United States and around the world would come to see him about financing their companies. He did not have an office and worked on the trading floor.

When I finished this explanation, Peter said, "What you're telling me is that the trading floor is Michael's home and that if we moved him off the trading floor, we'd be asking him to leave home." I told Peter he understood exactly what I was saying. As it turned out, this conversation was only an exercise between Peter and me, since there was no way the government was going to allow Michael to have any role at Drexel as part of any settlement. Peter was a decent person, an outstanding lawyer, and a friend, and I appreciated the position he was in and his efforts.

On December 21, 1988, Drexel acknowledged it had reached a settlement with US Attorney Rudolph Giuliani, contingent upon making a separate agreement with the Securities and Exchange Commission by early 1989. Drexel did reach a settlement with the SEC in the first quarter of 1989. The settlements required Drexel to plead guilty to six felony counts of mail and securities fraud and pay $650 million: $300 million for criminal fines and penalties and $350 million to an SEC disgorgement fund. Drexel announced at the time it had over a billion dollars of unencumbered capital after the settlement and that it was in excellent financial condition.

As part of the SEC settlement, Drexel agreed to extensive remedial measures and managerial and structural changes. The settlement was to resolve all allegations of misconduct related to securities trading or transactions involving the High Yield and Convertible Bond Department for the period from January 1, 1978, through January 24, 1989. Drexel agreed to add three new directors to its board of directors, all to be approved by the SEC, including former SEC chairman John Shad, who was to become the new chairman of Drexel.

Drexel agreed to no longer employ Michael Milken and place any other employee who was indicted on a leave of absence. The settlement also provided that Drexel "could not be involved with

Michael Milken directly or indirectly in any business transactions or activities in the future." Clearly, the idea that Peter Fleming discussed with me would never happen. (At that time, Michael Milken had not been indicted, let alone convicted.) Clearly the principle of someone under investigation being presumed innocent until proven guilty was not recognized by the SEC, nor for that matter the US Attorney's Office for the Southern District of New York. Not only did Drexel have to fire Michael Milken before any determination of any wrongdoing, but no employee was allowed to even discuss business with Michael Milken without Drexel's being in violation of its settlement. I called this the "you are not allowed to talk to Mike" provision.

In late 1988, while Drexel's settlement discussions were going on, Fred Joseph, the chief executive officer of Drexel, asked to meet with Michael with lawyers present. Michael and I met at Fred's home in New York with Arthur Liman and Irv Schneiderman, the partner at the Cahill Gordon law firm who had been responsible for the Drexel account at Cahill for many years. We knew going into this meeting that Fred Joseph was looking for Michael's "blessing" to their settlement. I asked Michael not to give them any comfort about such a settlement. At the end of the meeting, Mike indicated the settlement was going to hurt him but that he understood Fred Joseph had to do it. Not confrontational.

With Drexel now settled, Michael and Lowell indicted, and the emotional toll of this now two-and-a-half-year investigation mounting, Michael again wanted to explore the option of ending this ordeal and reducing the risk. He really did not want to confront the prosecutors and witnesses in a courtroom for months. That would be a process he had never encountered or understood, and he would be facing a substantial risk that he had no control over.

Drexel's plea agreement stated that Drexel was not in a position to dispute the charges that its employees were engaged in criminal activities. Edward Bennett Williams had always said Drexel would settle sooner or later. But the longer it held out, the greater the chance "the horse might fly." I had asked Ed Williams early in the investigation what we could do to accelerate the process and force the government to take action. Ed's comment was "He who chases justice often catches it." This was Ed's way of telling me that since all the power is with the government, the defendant does not want to precipitate action before the defendant has all the knowledge available to mount an effective defense. As for that "horse," he told a story about a prisoner in medieval times sentenced to death at the guillotine who asked to speak to the king. When the king granted the prisoner an audience, the prisoner told the king that if he would commute the sentence for one year, the prisoner would teach the king's horse to fly, and if the king's horse did not fly, the king could make an example of the prisoner by subjecting him to torture. The king agreed, and the prisoner returned to his cell. A fellow cellmate asked the prisoner why he would subject himself to possible torture when the scheduled execution would be quick and painless. The prisoner's response was that three things could happen during this one-year period: (1) the king might die and another king might come in and commute the sentence, and (2) the prisoner himself might die from natural causes. When asked about the third possibility, the prisoner replied, "Who knows, that horse might fly." Up to that point we had not seen any flying horses, and it was a bet Michael wanted to avoid if reasonably possible.

The ninety-eight-count indictment against Michael Milken mirrored the SEC charges, though there were some SEC allegations not included in the indictment, and vice versa. The only significant difference between the SEC complaint and the indictment was that the indictment included the Princeton/Newport relationship. The indictment numbered 111 pages. The first count alleged a racketeering conspiracy and consumed the first eighty-four pages. It described Michael Milken's business as a racketeering enterprise and listed fifteen transactions the government alleged formed part of a conspiracy with Ivan Boesky or the Boesky organization, or with Princeton/Newport.

Count two of the indictment alleged participating in a racketeering enterprise. Counts three through fifty-seven alleged mail and wire fraud relating to every confirmation and every phone call made with respect to the fifteen transactions. Counts fifty-eight through ninety-eight were more allegations relating to the same fifteen transactions—fifteen transactions and ninety-eight counts.

Page 2 of the indictment listed Michael Milken's and Lowell Milken's compensation from 1983 to 1987. That compensation is never referred to again in the 111 pages. Michael made over $550 million in compensation in 1986. As Ed Williams warned, How could a jury believe someone who made that much money was not guilty of something? It did not matter that Mike's compensation was determined by a formula agreed to between Michael and Drexel in the early 1970s based upon the performance of the High Yield Department. So compensation was on page 2 of the indictment to make it easy for the media to highlight.

Based on the indictment and the SEC complaint, Boesky claimed he had certain agreements with Michael that violated the securities laws. These alleged "agreements" were all based on telephone conversations. Every call Michael had with Boesky or others relating to the fifteen transactions in the indictment or otherwise could have been overheard by fifteen or twenty other people in the High Yield Department, since Michael conducted business from the center of the trading floor. He did not have a separate office and took all his calls at his desk.

The Boesky allegations all related to the payment of that $5.3 million fee by the Boesky organization to Drexel on March 21, 1986. The government's theory was that the settling up of all the illegal transactions between Michael and Boesky was paying a $5.3 million fee. Charles Thurnher put a handwritten memo in the file on March 21, 1986, that said,

> Ivan Boesky 3/21/86
>
> Corporate Finance NY $1,800,000
>
> Equity Research NY $2,000,000
>
> High Yield Department Research $1,500,000
>
> As per MM.

Michael Milken was recommending this fee be split up among the various departments of Drexel that had done work for Boesky over the years. And it was not a payment to Michael Milken or just his department but to Drexel Burnham.

Just as Oppenheim, Appel, Dixon & Co. had requested Lowell to sign a letter, they requested Ivan Boesky to sign the following:

> There was an oral understanding between yourself, on behalf of the Ivan F. Boesky Corporation, and Drexel Burnham Lambert Incorporated that Drexel Burnham Lambert Incorporated would provide consulting services. There were no formal records maintained for the time devoted to such consulting services. There were no prior agreements as to the specific value of such consulting services to be performed. There was no prior determination of the specific value for such consulting services until March 21, 1986, which amounted to

> $5,300,000 due to Drexel Burnham Lambert Incorpo-
> rated. Such amount was mutually agreed upon.
> If you agree with the above, kindly sign
> where indicated.

The document was signed after the statement, "I have examined the above and found it to be correct." It is signed by an attorney-in-fact for Ivan F. Boesky.

John Carroll suggested to me in 1990 and confirmed again in 2020 that had Lowell Milken never signed this letter, he probably would never have been indicted. I say "probably" because I believe Rudy Giuliani would have still wanted Lowell in the case to put pressure on Michael. Such a de minimis fee in the scheme of the Drexel and High Yield and Convertible Bond Department business ended up being such an important matter in the government's investigation and eventual indictment. On March 21, 1986, Michael Milken was a brilliant thirty-nine-year-old financier who had changed the way small and medium-size companies were financed. He had tremendous confidence in his ideas and his ability to deal with people. He was naive about a lot of things, including how many people despised him and his business and how this relatively insignificant fee with this individual would have such an important effect on his life.

The indictment refers to the evidence of the so-called Boesky arrangement by stating that in early 1984, Michael Milken and Boesky commenced a "secret arrangement" involving a series of unlawful securities transactions whereby the Boesky organization agreed to participate in various illegal transactions in which it bought and sold securities at the direction and for the benefit of Drexel and defendants without disclosing the true ownership of the securities as required by law. It further alleges that the Drexel enterprise bore the risk of all or part of the losses incurred and that defendants caused Drexel to pay the Boesky organization interest on funds used in buying and holding securities.

The indictment states that Drexel raised $800 million for the Boesky organization in March 1986 and did not disclose its arrangement with Boesky to the purchasers of the securities issued by the Boesky organization. And as proof of this arrangement, the indictment states the parties kept a running tally of the trades and periodically met to reconcile profits and losses and that Drexel received a direct payment of $5.3 million from the Boesky organization to balance the unlawful account. No matter how unimportant this "running tally" may have been to Michael Milken, it formed the basis of this whole investigation and changed his life.

Though Michael and Lowell were indicted under RICO with a focus on the Boesky relationship, the government investigation also focused on other relationships and on members of the High Yield Department who could help the prosecutors understand those relationships. Each employee of Drexel, whether a member of the High Yield and Convertible Bond Department or another department, was being subjected to extreme pressures. Every person questioned felt the pressure of being part of the criminal investigation. As various individuals received immunity from the government, there was a realization that if you could find a way to make a deal with the prosecutors, you could lessen the pressure. The possibility of going to prison and losing all your money put enormous pressure on many of these employees.

With everyone from Ivan Boesky to Marty Siegel to Boyd Jefferies to Drexel employees making deals with the government, it was natural that Mike wanted to explore the possibility of reducing his personal risk. When Michael and I had that conversation with Ed Williams late in 1987, Ed was very clear. Unless Mike could provide evidence that would allow the government to bring criminal cases against a number of his high-profile clients, this was not the time to enter into those types of discussions. Ed said that if Mike was willing to set up his clients like bowling pins and knock them down like a bowling ball, Ed could make a very attractive deal with Rudy Giuliani. Since Mike could not and would not provide such evidence, we did not pursue the discussion at that time.

Over a year later, Mike and I were meeting late one evening. He once again commented to me that everybody was making a deal except him. It was clear the pressures and stories were affecting him. My highly optimistic, nonconfrontational friend was showing the effects of the strain. I reminded Mike of Ed's comment about the bowling pins and how he would have to "give up" others. His voice cracked with emotion as he looked at me with tears in his eyes and whispered, "So instead, I am giving up my brother." Mike was so emotional, so frustrated, and so agitated. Yet he continued to persevere and hide all that from the world.

After Ed passed away in August 1988, the lead lawyer for our case at the Williams & Connolly firm was Vincent Fuller. Vince was also an accomplished criminal defense lawyer and had been associated with Ed Williams for many years. Vince had been the lawyer for John Hinckley, who had attempted to assassinate President Ronald Reagan in 1981 and was found not guilty by reason of insanity. Though Mike liked Vince very much and felt he was a very accomplished lawyer, he was not Edward Bennett Williams. After Ed's death, Arthur Liman clearly became the lead counsel for our defense and was the person Mike knew best and relied on most.

Vince Fuller could see the effect the case and all the publicity were having on Mike. After the indictment, he thought we should again explore the possibility of reaching a settlement with the government. Giuliani had left the US Attorney's Office to pursue his political career. Arthur Liman encouraged Vince Fuller to explore a settlement with the prosecutors away from Arthur while Arthur was aggressively preparing the defense.

Lowell and Michael appeared in court on April 7, 1989, to plead not guilty to the charges. I can only imagine how difficult that day was for them, since I know how difficult it was for me. First, they both had to be processed as individuals indicted for committing crimes. I could never have imagined either of them ever doing anything that could result in this moment. There I was, sitting in court and realizing that the US government was charging these two individuals whom I had known almost my entire life with committing crimes I knew made no sense. I had come to understand the process and why Michael was a target because of his success and notoriety. I could not believe that my childhood friend, Lowell Milken, who avoided notoriety like the plague, who had no interest in doing business with Ivan Boesky, and who would never come close to violating any rule, let alone the law, was being charged by the US government.

> **The case was now in the hands of a recently appointed judge presiding over her first high-profile criminal case. In addition, she was married to a *Time* magazine editor.**

It was also my first exposure to Judge Kimba Wood. Judge Wood gave the impression she was in command of the courtroom. She asked both Michael and Lowell a number of questions about their health, how they felt, whether they were taking medication or seeing a doctor. Since I was new to this process, I assumed those were the kinds of questions that were asked before a plea was taken. I later learned from our attorneys that Judge Wood was reading from the incorrect pages on a manual. The questions she was asking were questions you ask someone about to plead guilty to make sure they are fully aware of what they are doing. The case was now in the hands of a recently appointed judge presiding over her first high-profile criminal case. In addition, she was married to a *Time* magazine editor, raising an additional concern that she would be someone sensitive to the media in the most media-attention-getting case in the courthouse.

The following is from the transcript of the hearing:

> Are you Michael R. Milken? Are these your attorneys standing next to you? How old are you? What is your educational background? Are you currently or have you recently been under the care of a physician or a psychiatrist? Have you ever been hospitalized or treated for narcotics addiction? How do you feel today physically? Have you received a copy of the indictment naming you which is indictment S89CR.41? Have you had time to consult with your attorneys? Do you waive a formal reading of the indictment? Mr. Milken, how do you plead to the charges contained in the indictment?

Mike answered each question as expected, including the fact that he was not under the care of a physician, had never been hospitalized or treated for a narcotics addiction, and that he felt "Okay, Your Honor." As to the last question, he clearly stated, "Not guilty."

The judge then asked similar questions of Lowell Milken, who answered similarly, including to the final question: "I plead not guilty."

The court asked if the parties had agreed upon an appropriate bail. John Carroll replied,

Your Honor, over the course of the past week, the Government has been meeting with counsel and talking to counsel for all the defendants and attempting to work out both the bail issues and the forfeiture issues. I would tell the Court that we have made substantial progress with regard to both. What I would propose to the Court is that the Court calendar us for next Tuesday or perhaps next Wednesday. At that time, I expect we will be able to present to the Court consented to Orders with regard to both bail and the forfeiture issues.

The government consented to Michael and Lowell being released ROR (released on own recognizance).

The court directed further questions to both Michael and Lowell:

Do you understand that if you violate any condition of release, a warrant for your arrest may be issued and you may be jailed until your trial and you may be prosecuted for contempt of court? Do you also understand that it is a crime to try to influence a juror or to threaten or attempt to bribe a witness or other person who may have information about the case, or to retaliate against anyone for providing information about the case, or to otherwise obstruct the administration of justice?

Clearly Michael Milken and Lowell Milken were now within the criminal process, and though released on their own recognizance, they were no longer free citizens.

We were back in court a week later, on April 14, 1989, to finalize the agreements regarding forfeiture and bail. John Carroll had indicated that three separate agreements were reached with each of the three indicted individuals. Michael Milken had agreed to set aside assets, set up a cash account in liquid assets, and sign a note secured by illiquid assets. The illiquid assets were his interest in certain investment partnership interests. Finally, he had agreed to provide as additional security: his interest in Drexel, which if redeemed would also be paid into the cash account. Mr. Carroll represented to the court that he believed that the security Mr. Milken was putting up was sufficient.

Mr. Liman stated,

> I would just like to point out to Your Honor that the defendants are not only contesting the indictment, that they very specifically and expressly contest the Government's theories of forfeiture, and we have reserved our rights on that, and the agreements are without prejudice.

The court then signed the order, and then the discussion turned to bail.

Mr. Carroll indicated with regard to Michael Milken that the government proposed bail be set at the amount of $250 million in the form of a personal recognizance bond secured by Mr. Milken's residence and further secured by the monies that he was already setting aside in connection with the pretrial restraints on forfeiture. Mr. Carroll made it clear they were not asking for new money but would look to the monies that were being deposited as part of the forfeiture agreement.

Mr. Liman on behalf of Mr. Milken objected to such bail amount. He handed over Mr. Milken's passport and explained that Michael was not at risk to flee the jurisdiction. After argument, the court concluded,

> With respect to Mr. Michael Milken, I believe he has all of the roots in the community that anyone can have and

that he is an excellent candidate for bail. I find that the following conditions will reasonably assure the appearance of Mr. Michael Milken as required and will not endanger the safety of the community. I hereby release Mr. Michael Milken on the following conditions: That by April 17, 1989 he post a personal recognizance bond of one million dollars secured by one million dollars in real or personal property and that by April 21, 1989, he post his home as collateral.

I was always impressed with Arthur's ability to think on his feet. Nothing that was said or happened in court throughout the investigation ever escaped Arthur's attention or analysis as he protected Michael. As a result of Arthur's arguments, Judge Wood realized that the government's bail request was not reasonable.

We now knew exactly what the government was charging, and our legal team began preparing the defense in earnest. We reviewed every transaction referred to in the indictment and the SEC complaint. We had access to summaries of testimony that various witnesses had provided to both the SEC and the grand jury as well as Michael's own recollections and analysis of the transactions. We hired an economic consulting firm out of the University of Chicago, Lexecon, and worked closely with Andrew Rosenfield and Daniel Fischel, attorneys as well as principals of Lexecon, who believed that Michael was innocent of all charges. We were confident we could defend each and every transaction, though we knew at the same time the government was preparing its case and its witnesses to support its allegations. And we knew the risks were huge. The government had only upside—winning—and the defendants had all the downside. This fact, plus the constant press leaks and negative articles, kept weighing heavily on Michael. Nevertheless, Michael never wavered in his belief of his innocence of all the charges and never stopped strategizing with his lawyers on how to prove that innocence and reduce his risk.

It soon became clear that the government was not going to rely solely on Ivan Boesky. It started bringing pressure on a number of employees in the High Yield Bond Department, and these individuals were incentivized to try to make some kind of deal with the government. You had individuals who probably were making more money than they ever dreamed they would make and all of a sudden were faced with the possibility of losing their freedom and losing their income and lifestyle. And they could eliminate all that risk if they could be helpful to the government and receive immunity.

This ability to grant immunity is such a powerful tool. It can be used to get the testimony of a witness who could otherwise refuse to testify, even if the government does not know what the witness might say in advance. It is more often used after a witness's attorney gives the prosecutor a "proffer" of what the witness is prepared to say. In the latter situation, the witness is bargaining for the grant of immunity and protection from prosecution.

Lowell's attorney, Michael Armstrong, explained to me early in the process: in white-collar cases, there is no question the transactions took place. The question is, Were there any illegal arrangements or motives behind the transactions? And the securities regulations are vague and subject to different interpretations. In addition, in a white-collar case, a witness does not have to necessarily lie about everything. If 80 percent of what a witness is saying is accurate but he or she states that the purpose of a legitimate transaction is not legitimate, they can be an effective government witness lying only about a few things. And when you are talking about individuals who were involved in literally thousands of transactions and trades over several years, they may not even recollect what happened. That makes it very easy to rationalize telling the government what it wants to hear. I cannot emphasize enough that none of these individuals ever thought they would be put in this situation. In addition, some of these employees might have done things on their own that they might have wanted or needed protection from. When a witness is faced with a grant of immunity versus the possibility of being indicted, the ability to grant immunity is a powerful tool in the hands of prosecutors.

Over the ensuing months, several members of the High Yield Department and former members of the department made deals with the government. So, in addition to Charles Thurnher and Cary Maultasch, Jim Dahl, who was responsible for one of Drexel's largest clients, Columbia Savings & Loan Association, was granted immunity. Also, Terren Peizer, who came to Drexel from another firm where he was the contact for David Solomon of Solomon Asset Management, also a Drexel client, was granted immunity.

> Over the ensuing months, several members of the High Yield Department and former members of the department made deals with the government.

Then one day I received a phone call that Gary Winnick, a former member of the High Yield Department and family friend who had left to start his own investment company years earlier, and to my knowledge had no involvement in what the government was investigating, made a deal with the prosecution and was granted immunity. When Michael learned about this, he was stunned and told me that there was no telling how many witnesses there would be or what they would say. Every such witness made the defense of the charges more difficult.

Our team was prepared to attack the credibility of each government witness. Yet, as our lawyers explained, the prosecutors would respond at trial, "These witnesses are his friends" or "his colleagues" or "his employees and not ours."

As John Carroll stated to a class at Stanford Law School on April 16, 2012,

> Cooperators are seductive because they can help you. They are expert in what they are talking about and you are not, so they have an extraordinary informational advantage. The criminal justice system is basically an exercise in raw power. It is very much an uneven game where the Government has enormous power exercised by very young and very inexperienced people. You are developing a personal bond with your witness. Boesky is a rotten guy, but in the early stages of the case, prosecutors and the cooperators are bonding. The prosecutors' view of the defendant is being drawn by the cooperator, in this case by the press, forces outside the defendant himself. A defendant can't have that sort of interaction with a prosecutor.

Michael Milken was daily, if not hourly, assessing his situation and what the options before him were. Clearly, he was the major target of this intensive multiyear investigation. Our legal team and economic consultants were researching every allegation and theory. Their conclusion was that Michael had not committed any crimes and that every allegation could be defended. At the same time, many of the transactions being investigated were complex, and securities laws are often vague and also complex. We had seen what had happened in the Princeton/Newport case. So Michael was at extreme risk. And as

John Carroll said, Michael was being defined by cooperators, by the press, and by other forces outside his control. Whatever cooperating witnesses were telling the government, prosecutors wanted to believe the worst and clearly proceeded on that basis. That blank canvas was blank no more.

Michael had made it very clear to me that he would get no pleasure sitting in a courtroom day after day watching his lawyers present his case or pick apart government witnesses. Sitting in a courtroom at a defense table was something Michael Milken would find painful, even if he were acquitted. There was no "winning" to him.

> **Our legal team and economic consultants were researching every allegation and theory. Their conclusion was that Michael had not committed any crimes and that every allegation could be defended.**

We knew the charges. We knew the government was going to try to expand the charges through witnesses it was immunizing. We understood the power and advantages the prosecution had and how committed they were to winning this much-publicized case against a wealthy man who was being vilified in the press. We knew the risks were getting greater.

Vince Fuller and Bob Litt from the Williams & Connolly firm had been having meetings with the prosecutors. The prosecutors seemed interested in pursuing a settlement discussion. The indictment was mostly about Boesky and insider trading. Whatever Michael Milken was or was not, he was not an insider trader. The prosecutors still made it clear there was no settlement without Michael's making cases against others. They said we should think of the discussions as alphabet soup—the more letters Mike could provide to spell out names, the better deal he could make. No matter how nonconfrontational and risk adverse Michael was, he would neither admit to anything he did not do nor ruin other lives with such stories.

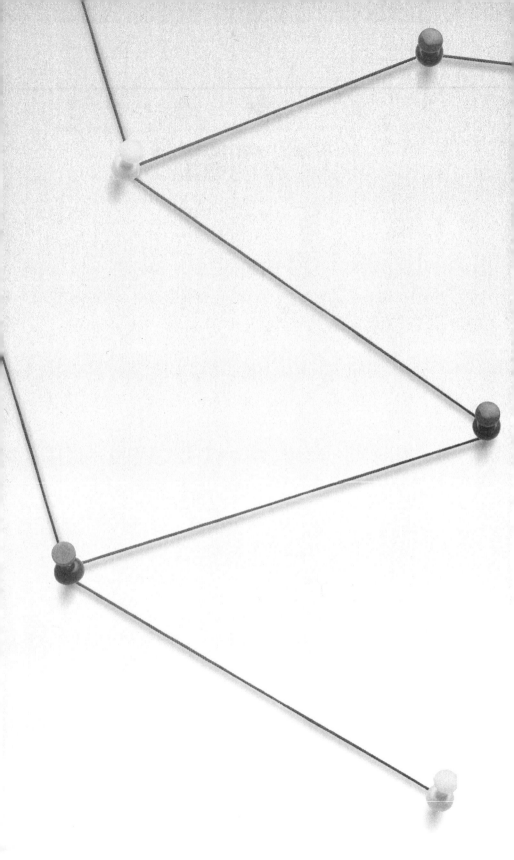

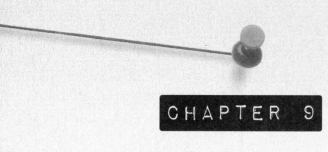

CHAPTER 9

The Plea Negotiations

For over three years we had all been removed from our normal routines. We were defending against a RICO prosecution the best we could. I was making almost weekly trips to New York or DC. Now Michael was out of the business he had built and that used to occupy over a hundred hours a week of his time. The toll it was taking on Michael and his family manifested in different ways.

On one trip, Michael and I were with our families in New York. One evening while we were working late, Ellen and Lori and our children were at a concert at Radio City Music Hall. At the end of the concert, Michael and Lori's eight-year-old daughter, Bari, collapsed in the lobby. Ellen and Lori immediately tended to Bari as someone called the paramedics. Fortunately, Bari did not have to go to the hospital, but it certainly was a frightening reminder to Lori and Michael, as well as the rest of us, of the effect this process was having on the entire family.

It was now clear the government was pursuing matters beyond the Boesky case. More witnesses were being questioned and even threatened with "target letters" saying they were likely to be indicted. And more witnesses were granted immunity in exchange for testimony. And Drexel was proceeding to do transactions without Michael's input for the first time in twenty years.

Though Drexel announced after its settlement that it had more than adequate capital to remain in business, it started using that capital to engage in transactions differently from the manner in which Michael Milken had invested the firm's capital. If Drexel had trouble completing a financing by finding buyers for securities being issued, it would buy the securities into its own inventory and borrow from the commercial paper market to do so. It was borrowing short term in the commercial paper market and lending long term by purchasing bonds with longer maturities, a very risky strategy. When Drexel's financial position deteriorated to the point where it was unable to borrow in the commercial paper market, it did not have the liquidity to pay its short-term debt. The CEO at Drexel, Fred Joseph, called the secretary of treasury, Nicholas Brady, for assistance. Mr. Brady had previously been the chairman of Dillon, Read & Co. and had been critical of Drexel Burnham and its role in takeovers. I do not know whether that had anything to do with the US Treasury Department's decision not to lend any assistance to save Drexel, but assistance was not forthcoming.

> More witnesses were being questioned and even threatened with "target letters" saying they were likely to be indicted. And more witnesses were granted immunity in exchange for testimony.

I received a call in January 1991 from Leon Black, who headed the Corporate Finance Department at Drexel. Leon explained to me the precarious situation Drexel was in. Leon was a friend and was supportive of Michael. He inquired as to whether Michael would be willing to lend money to Drexel to help prevent it from going bankrupt. I told Leon that based on the SEC settlement, there was no chance that the SEC would allow Drexel to enter into a transaction with Michael Milken. In any event, it was not something I could advise Michael to do.

One year after announcing it was well capitalized and agreeing not to consult with Michael Milken, Drexel filed for bankruptcy. Princeton/Newport and Drexel Burnham, two highly respected and successful firms, were now both out of business due to this investigation. Never again would a financial institution dare to defend itself from a government investigation. (An accounting firm, Arthur Andersen, was convicted of obstruction of justice related to its representation of Enron in 2002. Though the United States Supreme Court reversed the conviction of Arthur Andersen, by that time it, too, was effectively out of business.)

Over time, I would find myself participating with our lawyers in conversations with John Carroll and Jess Fardella regarding various processes and procedures in the case. This had two effects on me: (1) I came to see them more as people than villains—two talented young lawyers employed by the government who had been trained to use the power of the US Attorney to obtain convictions of individuals in cases assigned to them. They had no idea who Michael Milken was or what his business was. (2) It also became clear to me that they would welcome a reinstitution of settlement discussions. At this point they knew Michael Milken was not willing to make cases against others.

When the government indicted Bruce Newberg for a second time under RICO for arguably the exact same activity, it also sent a different message, whether intended or not. Bruce Newberg was charged twice for something that had never before been the subject of criminal prosecution. Still, the prosecutors indicted him a second time. The message it sent to me was that even if Mike Milken was successful in a trial before Judge Wood in the Southern District of New York, the US Department of Justice could, and most likely would, try to justify its highly publicized investigation by indicting Michael Milken again, whether in New York, California, Florida, or some other state where he had significant clients doing significant business. By this time I understood the power of the government and how the system could be made to work. And now the words of Aubrey Harwell, the lawyer who used to work in the Justice Department and now represented a Drexel employee, had new meaning: "If the government really wants to get you, it will get you."

So Arthur Liman, Steve Kaufman (a respected attorney who we had asked to join our legal team), Marty Flumenbaum, and I began discussions with John Carroll and Jess Fardella about a possible plea agreement. We began meeting in rooms in the courthouse rather than in the US Attorney's offices to avoid drawing attention to the meetings. There were no leaks to the press about those discussions.

> By this time I understood the power of the government and how the system could be made to work. ... "If the government really wants to get you, it will get you."

Carroll and Fardella made it very clear from that first meeting that just as Drexel had pleaded to six counts, Michael would need to plead to six counts. The number of counts was a requirement, since Michael had not cooperated and would not "make" cases. The six counts would include five transactions, and the sixth count would be for conspiracy to engage in five transactions. Boesky had to be involved in three of the counts. We understood these parameters for reaching a settlement. When the prosecutors said one of the five counts had to be insider trading, we responded that in that case there was no reason to continue the discussions. Michael Milken had never been involved in insider trading and would not plead to anything that even suggested he was involved in insider trading. Carroll and Fardella understood we were firm about insider trading, and we understood they were firm about six counts. We proceeded to try to figure out what five transactions Michael could admit to as being "wrong" that would satisfy the government. It was made clear that Michael did not need to acknowledge he knew he was committing a crime. He only needed to say he knew something was "wrong."

And there was another rather significant issue to be addressed: the indictment of Lowell Milken. As Lowell's lawyer, Michael Armstrong, would often say, "I do not believe Michael Milken did anything wrong, but Lowell Milken did not do anything." The prosecutors said they were willing to discuss the matter and suggested they enter into a deferred prosecution agreement with Lowell's attorneys in which they agreed they would put Lowell's case on hold for a year. Our lawyers suggested that once Mike had pleaded and a year had gone by, there would be little interest in prosecuting Lowell, especially with such a weak case. On the other hand, if Lowell was still under indictment while Michael was being interviewed by the government, the prosecutors could continue to use Lowell as leverage against Mike.

Lowell's position was very clear: Mike should do whatever he felt was in his best interest to do. Lowell had no trust whatsoever in the prosecutors. He knew he had done nothing wrong, and he was willing to defend his case. Lowell was emphatic that Mike's decision should not rest in any manner whatsoever on Lowell. I respected

Lowell's position but could never get comfortable with this idea of a deferred prosecution. Michael's legal team continued negotiations with the prosecutors.

After several meetings and intense conversations with Michael, our legal team was finally able to identify five transactions, three with Ivan Boesky and two with money manager David Solomon. Mike could say these were "wrong." He could not say he ever thought he was committing a crime when he agreed to these transactions, and he did not have to. None of these transactions involved the kind of venality alleged in the ninety-eight-count indictment nor had any such transactions ever before been the subject of a criminal prosecution.

We next negotiated the "allocution," which was the exact wording Mike would recite in court describing precisely what he had done in each transaction. I have negotiated hundreds of business transactions and settlements of disputes in my career. The negotiations with the prosecutors were the most intense and difficult negotiations I have ever participated in.

We also agreed with the prosecutors that the money Michael would pay would be $500 million—$200 million as the criminal fines and penalties and $300 million to be a disgorgement fund as part of the SEC civil settlement. The "disgorgement fund" was a fund controlled by the SEC that would be available to settle civil suits brought against Michael. We knew there would be civil suits, and Arthur Liman believed this amount would be more than enough to settle them—another valid belief based upon years of experience that proved incorrect. We had an understanding that the monies paid had nothing to do with amounts involved in the five transactions or the seriousness of the plea—Drexel paid $650 million to settle, and if there was to be a settlement, there was a financial price to pay. Alan Cohen, the head of the fraud unit at the time in the US Attorney's

Office for the Southern District of New York, said he would meet with the SEC attorneys and confirm the terms of our settlement with them. The SEC settlement should be much easier, since Mike could settle with the SEC without admitting or denying any of the allegations of their complaint. He did not have to acknowledge any wrongdoing to settle with the SEC.

The chairman of the SEC at the time was Richard Breeden, an outspoken critic of Michael and Drexel. Like Rudy Giuliani, Breeden seemed to enjoy publicity and was very public with his opinions. It seemed that with Mr. Giuliani now out of the picture, Mr. Breeden wanted the publicity from this case.

Usually in cases when the US Attorney and the SEC are both involved, the US Attorney controls the terms of a settlement, especially in such a high-profile case where everyone could declare victory on behalf of the government. Unfortunately, this was another situation where Mike would be the victim of circumstances beyond his control. Rudolph Giuliani had left the US Attorney's Office to pursue his political career. The US Attorney for the Southern District of New York was Otto Obermaier. Mr. Obermaier's old firm was representing certain key individuals in the government's investigation of Drexel Burnham and other financial institutions. Therefore, he recused himself from participating in any discussions having to do with any of these cases. He appointed Roger Hayes, a prosecutor in the office, to be the acting US Attorney for these purposes. In a criminal matter, it is the US Attorney who is supposed to represent the government. With an acting US Attorney, Commissioner Breedon saw an opportunity to play a more active role.

Assistant US Attorney Alan Cohen reported that Commissioner Breeden refused to accept the settlement as we had negotiated it. Breeden objected to a key provision: the total payment of $500 million. He felt Mike should pay exactly what Drexel paid; therefore, the SEC would go along with the settlement if the total payment was $650 million. Alan Cohen said that if Michael agreed to pay the additional $150 million, it could all become part of the disgorgement fund so that it could be used to settle civil cases.

The question of why someone who did not feel they had done anything that justified the investigation would pay this kind of money to settle has always been misunderstood. Since the Ivan Boesky settlement was for $100 million, the amounts paid by Drexel and Michael to settle were extremely important to the government. Once Michael decided it was in his and his family's interest to try to minimize the risk and settle, the amount of money was not going to be a determining factor as long as it was an amount he was capable of paying. To Michael, money was the by-product of success in the investing and financial services arena in which he was engaged. As he told Ed Williams and Arthur Liman at the beginning of the investigation, he was confident he could rebuild his wealth if he needed to due to his understanding of credit, capital structures, and the financial markets.

> **This process was extremely difficult for Michael. The lawyers advised him that they believed it was almost a certainty he would have to spend some time in prison.**

This process was extremely difficult for Michael. The lawyers advised him that they believed it was almost a certainty he would have to spend some time in prison. He had been gone from Drexel—or, as Peter Fleming termed it, his "home"—for a year and had watched

Drexel operate itself into bankruptcy, one more thing the media and the prosecutors could falsely blame on him. The issue of what would happen to Lowell was still unresolved, and a government agent visited Michael's ninety-plus-year-old grandfather to ask him about a high yield bond in his portfolio. Now the SEC wanted him to pay significantly more money than what the US Attorney was prepared to agree to. He literally could not buy a break and was about to break himself.

Stephen Kaufman was a former Assistant US Attorney who had worked with Robert Morgenthau in the US Attorney's Office with Peter Fleming, Michael Armstrong, and Arthur Liman. Stephen was one of the most respected lawyers in New York, and we asked him to join our team. Everybody spoke highly of Steve, whether other defense counsel or prosecutors. He is an individual of impeccable judgment and integrity. Arthur Liman brought Steve in as a member of the team because of his credibility and judgment. Steve was extremely valuable in this process.

Steve, Arthur, and I met at the US Attorney's Office with John Carroll, Jess Fardella, and Alan Cohen after the SEC "amended" the terms of the settlement. Cohen encouraged us to give him authority to agree to the $650 million, with an understanding that he would negotiate an amount that would be less. Both Steve and Arthur encouraged me to authorize Cohen to proceed in that matter. They felt we had a settlement and, since Mike had the resources, should not let the money stand in the way. Though Michael was kept informed of the negotiations by Arthur and me, he had not finally agreed to anything. Everyone knew there would be no final agreement until the final terms were presented to Michael and he agreed to accept them.

I did not believe the government was going to allow this settlement to fail because of Breeden and the SEC, and it was not fair for Mike to take another "hit," whether he could afford it or not. I also did not believe Alan Cohen would be successful in negotiating a lesser amount, assuming he even tried. Therefore, I insisted the maximum amount Mike would pay not be the $650 million that Drexel paid. That was Drexel's decision. In addition, I explained to John Carroll and Alan Cohen that I had grown up with Michael and Lowell. Their father, Bernard, and their mother, Ferne, were like second parents to me. Bernard Milken had passed away from cancer approximately a dozen years earlier. He was a man of impeccable integrity. How could I explain to Ferne that in this complicated and distressing process, her oldest son was probably going to go to prison and her other son would still be exposed to prosecution?

John Carroll privately suggested to me that they had probably made a mistake in indicting Lowell Milken. He said that Lowell, at most, had a secondary role in the Boesky relationship. All he had really done was sign a letter and was probably in no different position with respect to that relationship than was Charles Thurnher, who the government had immunized early on in the investigation. Charles Thurnher kept records, and Lowell was not even aware such records were kept. His only relationship with this matter was that he signed a letter—and, of course, he had the last name "Milken."

Several days later, Arthur, Steve and I, together with Marty Flumenbaum, were called to a meeting at the US Attorney's Office with Carroll, Fardella, Cohen, and Louis Freeh, who was then head of the criminal division and later became a federal judge and the director of the FBI. I had never met Louis Freeh, but I understood he was very respected. Our legal team sat at a conference table when Fardella, Cohen, and Carroll came in and sat down. Cohen first apologized on behalf of Louis Freeh, who apparently had to attend an arraignment and could not make the meeting. Cohen said they had reached an agreement with the SEC to proceed with the plea agreement on the six counts we had agreed to and for Michael to pay a total of $600 million—$200 million in fines and penalties and $400 million to the SEC disgorgement fund. In addition, all charges against Lowell would be dropped nolle prosequi. A nolle prosequi is a dismissal of all charges by the prosecution. This was almost unheard of in the Southern District of New York after bringing a high-profile indictment.

We got up and said we would talk to our client and get back to them. We gave no indication at all as to what our thinking was. As we got up, I turned to Steve and said, "Lowell truly was a hostage." As I was about to walk out the door, John Carroll came up to me, put his hand on my shoulder, and whispered in my ear, "Come back," which to me meant he was suggesting we settle on those terms.

We left the building and went back to Arthur's office with a very uneasy feeling. I found it distressing to be involved in a process where the enormous power of the government of the United States of America was being used to force Michael to make such a difficult choice when I knew he had not committed any of the crimes he was being charged with and yet the risks to him were so great that he had so few options. The offer of nolle prosequi regarding Lowell was a major concession. I was later told by John Carroll that the decision to dismiss the charges against Lowell was made by Louis Freeh, whom I had never met. He told John Carroll that if the SEC changed the terms, the US Attorney should offer something of value to Michael Milken.

Prior to this offer of dismissal of charges against Lowell, Michael Armstrong had met with the prosecutors in an attempt to assist in our negotiations and negotiated the following terms: (1) there would be a deferral of any prosecution against Lowell for a year; (2) at the end of that period, if the prosecutors were planning to proceed with the case, Lowell would have the option to plead to a single count of being an accessory after the fact, contemporaneous with the action; and (3) Lowell Milken would not be mentioned in the sentencing documents filed by the prosecutors with the court in the Michael Milken case.

Michael Armstrong believed he had a general agreement with the prosecutors with respect to these points. Before Lowell responded to this proposal, the prosecutors changed their position and informed Michael Armstrong that any future plea with Lowell Milken would have to be to two counts, not one. Since Michael Armstrong felt he had an understanding on one count, he rejected the offer outright. Lowell Milken acknowledged he was not interested in any such offer and that there should be no further conversations between his lawyers and the prosecutors. Lowell would never have ever pleaded to anything. Now it was a moot point.

We had the opportunity for Lowell to be dismissed without any agreement with the prosecutors. Michael had to make the most difficult decision of his life. Was he going to agree to plea to six counts, pay criminal penalties, pay funds into the disgorgement fund, and most likely spend time in prison? If he agreed, the risks of a trial and further indictments would be eliminated and the indictment of Lowell Milken would be dismissed, but he would be a convicted felon.

One of the more intense discussions we had with Michael regarding the pros and the cons of agreeing to this settlement took place in a conference room off Arthur Liman's office at Paul, Weiss, Rifkind, Wharton & Garrison. Arthur had introduced both Michael and me on a number of occasions to one of the named partners of the firm, Judge Simon Rifkind. Judge Rifkind had been a United States district judge who had returned to the practice of law and was the person in the Paul, Weiss firm whom Arthur Liman looked up to as a mentor. Michael's wife, Lori, was also with us that day when Arthur suggested that we get Judge Rifkind's opinion.

Judge Rifkind came into the conference room. Arthur explained to Judge Rifkind the offer that the prosecutors had made after our negotiations. Judge Rifkind was familiar with the case from prior meetings. He thought for about a minute and then looked to Mike and Lori and exclaimed, "You have no choice. You need to settle. The risks of going to trial, assuming you are innocent, are too great. This is an offer you need to accept."

Judge Rifkind then got up and left the room. Lori turned to Michael and me and said somewhat facetiously, "I guess that settles it." She commented that we had been wrestling with the most important decision of Michael's life for over an hour and that Judge Rifkind, then almost ninety years old, had walked in and in ten minutes summed the whole thing up and left. In retrospect, it was clear to me that Judge Rifkind, an experienced trial lawyer and district court judge, was telling us that no matter what we knew or what we believed, in the atmosphere that had been created around this case and around Michael Milken, he could not and should not take the risk of trying to prove his innocence, even if he was innocent, as opposed to settling on the terms before us.

Carroll and Fardella told us they were preparing a new superseding indictment, so we had to either agree to settle or this deal was off the table. They gave us a deadline by which we had to inform them of the decision.

The night before we had to give the prosecutors our decision, I was in New York and Michael was home in Los Angeles. I had a long telephone conversation with both Michael and Lowell that evening. Because I represented both Michael and Lowell, I had confidential privileged conversations with both Michael and Lowell from the beginning of the investigation. This particular evening we had our most extensive conversation together as we discussed each of the counts of the plea and the pros and cons of settling.

Toward the end of the conversation, I told Mike that having learned all that I had over the past three-plus years and knowing him as I knew him for over thirty years, if he were to settle I believed he needed to accept four things: (1) he was pleading to felonies and would be considered a convicted felon, no matter how unfair; (2) he would wind up going to prison for some period of time, which I thought would be between two and three years; (3) books and articles about this period would mention him together with Ivan Boesky and the insider trading investigation; and (4) for his own peace of mind, he needed to accept responsibility for allowing this to happen to him, no matter how unfair—not because he ever knowingly violated the law or committed a crime, which to this day I believe he did not, but because he voluntarily did business with this individual, which allowed this to happen. This last point was the most difficult. I knew Mike would never do anything consciously to hurt his family or put his business at risk.

The legal team assembled in Arthur Liman's office the next morning. We called Michael in Los Angeles. Mike was very subdued as he said we appeared to have done the best we could in these negotiations. Certainly if he were going to plead to anything, these were charges he would plead to.

Then he said, "Tell them we'll accept their deal." I knew that was the right decision, but it broke my heart.

We informed John Carroll and Jess Fardella, took a deep breath, and then headed to Washington, DC, to meet with the Securities and Exchange Commission to discuss the exact terms of the final judgment in the SEC case. Though Michael would not admit to any allegations, he would be subject to injunctions against activities in the future, including a lifetime bar from participating in the securities industry. He would be prohibited from "being associated with a broker, dealer, investment company, investment advisor, or municipal securities dealer." Mike had no desire to return to the securities business. Arthur explained to him that he could be a business consultant to companies and individuals in the future. He could also pursue his own investments.

We were in Washington all day arguing over the language of what sanctions would be instituted against Mike. The SEC lawyers wanted the language to be as draconian as possible. At one point Arthur walked out, reminding everyone that the SEC is a government agency bound by the US Constitution. We finally agreed to the language of the settlement.

Lowell Milken also had to settle with the SEC. Michael Armstrong had to meet with the SEC, and Lowell, too, had to take a lifetime bar from being in the securities industry. Lowell did not have to pay any fine or penalty. He was willing to take the bar to help Michael settle. Lowell was not in the securities industry, had never been in the securities business, and had no desire to be in that business. But it was important to Lowell, who had been a practicing lawyer many years earlier, that nothing he agreed to would result in his being disbarred, whether he ever again wanted to practice law. When that final piece was resolved, we had a settlement.

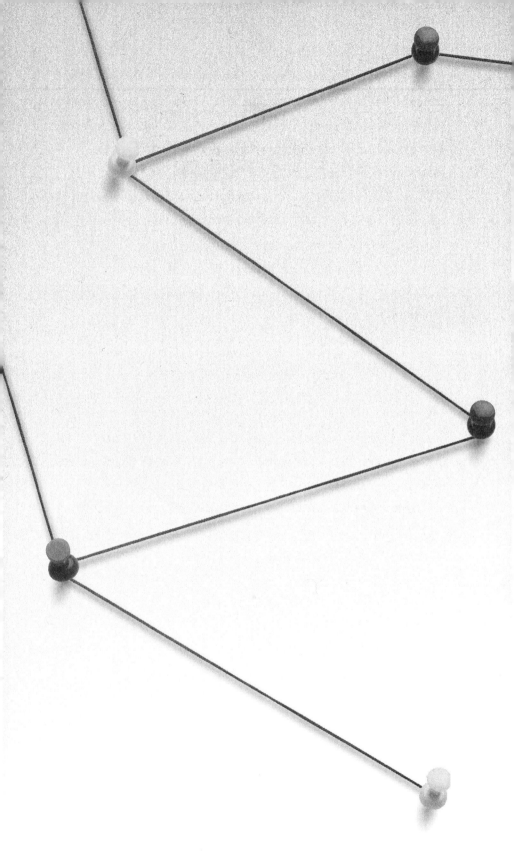

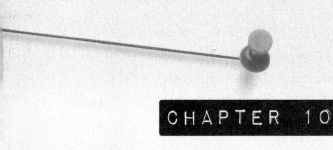

CHAPTER 10

The Plea

In a personal letter to Judge Kimba Wood dated November 5, 1990, Michael Milken discussed some of his thoughts and feelings about the toll that the then four-year investigation had taken on him and his family. Since he had not testified at the Fatico hearing conducted by Judge Wood and discussed in the following chapters, this was his only direct contact with Judge Wood:

> I have always attempted to be a shield for my family. Unfortunately, my actions have turned my shield into a reflector. The burden I have put on them is now almost unbearable. One of the most difficult things during this period has been the attack on my ideals, my beliefs and motives, the assault on my inner self. People can challenge what a person has done. I can understand the right and need of some people to condemn me for the offenses I committed. What I have not been able to accept, and what has been the most painful during the past four years, has been the assault on the sincerity of my beliefs, my moral system, and my basic inner being. To some it might sound ironic, but I have spent a lifetime trying to avoid publicity, even accolades. My

parents taught me if you worked hard and knew you did a good job, you should not need recognition from others. My father lived his life exactly that way. He was happy to let the other guy receive the credit. For the entire time my family and I lived in New Jersey, we were able to live a life of simple, quiet anonymity. After moving to California, this anonymity continued until the mid-1980s. Then as I tried to avoid publicity, that fact alone received public attention.

So much written about Michael Milken over the past thirty-five years is based on conjecture, rumor, assumption, or simply lies. The next four chapters discuss in some detail the actual public record of what Michael did and did not do. Understanding what Michael actually did starts with the plea. The plea agreement with the US Attorney's Office included the allocution—Michael's accounting of what he did. The government and Michael agreed to each word Michael would recite under oath in court. Everything that transpired after Michael pleaded confirmed that Michael did only what he said he did in the allocution and nothing else. The quotation from Michael above provides a glimpse of his state of mind at the time he reached the difficult decision to plead.

After the plea, the government and Michael's attorneys on his behalf

> "I have always attempted to be a shield for my family. Unfortunately, my actions have turned my shield into a reflector. The burden I have put on them is now almost unbearable."

filed their respective sentencing memoranda with the court, which is standard process. The government set forth its claims of what Michael did in addition to what he pleaded to and why he should be punished severely. Michael set forth that his plea was the total of any wrongdoing on his part, amounted to actions that had never before been the subject of criminal prosecution, and represented a rare departure from an exemplary life and that therefore he deserved lenient treatment. Judge Wood, receiving such disparate descriptions, held a Fatico hearing, or minitrial, to resolve the issue. After the hearing, she issued findings, handed down her sentence, and explained her reasoning for the sentence in a series of opinions, findings, and comments over the next several years. The plea agreement, sentencing memoranda, Judge Wood's findings and conclusions following the Fatico hearing, and her sentence represent the objective public record. They represent what Michael Milken did and did not do.

The plea agreement is a letter dated April 22, 1990, and is addressed to Arthur L. Liman and signed by Roger S. Hayes, acting United States Attorney. It is also signed on April 23, 1990, by a representative of the US Department of Justice and, on April 24, 1990, by both Arthur Liman and Michael R. Milken. The agreement has eighteen paragraphs. Paragraph one states the following:

> On the understanding specified below, the Department of Justice will accept a guilty plea from Michael R. Milken to a six-count information SS89CR0041(KMW) charging (1) conspiracy to violate the laws of the United States; (2) aiding and abetting the failure to file a truthful and accurate Schedule 13D with the Securities and Exchange Commission; (3) securities fraud; (4) aiding and abetting the violation by a registered broker-dealer of the SEC's reporting requirements; (5) mail fraud; and (6) assisting the filing of a false tax return.

It is important to note that the agreement was with the Department of Justice as well as the United States Attorney for the Southern District of New York. Often plea agreements are made with the particular US Attorney's office prosecuting the case. In this case, because of the potential for US Attorney's offices to conceivably conduct further investigations, especially after Bruce Newberg was indicted twice, it was agreed that Michael could not be indicted again in the federal system. Michael's plea agreement was binding on all US Attorneys' offices in the United States. Three of the charges—aiding and abetting failure to file an accurate 13D, aiding and abetting a violation by another of SEC reporting requirements, and assisting another in filing a false tax return—were regulatory violations involving other parties and also had never before been charged as crimes.

Paragraph two states,

> Each count of information SS89CR41 carries a maximum penalty of (a) five years imprisonment, except for count six, which specifies a maximum imprisonment term of three years; (b) fines and restitutions as described by [US Code]; and (c) a mandatory $50 assessment.

The reference in both the first and second paragraph to SS89CR.0041(KMW) is to the superseding information to which Michael was pleading guilty. This information superseded the ninety-eight-count indictment. He was not pleading to any of the counts set forth in the original indictment but only the five acts set forth in the information and the plea agreement.

The maximum prison term of twenty-eight years became a major focus of discussion and understanding with the prosecutors during the plea negotiations. John Carroll and Jess Fardella understood we needed to discuss how to limit any potential term of sentence. The process in the Southern District of New York when Ivan Boesky pleaded allowed the prosecutors and defendant to agree to arrange to plead in front of a specific judge. This process had been discontinued and was not available to Michael. There was criticism about Boesky being able to choose a judge; therefore, the rules were changed so that neither the prosecutors nor a defendant could arrange to plead before a specific judge. At one point during our settlement discussions, John Carroll said to Arthur Liman, "It's hard to believe that in the year 1990 a group of intelligent and creative lawyers cannot figure out how to limit the sentence."

After discussing this issue with his colleagues and some judges, Arthur Liman came up with what appeared to be a brilliant solution. Arthur recommended that at the time of the plea, he would address the court and state, "The government has agreed that it will make no specific recommendation as to the sentence of incarceration. That means the government will not ask the court to impose consecutive sentences in this case." John Carroll would then state, "Your Honor, that's correct. It is the general practice of our office not to recommend specific sentences, including consecutive sentences, although on certain occasions we have done so. In the light of the entirety of this plea agreement, we think it's entirely appropriate to adhere to that practice in this case."

The prosecutors agreed to this language as a solution to our problem. Arthur advised that based upon his own experience, that of Stephen Kaufman, and that of all the experienced lawyers and judges he spoke to, this would send a clear message to Judge Wood to cap the maximum sentence at five years, given there would not be any consecutive sentences. Michael would not have settled if he'd believed he could be sentenced to more than five years.

The third paragraph of the plea agreement stated the following:

In consideration of this plea and subject to the conditions of paragraph six below, Michael R. Milken will not
be prosecuted further by the Department of Justice for
any activities relating to or arising from Drexel Burnham
Lambert Inc.'s or Milken's business or investments
during the period of his employment with Drexel or
his association with Drexel's affiliates, up to the date of
the signing of this agreement by Michael R. Milken. …
Further, at the time of sentencing, the Government will
consent to the dismissal of all outstanding charges as to
Michael R. Milken in Indictment S89CR0041(KMW).

This was a final settlement with the Justice Department for
anything and everything that had happened during Michael's entire
Drexel career. The original ninety-eight-count indictment was being
dismissed in full.

The agreement continues as follows:

It is understood that Michael R. Milken's Allocution at
the time of his plea shall incorporate, *in haec verba*, the
statement of Michael R. Milken identified as Exhibit
A, the accuracy of which Michael R. Milken hereby
affirms. It is further understood that the Department of
Justice is not bound in any way by any factual or legal
assertion set forth in Exhibit A.

Even though the government was not bound by factual or legal
assertions in exhibit A, it did require Michael R. Milken to recite
the allocution in exhibit A *in haec verba*, or "word for word." The
government agreed that the allocution was exactly what Michael was
pleading to. Michael recited the allocution, under oath, in court, and
the government never accused him of violating that oath.

Another provision of the agreement is the following:

> The Department of Justice cannot and does not make any representations or promises as to what sentence of incarceration Michael R. Milken will receive. It is understood that any sentence of incarceration to be imposed on Michael R. Milken is within the sole discretion of the sentencing Judge. In connection with that sentence, the Department of Justice will not make any recommendation as to a specific term of incarceration. It is further understood that, in connection with sentencing and in consideration of the fact that Michael R. Milken will not be further prosecuted by the Department of Justice for Drexel related activities, the Department of Justice retains the right (i) to present to the Court and Probation Department, either orally or in writing, any and all facts and arguments relevant to sentencing, including the facts and circumstances of other pertinent cases, and (ii) to make any recommendation regarding any sentence it deems appropriate, except as otherwise provided herein. … To limit any factual disputes to the extent possible, the parties agree to exchange draft sentencing memorandum sufficiently before sentencing.

This paragraph covers three main issues:

1. The government is not responsible for what the sentence may or may not be, but the government will not make any recommendation as to a specific term of incarceration.

2. The government has the right to present to the court any and all facts and arguments that it wishes, and Michael

Milken retains the right to contest any facts asserted or arguments advanced. The reason we had to agree to let the government present other allegations to the court resulted from what happened in the Robert Freeman case. The prosecution had filed a lengthy sentencing memorandum alleging Freeman had committed more crimes than the one count he pleaded to. Judge Pierre Leval indicated he would not accept such a memorandum and stated that if the government felt Freeman should be punished for more than the one count, then it should have charged him with more than the one count to which he pleaded.

3. We would exchange draft sentencing memoranda before they were submitted to the court. Unfortunately, the government and Michael's legal team never exchanged draft sentencing memoranda before sentencing. This may have been the biggest mistake we, as the defense, made in this case. Between the time of the plea and filing of sentencing memoranda, we met with the prosecutors about what Michael's cooperation might look like. This resulted in disagreements among lawyers, and we never exchanged drafts. The government sentencing memorandum was a vicious, if not devastating, document in its attack on Michael's character and allegations of wrongdoing in addition to what he had pleaded to. The government memorandum could only have been improved by an exchange of drafts before filing.

Another paragraph of the plea agreement provided that Michael would cooperate and meet with the government after sentencing. We

8

knew Mike would be truthful and would not accuse his customers and colleagues of wrongdoing. We also knew that the prosecutors had made up their minds and believed Michael could provide incriminating evidence against others. It is unfortunate that this process did not allow for the prosecutors to know Michael Milken, the human being, before sentencing.

The last key provision of the plea agreement was quite short: "In consideration of this agreement and upon the terms and conditions set forth in a letter to Michael Armstrong, Esq., dated April 23, 1990, the government will file a nolle prosequi with regard to the charges against Lowell J. Milken in Indictment S89CR.0041(KMW)."

Clearly this short sentence in this six-page agreement was the only positive thing in this document.

Michael read exhibit A, the allocution, in court under oath on the day of his plea, April 24, 1990:

> I was the founder and head of the High Yield and Convertible Securities Department at Drexel. In pioneering the creation of new instruments for the financing of companies, most of which did not have access to capital markets because they did not have investment-grade ratings, and in making markets in such securities, we operated under unique, highly demanding, and intensely competitive conditions. But I do not cite these conditions as an excuse for not conforming to all of the laws that governed our highly regulated business. I am here today because in connection with some transactions, I transgressed certain of the laws and regulations that govern our industry. I was wrong in doing so and knew that at the time and I am pleading guilty to these offenses.

Michael acknowledged he transgressed certain laws and regulations in some transactions and was "wrong" in doing so.

With respect to his relationship with Ivan Boesky, he stated,

> One of the accounts we did business with was the Boesky Organization, which also did business with many other firms. Drexel did some financings for and trading with the Boesky firm, but Drexel's business with the Boesky Organization never approached one percent of the business of our department. We were not social friends, and had little in common. He traded in stocks; I traded primarily in bonds, or their equivalent. His philosophy of business was different from mine. The relationship started as an arm's length and correct one. Unfortunately, however, certain of our transactions involved reciprocal accommodations, some of which violated the law, including those that are referred to in this allocution.

Michael then discussed the five transactions he was pleading to:

1. **Fischbach**: In 1984, Drexel owned securities of a company called Fischbach. Victor Posner, who had been a client of Drexel, had an interest in acquiring Fischbach, which he publicly announced. Boesky, as an arbitrageur, was familiar with Fischbach and told Michael he wanted to purchase Fischbach securities, which Michael encouraged him to do. Boesky started buying securities of Fischbach and filed a 13D and called Michael incessantly, complaining that the stock was dropping and saying Drexel was responsible for

the losses. "I do not remember exactly what I told him almost six years ago, but I indicated to him that he would not lose money. I assured him that Drexel would make good on his losses. I did not expect that they would be reflected in any 13Ds filed by the Boesky organization, and, in fact, they were not. Thus, I assisted in the failure to file an accurate 13D."

This was the first time anybody was criminally prosecuted for committing a crime relating to a 13D filing of another person. I doubt the issue of whether Boesky should amend his 13D ever crossed Michael's mind.

2. **MCA Stock**: Also in 1984, Golden Nugget, a client at Drexel, held a substantial amount of MCA stock that it decided to sell quietly in one or more blocks without identifying the ultimate buyer or seller of the stock, which is a legitimate practice. Since Michael knew Boesky bought large blocks of stock and had an interest in entertainment stocks, he offered the MCA shares to Boesky. Boesky again complained he had lost money on his purchases, and "I promised that we would make up any losses the Boesky organization suffered" and "this promise was not recorded on Drexel's books nor made public, and it was wrong to do so." The government required one of the counts that Mike was to plead be a securities fraud count. This was that securities fraud, since "the promise was not recorded on Drexel's books or made public." This was another instance where Michael said he would make up any losses rather than confronting Boesky and arguing or prolonging the conversation.

WITNESS TO A PROSECUTION

3. **Helmerich & Payne**: In 1985, the Boesky organization asked Drexel to purchase approximately a million shares of Helmerich & Payne stock with an agreement that the Boesky organization would repurchase the stock in the future and make up any losses Drexel may have incurred. "Although I was not involved in the purchase of these securities, I later learned of this understanding. I approved this understanding. I also gave instructions to sell the stock back." The Boesky organization, as a broker dealer, had to maintain a certain amount of net capital. The understanding that the Boesky organization would make up any losses was an oral one, as the stock was not charged to the Boesky organization's net capital while held by Drexel. Therefore, Michael pleaded to aiding and abetting another in a net capital violation.

   Michael also stated in his allocution that he caused Drexel to execute certain bond trades with the Boesky organization that resulted in profits to the Boesky organization, and a Drexel employee "tried to keep track of how the Boesky organization stood, in terms of profits and losses, on these and certain other transactions, though so far as I know, the scorekeeping was never exact." No one ever suggested there was anything wrong or improper about the bond trades that resulted in those profits.

4. **Finsbury Fund**: The next two transactions were with David Solomon, a portfolio manager who specialized in high yield securities. Unlike Boesky, Solomon was a large customer of Drexel's as well as of other firms. He managed a high yield portfolio called the

Finsbury Fund. This was an offshore fund underwritten by Drexel, which paid an annual commission to its salesmen. Drexel charged the commissions to the High Yield Department. Michael agreed with Solomon and the management at Drexel that his department could recoup this 1 percent commission:

> We charged Solomon a fraction of a point more on certain purchases he made for his clients or a fraction of a point less on certain sales he had made for his clients to help recoup the 1 percent commission. All adjustments were to be made within the bid-ask range for the particular security at the time of the transaction. These adjustments were not disclosed by Drexel or me to the shareholders of Finsbury. The confirmations for Solomon's purchase of securities were mailed by Drexel and did not disclose the adjustments or that they were made to reimburse Drexel for the selling expenses. This failure to disclose was wrong.

In every purchase or sale of a high yield security, there is a spread between the bid price (the price the market maker is willing to pay) and the ask price (the price the market maker is willing to sell the security at). A sophisticated investor like David Solomon would usually negotiate the price somewhere between this spread. In this situation, Solomon in effect would pay the ask price if he were buying or accept the bid price if he were selling without negotiation. The government insisted there be a mail fraud count in the plea, and as these "adjustments" were not identified on confirmations mailed to Solomon, this was a mail fraud. I was originally concerned Judge Wood would not accept this description as a crime, since the confirmations were sent to Solomon and not to his clients and Solomon was aware of the adjustments. Arguably, it was Solomon who should have disclosed the adjustments to clients. I am also sure Michael never thought about what was and was not disclosed in confirmations. Ironically, Judge Wood later found the total economic effect of these adjustments was $318,082, and this was the only count of the plea where Judge Wood found any economic effect.

5. **Tax Trades**: In December 1985, Solomon asked Drexel if it could help him generate short-term losses for his personal income tax purposes. "In light of the customer relationship between Mr. Solomon and Drexel, I assisted him in purchasing from Drexel certain securities that traded at a significant spread between the bid and the ask price. Drexel thereafter repurchased these securities at a substantially lower price, thus generating a loss for him and a profit for Drexel. I either told them we would provide him with an investment opportunity to make up his loss, or that was implicit in the conversation."

The most interesting aspect of this particular transaction is that Solomon actually did incur the losses he claimed on his tax return. Michael Milken did provide Solomon with an investment opportunity at a later date that turned out to be profitable, did make up for the losses, and created a gain that Solomon also reported on a later tax return.

Another Drexel employee who was responsible for the Solomon relationship, Alan Rosenthal, was indicted by the government in May of 1991 and charged for the same tax transaction. As described in *United States of America v. Alan E. Rosenthal* (9F.3d 1016 [2d Cir. 1993]), Rosenthal was charged in an eleven-count indictment, but prior to trial the government dismissed four of the counts, and on defendant's motion the trial court dismissed another count. A charge of aiding and assisting another in filing a false tax return for the exact same transaction Michael pleaded to was included in the indictment. That charge was dismissed by Judge Louis Stanton, the trial court judge, on a motion by Mr. Rosenthal at the close of the government's case. Judge Stanton decided there was insufficient evidence indicating Solomon's losses were compensated by "insurance or its equivalent." Judge Stanton stated that reimbursement through a promised investment opportunity at a subsequent time was not enforceable and was not certain enough to qualify as some kind of compensation or assurance to Solomon that he would not lose money. Judge Stanton did recognize an anomaly: David Solomon and Michael Milken, the two people most directly involved in the trades, both acknowledged they were wrong. Yet Judge Stanton found nothing illegal about the transaction since Solomon lost money, and the mere promise to make something up is not enforceable. Alan Rosenthal was convicted on a single count, for which he paid a fine and served no prison time.

Every "promise" Michael Milken pleaded to with respect to either Ivan Boesky or David Solomon was not certain enough to be insurance or its equivalent.

The end of Michael's allocution was very emotional as he broke down and barely was able to speak:

> Because of the tremendous amount of publicity that has surrounded this case, I wish to make clear that my plea is in acceptance of personal responsibility for my own failings and actions and not a reflection on the underlying soundness and integrity of the segment of the capital markets in which we specialize and which provided capital that enabled hundreds of companies to survive, expand, and flourish. Our business was in no way dependent on these practices. Nor did they comprise a fundamental part of our business, and I regret them very much. This investigation and proceeding are now in their fourth year. This long period has been extremely painful and difficult for my family and friends as well as myself.
>
> I realize by my acts I have hurt those who are closest to me. I am truly sorry. I thank the Court for permitting me to add this apology and for its fairness in handling this complex case.

Michael slumped into his chair as he barely finished the last sentence. Michael was released on his own recognizance, and sentencing was scheduled for October 1, 1990, with the sentencing memoranda to be filed with the court three weeks prior to that. As we left court that day, I was overwhelmed by what had happened. After all that work and all that time, my friend left court as an admitted felon. Moreover, though he was "released on his own recognizance," he had lost his freedom. This was very difficult to process for Michael and for me. I had no idea how much longer this ordeal would be extended nor how much more difficult it would become.

Now it was time for me and Michael to prepare for sentencing and to work on securing a fair sentence. Since I had been so involved in the negotiations with the prosecutors on the plea, I was hopeful we could negotiate a fair sentencing memorandum and try to make a case for the sentence to be no greater than three years. Under the rules of the Bureau of Prisons, Michael then would have to serve approximately two-thirds of any sentence. Whatever the sentence, it was all so painful.

> After all that work and all that time, my friend left court as an admitted felon.

The reason I have quoted so much of Michael's allocution is that, in spite of all that has been written over the years, this allocution reflects exactly what Michael did and did not do, and the court later confirmed that Mike did what he said in the allocution and nothing else.

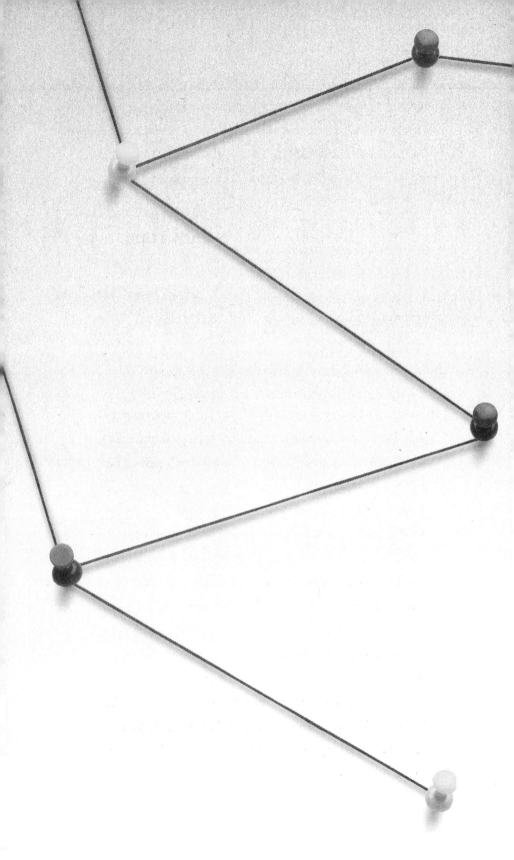

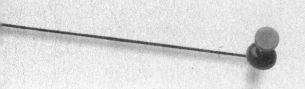

CHAPTER 11

Sentencing: Contrasting
Memoranda and Boesky Tape

Michael further reflected in his letter to Judge Wood,

> I do feel that much of my life during the past four years
> has been like a ping-pong ball, with every cause on either
> side of the issues using me as a symbol for their own
> uses. To everyone who has ever felt that their privacy has
> been invaded by the government or unjustly accused, I
> have asked, "Please, don't use me as a symbol." To those
> who I don't even know, whom I've never met, who call
> me a symbol of the 1980s or a symbol of money and
> power, I say I've never sought notoriety. I have asked
> both sides not to use me as a ping-pong ball. Let me
> return to a life of anonymity if humanly possible for
> myself and my family. I think I can accomplish more
> by blending back into society and quietly seeing what
> I can do. I am a person, not a symbol. I, like other
> individuals, have strong beliefs and ideals and as I have
> acknowledged by my plea before Your Honor I have
> made mistakes.

Between the time of the plea and the scheduled sentencing on October 1, we were busy. Mike needed to meet with his probation officer, who would make a report to the court at sentencing regarding his background and what he pleaded to. The legal team began an ill-fated series of meetings with the prosecutors to see if we could narrow the issues for the sentencing memoranda. We also began the process of assembling letters of support from dozens of people who wanted to write to Judge Wood to present a true picture of who Michael Milken really was and what he had done in his lifetime. We continued our analysis of the government's claims we knew would be presented in the government's sentencing memorandum. The Paul, Weiss team began work on Michael's sentencing memorandum with input from Michael Milken.

> The prosecutors told the judge at the plea hearing that they had every reason to believe Michael's cooperation would be truthful. They indicated otherwise in their sentencing memorandum. And they still had never met with Michael.

After our first postplea meeting with the prosecutors, it was clear that the decision to delay cooperation until after sentencing had been the right decision. On the other hand, the decision for the lawyers to meet with the prosecutors to discuss anything other than the plea and the sentencing memorandum was a mistake. The prosecutors told the judge at the plea hearing that they had every reason to believe Michael's cooperation would be truthful. They indicated otherwise in their sentencing memorandum. And they still had never met with Michael. Since we had agreed that cooperation would start after sentencing, we should not have "previewed" cooperation. We should have tried to narrow the issues rather than highlighting the differences.

Not surprisingly, Michael developed a good relationship with his probation officer, Michaela Bracken. Ms. Bracken was a very experienced probation officer who came to truly understand Michael Milken and what this process had done to him. She became a person Mike could talk to. Unfortunately she was not the judge, and she had no influence on the prosecutors. Ms. Bracken was the first government official who actually spent time with Michael. Her reaction to him validated my belief: the best advocate for who Michael Milken really is, is Michael Milken. Unfortunately, the prosecutorial system creates too many risks to a person under investigation to spend time with the prosecutors. The prosecutor does not have the opportunity to get to know his or her target before taking action, and that only hurts the target.

Judge Wood did receive hundreds of letters from friends, colleagues, clients, and customers trying to explain what a talented, caring, and decent man Michael Milken is. These letters were very different from the picture the government painted. Still, a judge normally gives deference to the government in these situations.

The sentencing memoranda were filed with the court on September 10, 1990. The government's sentencing memorandum was a 216-page document, and the Milken sentencing memorandum was 137 pages. The two documents described two very different people.

The government's memorandum set its tone on the first page:

> In a highly sophisticated and systemic way, Milken endeavored to enhance his power and enlarge his wealth by willingly cheating clients, manipulating the markets,

and evading the laws and rules designed to safeguard the investing public. ... Milken developed and nurtured corrupt relationships with numerous clients and customers, including Ivan F. Boesky, David B. Solomon. The six charges to which Milken pleaded guilty provide but a sampling of a larger pattern of criminal activity that had permeated Milken's operation of the High Yield Bond Department.

It goes on as follows:

The Government does not contend that Milken's entire business was a sham or that he ran it in a wholly corrupt fashion. ... The Government does contend that two inescapable conclusions are established by the facts set forth below: Milken's criminal conduct was calculated and systemic rather than gratuitous and aberrational. ... The Government most strongly urges that he be sentenced to a period of incarceration that reflects the enormity of his crimes.

The government contrasts Milken with Dennis Levine, Ivan Boesky, Martin Siegel, and Boyd Jefferies, who they say accepted responsibility for a broad range of crimes, cooperated soon after receiving notice of the investigation, brought to light extensive criminal conduct unknown to the government, and took affirmative steps to clean up their industry.

In spite of his many post-investigation social and charitable and good works, Milken has not taken—and has indicated that he will not take—affirmative steps to clean up the industry he dirtied. ... [We] urge that Your

Honor recognize that Milken should be punished as the unreconstructed and unapologetic man that he is.

By contrast, the first page of the sentencing memorandum of Michael Milken states the following:

> As the probation report and the hundreds of letters received by this Court attest, Michael Milken's crimes stand in sharp contrast to the characteristics and values he has displayed throughout his life. These letters … as well as the probation report, paint a portrait of a family man in the most complete and traditional sense; an extraordinarily hard working and successful business-man; a modest individual who shuns personal publicity and material possessions; a passionate and involved member of the community; a person deeply concerned by the problems of society; a person of great conscience, compassion, and charity who has always been generous with his time, money, and spirit.

The memorandum continues,

> We urge this Court to consider what his [Milken's] offenses were not. Although inexcusable, Michael's offenses, as the probation report concludes, were neither venal nor motivated by greed. He did not personally profit by them. They did not involve trading securi-ties on the basis of inside information. Nor did these offenses infect the core of his business.
>
> Moreover, the majority of offenses to which Michael pleaded guilty had rarely, if ever, been subject to criminal prosecution at the time of Michael's acts.

Prior to 1986, no criminal prosecution had ever been brought for aiding and abetting the filing of a false 13D by another. Prior to 1986, no criminal prosecution had ever been brought for aiding and abetting a broker/dealer's avoidance of the books and records requirements imposed by the securities laws. And, to this day, we are unaware of any criminal prosecution that has ever been brought for a failure to disclose an attempt to recoup commission expenses from portfolio managers.

The novelty of the charges does not excuse Michael Milken's transgressions, but it does provide a framework for assessing the relative severity and culpability of his defenses.

The government makes reference to "postinvestigation" charitable work. The court specifically found these works preceded the investigation. The government also argued that Milken should be punished for defending his crimes for so long, since the government had to forgo prosecutions of other individuals who it claims committed crimes, such as James Dahl, Terren Peizer, Cary Maultasch, Peter Gardiner (each of whom were Drexel employees who testified against Michael), Gary Winnick, and David Solomon. The government complained it entered into nonprosecution agreements with each of these individuals to compel testimony. We will never know whether the government really would or could have prosecuted any of these individuals. What we do know is that it was their choice to forgo any prosecutions to "get" Michael Milken.

The government's memorandum goes on to cite the probation report:

Milken and his employees were trading in seven thousand securities and carrying two thousand positions each day. Ivan Boesky was not a major factor in the business and during his relationship with Drexel, Boesky called the High Yield Bond Department thousands of times yelling and screaming things of being his fault. Milken reports that on these occasions when he spoke directly with Boesky he frequently refused to answer questions about confidential material. Infrequently, however, Milken reports that the easiest thing was saying, "I'll make it up to you. Then I can get to the three or four calls on hold and the two people who were standing nearby waiting to speak to me. ... I just got him off the telephone and did not hurt anyone. I concentrated on what I wanted to do and thought, *Okay, if you want to make money I'll find you money*. I had a hard time not taking care of people. In my desire to please the customer, I went too far. It's hard to reconcile what I have said with my behavior."

The government then concludes,

Milken's criminal conduct is fully consistent with a master scheme to acquire power and accumulate wealth. Such an overarching plan pervaded Milken's lawful and unlawful business practices.

The prosecutors, unlike the probation officer, did not know Michael. As I have underscored, Michael Milken is nonconfrontational. He was also naive in believing his way of dealing with Boesky would not eventually be a problem. He had confidence in his ability to find solutions without confrontation. So, if he wanted to get someone off the phone without creating an argument, he would put the issue off to another day and find a way to deal with it later.

When Ivan Boesky was investigated by the SEC, he and his counsel, Harvey Pitt, who was a former general counsel to the SEC, clearly came to a conclusion at some point that he should explore a settlement. Mr. Boesky had engaged in insider trading in a manner that included buying material nonpublic information from others, who were also violating the law, and making payment by delivering suitcases of cash. He had to be aware that if he could "deliver" the most successful financier at the time, Michael Milken, at the most successful securities firm, Drexel Burnham Lambert, Mr. Boesky could make the best possible deal.

The settlement that Ivan Boesky made with the government was considered extremely favorable for him. When Mr. Boesky was sentenced, the prosecutors went out of their way to laud Mr. Boesky for his cooperation and asked the judge to impose a very lenient sentence.

The government memorandum goes on to state that at the time of the plea, it appeared the gulf had narrowed between the government's and Milken's views of the facts alleged in the conspiracy count, and the government fully expected Milken's cooperation would bear fruit.

> Unfortunately our confidence has waned. Milken stands before the Court for sentencing as a Defendant who has expressly bargained not to cooperate prior to the imposition of sentence and who has been less than forthright with the probation department regarding his criminal responsibility.

There is nothing inconsistent between the allocution that the government agreed to and Michael's discussions with Michaela Bracken. The only information the prosecutors obtained from the time of the plea until the filing of the sentencing memorandum came from Michael's lawyers. The prosecutors still had not spent one second with Michael Milken.

In a cover letter to the Michael Milken sentencing memorandum, Arthur Liman states,

> We are aware that some judges in this district have found it helpful in evaluating the Defendant to meet with him in the presence of the Government. We would be pleased to have such a meeting if Your Honor believes it would assist in formulating the sentence. Because the timetable did not permit the exchange of drafts of the Sentencing Memorandum before the submission to Your Honor, we would contemplate filing a reply brief after receipt of the Government's brief. Once we receive the Government's brief, we will ask the Court to fix the date for the reply.

These memoranda could not have been further apart in their depiction of Michael Milken and what he had done. That situation could never favor the defendant. Judge Wood certainly did not know Michael Milken. Unfortunately, she did not take Arthur up on his suggestion that she meet Michael with the prosecutors present.

The government memorandum claims there were meetings between Milken and Boesky after Dennis Levine was arrested during which Boesky and Milken discussed the effect of Levine's arrest on their dealings. Milken

> These memoranda could not have been further apart in their depiction of Michael Milken and what he had done.

denies ever having any such discussions and that the first and last he ever heard of such a claim was in this memorandum. The government also states that the two met again in October of 1986, when Wall Street was rife with rumors that Boesky was implicated in the Levine scandal. A meeting did take place in October after Boesky had already made his settlement with the government but weeks before it was announced. Boesky was wearing a wire, and there is a tape of that meeting. The tape is almost two and a half hours long. The meeting was at the Beverly Hills Hotel, which Boesky owned at the time.

At the beginning of the tape, a criminal investigator states that Mr. Boesky would be meeting with Michael Milken at approximately two o'clock in the afternoon and that Mr. Boesky voluntarily consented to the taping. After Michael arrives, he and Boesky begin discussing the Beverly Hills Hotel and some people Michael knew who might be interested in buying the hotel. They referenced owners of the hotels in Las Vegas as well as potential buyers from Japan or the Middle East.

> MILKEN: Then you have the people in the United States, the individuals—if I was selling, have a little talk with Donald Trump.
>
> BOESKY: Donald has already made the phone call.
>
> MILKEN: You might need his overall psychology.
>
> BOESKY: He seems to have some other ideas in the marketplace, too, if I can attract him.

They mention they will be meeting that day with Kirk Kerkorian, who was another potential buyer of the hotel.

> BOESKY: Michael, we're going to meet with what's his name later on, and I have got one guy that's got to say hello before I do, so after our meeting I have got seven minutes to spend with a guy, you can use the phone or something. Then we'll go do this other guy.

Obviously, Boesky is referring to getting rid of the wire before the meeting with Kirk Kerkorian.

Boesky and Milken discuss certain investment ideas, various industries, and the markets in general. Then Boesky says there are a number of things he wants to discuss:

> BOESKY: First of all, as you know, we have had some inquiry. That's not unusual. We always have inquiry. We had subpoena. Our lawyers were able to get that withdrawn. Maybe they'll come back at some point in time, maybe they won't. ... I might ask you, have you gotten any inquiry? Any subpoena? Nothing? That's good. We go back to a long time ago, right? And we talked about a little item of business that we had, that you raised last year. And we got to figure out what that is.
>
> MILKEN: It's done.
>
> BOESKY: That's good. Tell me what it is, because I'd like to know how should we handle that, what is it?
>
> MILKEN: The quality issue was how do we get to the negotiation of all the fees on the deal.
>
> BOESKY: Which deal, the funding or the $5.3 million?

MILKEN: Well, both. The $5.3 million obviously was the deal—and they have the [information] in New York. The corporate finance group in New York …

BOESKY: We have to have a story that's the same.

MILKEN: Well, of course, we have.

BOESKY: What is the story?

MILKEN: Well the same thing were all the charges. One, for the zero-coupon, all the work to be done on the zeros.

BOESKY: If I am asked, why did you pay Drexel for?

MILKEN: Well, the $5.2 to $5.3 million was due to the old partnership.

BOESKY: Which things, though, Michael? You've gotta have documentation, you send a bill for $5.3 million.

MILKEN: They have that in New York, that's where the fees are, they have it. … Let me give you the list. They have, and you'll be able to check in New York who has the list, but we had submitted the list to them because they had received the fees …"

BOESKY: So, in other words, when they wrote a letter to us and said there was nothing, no substantiation, it was just a bill, there was nothing. Okay. So they sent a bill. We paid the bill.

MILKEN: Well, there was an outline of things that had been discussed. …

BOESKY: Which things?

MILKEN: Well, first you have the work done on the things like Dart and Kraft by Alan. [Alan Greditor was in charge of equity research in New York.]

BOESKY: Yes.

MILKEN: Okay. The work on Allied Package Food Company, the industry, where it's going; we didn't receive any commissions on any trades you did, etc. So the work was done. The next piece of work that was done was like corporate finance, looking at restructuring the partnership, all the tax issues, the meetings, people flying back out to California back and forth. How can we restructure the thing? That went on for fifteen months ... then you have the study on the work done on savings and loans.

BOESKY: By whom?

MILKEN: The firm, the work done by our group, financial advisors, by corporate finance, by M&A. Should you buy an S&L. Shouldn't you buy an S&L. Should you invest what's going on in the industry.

BOESKY: When you say Dart and Kraft, you mean General Food, Dart, and Kraft. All these items that were analytically Alan Greditor.

MILKEN: You also owned stock and sold stock. ... This all falls into that financial services issues. ... Where is it going? What's the direction? I think you've had positions in Warner Communications, MCA, MGM, you know, etc., etc.

BOESKY: Now pause on that. Who helped with that?

MILKEN: Research coming, all the research done in New York.

BOESKY: Did I have MCA? I can't remember. Did I have MCA?

MILKEN: You owned at one time a million shares at MCA back in November of 1984.

BOESKY: Right.

MILKEN: Start thinking you probably used most of this work to make a decision to buy Warner. You also bought Gulf and Western, if I remember correctly. Basically, you were interested in the work we had done in the industry, what—where we thought the industry was going.

MILKEN: Next one was the energy field.

BOESKY: What about energy?

MILKEN: What our views were on energy.

This conversation continues, mentioning various companies Drexel did work or gave advice to Boesky on. As Michael told Lowell on March 21, 1986, he charged Boesky a fee on behalf of Drexel for "all the work" that had been done for years that Boesky never paid for.

Michael shows his recall for transactions as he recalls securities Boesky invested in and work various people at Drexel did for him. The same day the fee was charged, Charles Thurnher did create the note for the Drexel records in New York, suggesting the fee should be allocated between three separate departments at Drexel: $2 million to the Equity Research Department in New York headed by Alan Greditor for the work he did, $1.2 million to the Corporate Finance Department for all the M&A work they had done regarding companies and industries Boesky looked at and never pursued; $1.5 million to the High Yield Department for all the work and advice Michael and others in the department had given. Boesky never suggested that anything Michael said was incorrect. The conversation continued:

> BOESKY: What I would like to have, I would like to have in my file something that looks a lot like what's in your file, that's what I would like to have.
>
> MILKEN: In essence, you told me, "If I don't do some business I'll pay you."
>
> BOESKY: Right.
>
> MILKEN: So when you were disbanding the partnership you couldn't carry the thing forward, so you paid us.
>
> BOESKY: Okay, all right.
>
> MILKEN: Wasn't that our understanding?
>
> BOESKY: Okay, I've got nothing else.

They then talk about some other investment ideas and the market, Boesky's business, and the debt Drexel had issued for Boesky the prior March. It is now a few minutes before Mr. Kerkorian is to arrive. Mike asks Boesky about his children, and after that the discussion ends.

When John Carroll delivered the tape to Marty Flumenbaum, he said, "You'll probably be as disappointed in it as we were."

What certainly was not disappointing was the fact that Michael emphasized several times they had done a significant amount of work for Boesky where Boesky had not made investments and not paid fees. Michael was able to recount precisely what work was done and who did it, and he recalled specific securities Boesky did buy as a result of work and advice from Drexel. Michael also maintained they had discussed the fact that Boesky would pay for all the work Drexel had done for him over the years and that when the old entity was dissolving, that would be the time to pay. ("Wasn't that our understanding?" "That was our understanding.") Also, Michael's comment on the tape, "In essence, you told me, 'If I don't do some business, I'll pay you,'" was not disputed by Boesky, though he was a government witness wearing a wire at the time.

Alan Greditor, who headed the Equity Research Department, told Drexel's attorney Peter Fleming that Michael had told Alan at the time that Boesky paid the fee, that part of it would be allocated to Alan's department. Alan Greditor, unfortunately, tragically died in an automobile accident early in the investigation.

The tape was somewhat disappointing in that Michael did not just say, "What are you talking about?" But that was not Michael Milken's nature. It was easier for him to keep responding than to start an argument. I always believed Boesky and Milken had different motives for whatever recordkeeping Mooradian and Thurnher were doing. For Boesky it might have been a way to try to hold transactions such as Fischbach over Michael's head. Michael, on the other hand, asked Charles Thurnher to keep records since Boesky was keeping records and to make sure they included every possible situation where Boesky made money. On March 21, 1986, Michael collected the fee owed to Drexel, and the recordkeeping stopped.

I am sure that the prosecutors were disappointed that this two-plus-hour tape does not have a single mention of any of the transactions Boesky claimed violated the law. Boesky never said any of the transactions the government referred to in its sentencing memorandum were inappropriate in any way. Michael seemed very comfortable in explaining exactly what the fee was for. Both Seth Mooradian and Charles Thurnher were immunized government witnesses, and neither was ever called as a witness to substantiate the government's claims. The government never referred to the tape or cited any of the tape in the sentencing memorandum or otherwise. And the government never called on Boesky to testify or substantiate any of the allegations.

The government sentencing memorandum does discuss the payment of the $5.3 million fee on March 21, 1986, as a "reconciliation of accounts." It accurately states Boesky was winding down his corporate business and was now going to commence operations through a larger limited partnership, for which Drexel raised the financing. It further states the restructuring offered Milken an opportunity to balance outstanding accounts with Boesky since Boesky was dependent on Drexel to complete the financing, which gave Milken leverage. This $5.3 million fee was the basis of the government's entire investigation, and yet it became a nonevent in the memorandum and at the later sentencing hearing.

Michael Milken's sentencing memorandum was divided into four parts: (1) family, (2) philanthropic and professional values for which Michael Milken has stood throughout his life, (3) the offenses to which he pleaded guilty, and (4) the principles of punishment and the relevant sentencing precedents in the Southern District.

Part 1 is biographical and discusses Michael Milken—the individual, his business, his family, and his commitment to family and community. He first started working at Drexel in 1969. By 1972,

Michael had established the groundwork for what would evolve into Wall Street's first group devoted extensively to research and trading of high yield securities. This group became the High Yield and Convertible Securities Department when Drexel merged with Burnham & Company in early 1973. Mike's compensation arrangement was formalized in 1975, when he agreed his department would receive 35 percent of the net profits that it produced as a bonus pool, which Michael would be responsible for allocating to himself and members of his department. Mike never attempted to renegotiate the formula even as the profits of the department grew significantly due principally to Michael, and Drexel never questioned Michael's allocation of the bonus pool, which management approved each year.

The personal section cites the many letters the court received from people who knew Michael, including my father of blessed memory, Raymond Sandler, who was a very respected attorney and community leader in Los Angeles and who had known Michael since he was eight years old:

> Despite his reputed great wealth, Michael is a modest, unassuming gentleman. He and his family live quite simply. They indulge in none of the extravagancies that are commonly associated with people who are so affluent—no large parties, no fancy jewelry, no staff of servants.

Michael's client and friend, Steven Ross, who, when he passed away in December 1992, was CEO of Time Warner, having led Warner Communications since the 1970s, stated,

> Michael has made a great deal of money, but money does not drive him. He never talks about money and

no one knew that he was so rich until the investigation publicized his earnings.

And there was the head of the school where Michael's children went:

I know of no father who has been more supportive of his children's education than Mike Milken.

The memorandum continues as follows:

Michael Milken will live for the rest of his life with the knowledge that he has inflicted enormous emotional and physical pain on his wife and his children, whom he loves more than anything else in the world. For him, this punishment is more severe than any this Court could possibly impose.

There are quotes from his employees, including those who moved with him from New York to Los Angeles in 1978:

Michael was personally involved with everyone. He got involved with what community to live in, considering our various needs, where our children would go to school, where our wives could find employment opportunities, and almost every facet of our lives.

Once he made a commitment to you, he was with you all the way. ... Mike's family attitude extended to all he worked with.

There is a quotation from the probation officer:

Despite involvement in a fiercely competitive, time-consuming vocation, he managed to devote time to his

family and friends and to establish charitable foundations addressing what he sees as the major ills in society.
In addition to donating millions of dollars, [Michael]
has given hours of his own time and has established a
close rapport with many of the disadvantaged youth
with whom he works.

A local judge in Los Angeles who did not know Michael volunteered the following:

My son is a sixth-grade student at the Stephen S. Wise
School. I was quite surprised when Eric came home
one day and told me that Mr. Milken is now teaching
math to his class. ... One afternoon Mr. Milken noticed
that Eric appeared confused about the lesson he was
teaching and he called him to the blackboard. Mr.
Milken continued to work with Eric at the board until
Eric completely understood the concepts. Since that
time, Eric has changed his attitude toward math and
his grades have improved.

One of the more extraordinary letters was written by Monty Hall,
television personality and philanthropist, who created and emceed a
long-running television show called *Let's Make a Deal*:

I personally raise over twenty million dollars a year for
various charities and make over fifty appearances, all
without charge, for causes that range from children to
the elderly. ... I can say unequivocally and that in all
my years of working in the field of philanthropy with
heads of business, professionals in Government, I have
never met the equal of Michael Milken. This is a man

who deeply cares about the society in which he lives and about the contribution that he can make to it.

There is a whole section of quotations from clients about Mike's talents and capabilities as a financier but also about his dedication to his clients and to his business as well as his personal integrity.

The memorandum explains how Michael Milken and Drexel made capital available to companies that never had it before and how the department had grown from thirty-five employees in 1978 to over two hundred employees by the mid-1980s. The department had well over a thousand customers, traded in seven thousand separate issues of securities, and could execute as many as a thousand trades each day while carrying a trading position approaching $4 billion. Therefore, the five transactions Michael pleaded to were the exception and had nothing to do with the growth or scope of his business.

The third section of the memorandum recounts the nature of the offenses pleaded to and anticipates that the government would present allegations beyond the plea. The memorandum states,

> Michael should be sentenced based on the offenses to which he pleaded guilty. He should not be sentenced for crimes that he did not commit. He should not be sentenced on charges for which the Government expressly has forgone prosecution in return for his guilty plea.

The memorandum further explains that in the three transactions to which Michael pleaded guilty involving Ivan Boesky, Boesky was a willing buyer of the securities, and that it was only after his complaints to Michael that Michael agreed to make good on losses. With respect to the David Solomon offenses, the memorandum strongly disputes Michael Milken ever improperly induced Solomon to do business with Drexel. Michael did ask Solomon to reimburse Drexel for the

Finsbury commissions through certain fractional point adjustments on trades within the bid and ask of the market. Mike did this with the knowledge of Drexel's management. The wrongful act was not disclosing the adjustments as commission in confirmations mailed to Solomon's customers. With respect to the tax transactions, it is made clear that Michael Milken never improperly deferred or abated any of his own taxes. He accommodated Solomon to realize a loss for tax purposes, but it was a real loss. Though Michael gained very little from the crimes he pleaded to, the memorandum does state he did violate the law and that such course of conduct "was completely contrary to his value system." Again, the probation officer, Ms. Bracken, observed,

> Among Milken's strengths are his inability to accept defeat, his total commitment to causes he considers "just and right," and his vision concerning business and society. His weakness was that as creator and head of the high yield department at Drexel these convictions were more important than his responsibilities and obligation to conduct business fully within the parameters of the law.

The rest of the memorandum focuses on principles of sentencing, with an example of other sentences in comparable situations. A table setting forth sentences imposed on nearly one hundred securities fraud cases prosecuted in the Southern District of New York since 1978 was attached. The sentences ranged from probation to four years of imprisonment. In the history of the district, only two defendants who pleaded guilty and agreed to cooperate received prison sentences greater than one year and one day, and those were Ivan Boesky and Dennis Levine, both of whom were involved in insider trading compounded by employing secret foreign bank accounts, committing perjury, evading taxes, and obstructing justice.

The memorandum discusses the fact that since Michael Milken had been publicly pilloried in one of the most intensive and certainly most public criminal investigations in the history of the Southern District, the sentencing goal of retribution or punishment had already been achieved. He watched his entire world disintegrate as he was branded a racketeer as well as unfairly blamed for a multitude of excesses of the past decade. Michael's sentencing memorandum respectfully requests he be sentenced to a term of probation conditioned upon full-time community service, given he performed extraordinary community service before ever being the target of a criminal investigation and would continue to do so.

So there were two sentencing memoranda: one from the government depicting Michael as a person who effectively engaged in full-time violation of the law with his plea barely touching the tip of the iceberg, and one from Michael Milken denying any other wrongdoings, including dozens of quotations from people who knew him and had done business with him—consistently referring to him as an extraordinary visionary, businessman, friend, and colleague.

Of course, with such a divergence of views, each side felt compelled to file a reply sentencing memorandum.

The reply sentencing memorandum of Michael Milken was another 129 pages refuting each and every allegation of additional criminal conduct made by the government. Since the defense team was aware of the transactions the government was looking at, we had done extensive analysis of the trading of every security involved, the economics of every transaction, and the evidence of what was involved in each transaction.

We argued the court should not consider any evidence regarding unadjudicated offenses the government submitted in its sentencing memorandum. A court should receive dispassionate rhetoric, accurate and complete factual presentations, and an unbiased weighing of all relevant factors.

> The Government seeks to have the court punish Mr. Milken for a host of alleged acts which Mr. Milken has never acknowledged and has never committed. The Government's hostility is further evidenced by its improper attempt to have Mr. Milken punished less for his crimes than for his wealth and status. The Government's Sentencing Memorandum includes more than twenty-five references to Mr. Milken's "greed" and "wealth" in the first twenty-fives pages alone. It ignores the many letters to the Court that attest to the fact that he is not concerned with material possessions or the accumulation of wealth. If the Government had wanted Mr. Milken sentenced for these crimes, it should not have entered into the plea agreement which it did. It should not have represented to the defendant and the court that it would adhere in this case to its "general practice" with respect to sentencing, and it would "make no specific recommendation as to the sentence of incarceration" and that it would not "ask the court to impose consecutive sentences in this case."

Our reply memorandum underscores the fact that Mr. Milken pleaded guilty to discrete violations of rules and regulations governing securities markets. "They do not involve RICO, insider trading, bribery, corruption or obstruction of justice. Mr. Milken would not have pleaded guilty to those charges, and the government is aware of that fact." It argues that if the court were inclined to consider the government's evidence of other crimes, the defendant would be entitled to what was known as a Fatico hearing from the case of *United States v. Fatico*, which would entail live cross-examination as well as extensive defense presentation. In other words, we would have precisely what the plea agreement was designed to avoid: a costly and time-consuming series of motions, hearings, and trials of indefinite duration.

The reply then refutes each of the government's allegations and concludes by stating the following:

> The Government repeatedly stresses that equal justice requires that the wealthy not receive favored treatment in the courts because of their means. We agree with that proposition. But the Government ignores the corollary proposition that no one should be penalized in this country because of his or her wealth.

The government's reply memorandum was thirty-four pages of a continued attack on Michael Milken. They repeat their allegation that Michael Milken's crimes were serious and extensive, stating, "Milken's conviction of the conspiracy charge, in particular, stands as proof of the sweeping nature of his conduct."

This comment was disingenuous. During the negotiations of the plea, I raised concerns about the conspiracy charge, since I was concerned it suggested wrongful activities beyond the five transactions that Michael was pleading to. The prosecutors assured me that I should not be concerned. They said Michael was only pleading to those five transactions, and the count of conspiracy to commit the five acts added nothing to the admission regarding the five transactions. The government required six counts, and one of the counts needed to be for conspiracy.

The government's reply memorandum tried to distinguish cases the Milken sentencing memorandum cited. The government cited a case where the court imposed consecutive sentences on a defendant who pleaded guilty to racketeering and racketeering conspiracy charges but who also participated in a double homicide. Here was the government comparing Michael Milken to somebody who was involved in homicide and racketeering and received twenty-four years and received consecutive sentences. This argument was inconsistent with their agreement not to recommend consecutive sentences.

The government even stated that the fact Michael Milken agreed to pay $200 million in criminal penalties and $400 million in restitution "belies both his contention that he committed only the five enumerated crimes and his argument that even these crimes were aberrational and technical violations. ... Milken's agreement to pay these monies stands out as the most reliable measure of his criminal conduct."

This statement also violated our understanding with the government during the settlement negotiations that the amount of money agreed to be paid was not an admission of guilt beyond what Michael pleaded to. In a proceeding before the US Parole Commission post-sentencing, Judge Wood acknowledged this fact.

The government concluded its reply by asking the court to ignore a case cited in the Milken sentencing memorandum, where the defendant received a sentence of community service, and to consider instead the sentence imposed upon the defendants in a case where the lead defendant was sentenced to a term of fifteen years' imprisonment. The government was in effect suggesting the court impose a fifteen-year sentence after agreeing in the plea agreement not to recommend a sentence and stating it would not recommend consecutive sentences.

Michael was now dependent on Judge Wood to see that justice was done. The reply memoranda were filed on Friday, September 21, 1990. We reviewed the government's reply sentencing memorandum over the weekend, and Arthur Liman sent a letter to Judge Wood with a copy to John Carroll on September 26, 1990. The letter stated,

> While we regret burdening the Court with additional papers in connection with Mr. Milken's sentencing, we feel compelled to respond to four arguments advanced by the Government in its Reply Memorandum.

The government argued that by pleading guilty to a conspiracy count, Mr. Milken actually pleaded guilty to the other charges not referred to in the plea agreement or the allocution.

> There is a difference between a conspiracy charge and a substantive offense. The plea to the conspiracy is just an admission that there was an agreement. The substantive counts are not defined by the conspiracy, but by the five counts actually pled to. The Government was aware at the time of the plea that Mr. Milken disputed the charges now claimed that he admitted sub silentio. Pleas of guilty must be construed strictly and the admission of a conspiracy is not tantamount to an admission of responsibility for the complete recitation of deeds that the Government ascribes to that conspiracy.

The letter also objected to the government's effort to place before the court as "precedents" cases substantially dissimilar to this case representing very long sentences and in some cases outside the Southern District of New York. In fact, we could not find a single instance in a securities fraud case prosecuted in the Southern District where the government had ever asked a sentencing court to consider sentences imposed in cases outside the Southern District. Each district has its own practices with respect to investigations, charges, and plea agreements.

Most importantly, this letter states that the government had violated paragraph 8 of the plea agreement, which provided it would not make any recommendation as to a term of incarceration. In addition, the government had told us explicitly that if Mr. Milken agreed to the $200 million fine and the $400 million civil fund, the government would not use the amount of these payments against Mr. Milken at sentencing. It was now time for the court to react.

At this point, all that I could do was hope and pray Judge Wood would review our memorandum, look at the comments of the probation officer, and consider the arguments that our legal team was making. At that point in time—September 1990—I had known Michael Milken for thirty-six years. We had worked closely together for seven years. Every positive statement about Michael Milken referenced in Michael's sentencing memorandum came from people who knew him personally, worked with him, and/or had done business with him. The memorandum also quoted the comments of the probation officer who had spent considerable time with Michael. All the negative comments about Michael came from either the prosecutors, who had never met Michael Milken or spent any time with him, or witnesses who were cooperating with the prosecutors under agreements that provided these witnesses great incentives to provide the prosecutors with negative information about Michael Milken. Unfortunately, and as I was learning at the time, when there is a conflict between a defendant—especially a defendant who had pleaded—and the government, great deference is paid to the government.

CHAPTER 12

The Fatico Sentencing
Hearing and Sentencing

Back in Berkeley in the late 1960s, our fraternity successfully participated in intramural athletics. I can still feel the intensity that Michael brought to every event—whether flag football, basketball, soccer, or badminton. He always wanted to win by playing harder and better than the opponent. I witnessed this same intensity in the operation of the High Yield and Convertible Bond Department. Michael seemed familiar with every position held in the department trading portfolio. He was interested in every trade. He made sure that he understood each transaction, since to him every transaction was important, no matter how large or how small.

It was the same intensity that led Mike to finally decide to reduce risks by pleading. Even though he had a hard time accepting the intricacies of the criminal justice system, he knew there was risk in going to trial, and he knew that having to sit in court every day and listen to witnesses without being able to respond immediately would be a very difficult process for him. So he pleaded to end the nightmare and reduce the risks for himself and his family, which also meant avoiding the publicity and ordeal of a trial.

On September 27, 1990, Judge Wood called counsel into court, stating,

> I thought it might assist counsel to know in advance the Court's position on a number of points that had been raised in letters to the Court and in sentencing memorandum and I will take them up in sequence.

She first addressed our argument that the government's denigrating the potential value of Mr. Milken's prospective cooperation violated the plea agreement and that to punish Mr. Milken more harshly than it otherwise would in an effort to force his cooperation would be unconstitutional:

> Neither of these points need concern the defendant. I have no intention of lengthening Mr. Milken's sentence for the purpose of inducing him to cooperate, and I am ignoring anything the Government has said about how Mr. Milken's cooperation is likely to be of little value. … I'm assuming that Mr. Milken will do what he says he will do, that is cooperate fully.

Next, Judge Wood addressed the September 26 letter from Mr. Liman:

> Defense counsel is, of course, right that in pleading guilty to a conspiracy count, Mr. Milken has not pleaded guilty to committing each act he conspires to commit. Secondly, I had noted how relatively simple the Fatico evidence was in cases cited by the Government for the proposition that other courts have considered serious, unadmitted offenses in sentencing. Third, to

the extent that the Government Sentencing Memorandum could be read to make a recommendation as to a specific term of incarceration by stating that Mr. Milken deserves a more substantial penalty than Mr. Boesky, who received a three-year sentence—and I didn't read it as doing so, but I'm addressing that—I'm ignoring any such recommendation, and I am, of course, holding the Government to their agreement. … Similarly, I had already, in my own mind, rejected the Government's argument that the size of the fine and restitution fund are necessarily tantamount to an admission that Mr. Milken committed more serious crimes than those to which he pled.

The court then addressed the significant differences in sentencing memoranda.

Now I'd like to turn to the question whether unadmitted crimes are relevant and whether a Fatico Hearing is warranted.

Judge Wood asked John Carroll how long a Fatico hearing would take on all the allegations. Clearly, Carroll had not thought about that:

Your Honor, we think it's our duty and our burden to convince the Court that Mr. Milken's crimes were neither isolated nor aberrational, but we don't think that we would have to go through all of our evidence to convince the Court of that, so it's hard for us to evaluate at this time how long a Fatico Hearing would take without knowing what would be useful to the Court.

The court replied,

> I had understood you to be asking for much more, but
> I will take into account what you just said.

Judge Wood indicated she was going to consider many aspects of the defendant's character brought to the court's attention by the submissions and letters.

> For the most part, the Government does not dispute
> that Mr. Milken has engaged in many acts of charity
> and generosity. ... You have not disputed—I am
> speaking now to the Government—that Mr. Milken
> has been supportive to his wife, children, relatives,
> friends, neighbors, and coworkers when they needed
> his help. ... Although the Government has suggested
> in some of its language that Mr. Milken's work with
> disadvantaged children is a recent vintage and could
> have been prompted by the subpoena he received, I had
> the probation officer investigate the timing of his good
> works and contributions and I am satisfied that Mr.
> Milken worked with the disadvantaged and contributed
> money to assist them well in advance of this investiga-
> tion becoming known to him. It thus appears to be
> that the only matters seriously in dispute are whether
> Mr. Milken engaged in criminal conduct alleged by the
> Government and contested by Mr. Milken. Is that right,
> Mr. Carroll?

Mr. Carroll's response was disingenuous:

> Your Honor, I think it is largely correct. If there was
> some suggestion in our papers questioning when Mr.

Milken began working with disadvantaged children, that was not intended.

The government sentencing memorandum was not "some suggestion"; it specifically referred to this philanthropic work as "post-investigation."

The court recognized that the defendant disputed all the allegations made by the government in its sentencing memorandum and acknowledged only the conduct specifically set forth in the plea agreement. And then came the bombshell:

> I believe that fairness to the Government and to the defendant is best achieved here by following the traditional course of permitting the Government and defendant to present evidence concerning unadmitted conduct to shed light on the defendant's character, but limiting the amount of material to be presented. I believe that I may be able to obtain a sufficient sense of what light the unadmitted conduct sheds on Mr. Milken's character in an approximately two-week-long Fatico Hearing. To be fair to both sides, I will set time limits on how much testimony each side may elicit. I believe that giving each side about twenty hours in which to present direct testimony and cross-examine the opposing witnesses should suffice. ... Each side would be permitted to use its time allotment to present testimony and documentary evidence concerning as many allegations of unadmitted offenses as it wishes.

The court then asked counsel when they might be ready for a Fatico hearing, and a conference was scheduled for early the next week to address timing.

Mr. Liman told Judge Wood he was hoping that they would not get into disputed matters and the government might reflect upon the court's ruling and conclude we could proceed to sentencing. As Mr. Liman made clear, he would have to know what the government was proposing, and prolonging this process would only prolong extraordinary anguish and agony for Mr. Milken and his family. I was again impressed with Arthur Liman's ability to grasp all the issues raised by whatever was happening in court and to respond immediately and appropriately. Mr. Carroll responded that he would be meeting with Mr. Liman and would make every effort to find common ground.

This was all devastating and did add to the anguish and agony Michael Milken was experiencing. Since Michael had previously informed me that he did not want to take the risk of trial under the atmosphere we were then operating in, the decision to hold, in effect, a minitrial was devastating. Drafting the sentencing memorandum to reflect Mike's entire life was a difficult process for Michael. Having to read the government's sentencing memorandum absolutely infuriated and hurt him. Now I had to inform him that in spite of his plea to committing crimes and the risks he was facing at sentencing, the trial he thought he was avoiding would take place after all. Mike did not take the news well.

Unfortunately, there was not much we could do. We had shown the court how Michael was respected by coworkers, clients, and competitors and how devoted he was to serving the disadvantaged. Judge Wood knew the nature of what he pleaded to: acts that were regulatory violations at most and that had never before been subject to criminal prosecution. And now she wanted to know more about his "character" as the government continued to attempt to justify its intense investigation and all the publicity about this case notwithstanding the plea agreement.

The government violated the spirit and substance of the plea negotiations with its references to specific long sentences, claims about the conspiracy count, and claims about the money to be paid as part of the settlement. Though Judge Wood said she was ignoring all of that, she was still holding a Fatico hearing. All the risks and downside went to Michael—none to the government. All the power rested with the government—none to Michael. The prosecutors had an obligation to see that justice was done. Unfortunately, they were not trained to do so. The people who knew Michael Milken loved and respected him. Neither the judge nor the prosecutors knew him at all.

From this point until the beginning of the Fatico hearing, there were almost daily letters and conferences with the court. In a telephone conference on October 1, 1990, John Carroll indicated they would be starting with what they call the "Wickes April 1986 manipulation" and then presenting evidence with respect to an "MGM transaction with Boesky in 1985," the "Caesar's World transactions from 1983,"

> **The government violated the spirit and substance of the plea negotiations.**

and the "Storer Communications transaction," as described in their sentencing memorandum. The government also indicated that some of the witnesses it would call for a specific transaction might provide information with respect to other government allegations in addition to the four transactions the government would be attempting to prove. Arthur Liman again immediately objected. He argued that he would then need to be prepared to try the entire case. He would need to prepare to cross-examine the witnesses on everything they knew, meaning he would need the same extensive discovery he would have been entitled to in actual trial. In addition, Wickes and Storer Communications were very complex transactions that would require the review of voluminous documents.

Mr. Liman also made it clear, for the record, that he felt this process violated his client's rights and that he was very concerned about it. The government would choose the transactions, and the defense would have to prove a negative by defending whatever the prosecutors chose to present. The initial list of witnesses included seventeen witnesses, adding to Mr. Liman's concerns, especially with the Fatico hearing scheduled to begin the following week. Arthur was clearly making a record for a possible appeal of the entire Fatico process as applied to this case and for a possible claim that the government had violated the plea agreement.

Judge Wood indicated she did not want to deal with hypotheticals and would deal with the issue of possible continuances if the defense needed more time as it came up. Mr. Liman insisted the process was unfair, and he wanted the record to reflect that. Judge Wood remarked,

> Each time you come up with the universe of possibilities, it's going to be my task to bring you back to earth, which is that this is a Fatico Hearing. … So before we start finding that there are impediments to going forward, I want to explore the alternatives in a concrete context.

Judge Wood wanted to conduct this minitrial, and she indicated she was going to do that. Arthur had a responsibility to his client, and he was going to protect him as best he could. The chemistry between Arthur Liman and Judge Wood was not great.

On October 9, in a telephone conference, the prosecutors indicated they now intended to prove what it called the "Wickes,

Storer/SCI, and Caesar's World" transactions, in that order, and was no longer going to pursue "the MGM transaction." It also indicated that one of its witnesses who worked for the Boesky organization might be asked one or two questions relating to MGM. To this, Arthur Liman again quickly objected. We had studied MGM and knew allegations about this subject were easily defensible.

Judge Wood made it clear to the government that she shared Mr. Liman's concern about getting into transactions other than the three the government was now indicating it would be presenting evidence on. Arthur was effective in protecting the record.

The government also listed the witnesses it would call for each transaction and indicated that although Boesky was on the witness list, it had a "diminished expectation" that he would be called. From what we now know, the government never intended to call Ivan Boesky.

The Fatico hearing turned out to be everything I feared it would be. Even though we were successful in showing that Michael Milken did not commit the other crimes the government alleged in its sentencing memorandum, the hearing was still a minitrial with intensive press coverage. Michael, as he knew he would, had a terrible time sitting in court every day listening to witnesses deliver testimony whose veracity he disputed.

On the first break during the first day of the hearing, we went to a room in the courthouse. Arthur Liman was reviewing with the team notes of the testimony we'd just heard and preparing for cross-examination. Michael had three pages of notes regarding statements he found inaccurate, and he wanted to review each one of them in detail with Arthur. The problem was that we did not have evidence we could introduce in court to prove all these statements were inaccurate. Arthur turned to me and said, "I have to prepare for cross-examination. Please keep Mike away from me right now." When I explained the situation to Mike, he accepted it, though unfortunately he had a difficult time understanding this legal process of "courtroom truth," which increased the agony of the whole ordeal.

The Fatico hearing reinforced the fact that we were not playing on a level playing field. In its sentencing memorandum, the government had said one of the reasons Mike should be punished was that as a result of his defending himself, the government had to give immunity to numerous witnesses the government believed had committed crimes. Now we were at the sentencing stage after Mike had pleaded guilty. Based on the government's reasoning, there was no reason for it to continue to give immunity to witnesses to assist in the prosecution of Michael Milken. Nevertheless, the government continued to immunize more witnesses to secure their testimony for the Fatico hearing. It obtained a conviction of Michael Milken through the plea agreement, and Michael was to be sentenced. Why was it necessary to continue to immunize witnesses?

> The Fatico hearing reinforced the fact that we were not playing on a level playing field.

From a defense standpoint, the only way to refute the testimony of these government witnesses was to produce our own witnesses who were equally familiar with the transactions. That presented another problem. The government had informed a number of these potential defense witnesses that they were "targets" of the investigation— meaning the Government might indict them for crimes. Therefore, the lawyers who represented these witnesses would not let them testify. The government would not agree to immunize them, and we were not able to obtain their testimony. The government never indicted any of these potential defense witnesses. This was another reminder of how much power the government has and how little power the individual has in a criminal prosecution.

The Fatico hearing took place over several weeks, with the government choosing the three transactions to demonstrate to Judge Wood that Michael Milken had in fact committed crimes in addition to what he had pleaded to. Judge Wood issued detailed findings after the Fatico hearing. She commented in her findings that though she had allotted twenty hours to each side, neither party had used their allotted time. Arthur Liman had requested for the record that he be able to use part of this time to present evidence about the legitimacy of Michael's business to help inform the court about Michael's character. This request was rejected.

The government presented evidence on Wickes, Storer Communications, and Caesar's World. The government picked whatever it wanted to present. In addition to the three transactions, it could have indicated it would use some of its time to show obstruction of justice. It did not. Yet several of its witnesses testified that Michael indirectly made suggestions to them about possibly destroying documents, though each of them also testified that they had never destroyed a document. Judge Wood seemed especially interested in this testimony. In our posthearing memorandum on behalf of Michael Milken, we argued as follows:

> Although the Government did not choose to present obstruction of justice as one of its transactions, the Government nonetheless elicited testimony about events which they undoubtedly will claim constitutes obstruction. The Government's decision, however, not to make this claim one of its transactions, should be binding on the Government, and as a clear indication the Gov-

ernment did not believe its proof on this issue to be
strong. … None of the evidence, however, demonstrates
an effort to obstruct justice by Mr. Milken. No witness
was asked by Mr. Milken to destroy a document; no
witness was asked to give false testimony; no witness
was asked to withhold evidence from the Government;
no witness was ever intimidated.

The claim of obstruction came out of left field. Michael was
adamant that no obstruction or even suggestion of obstruction ever
took place. I was intimately involved in every facet of the investigation
and Michael's defense, and I am convinced that none of the claims of
obstruction are accurate.

Preliminary Fatico findings were released by Judge Wood the
morning of November 21, 1990, the day set for sentencing. I had
hoped to have an idea of what the sentence might be by reading those
findings. Notwithstanding our understanding that the court would
only consider evidence relating to the three transactions and not other
"background" testimony unrelated to the three transactions above, the
first finding was "attempts to obstruct justice."

One government witness, Terren Peizer, testified that Michael
Milken came to him shortly after Drexel was served with a subpoena
and asked him if he had a book containing entries evidencing transactions with David Solomon. Michael allegedly told Peizer to give the
book to Lorraine Spurge, another employee at Drexel Burnham. Mr.
Peizer testified he gave her this book and never saw the book again.
In fact, Ms. Spurge had testified in front of the grand jury that this
had never happened. We had wanted to call Lorraine to testify at the
Fatico hearing, but she was one of the witnesses who had been sent
a target letter. Her attorney, therefore, would not let her testify. We
asked the court to ask the prosecutors to grant her immunity, as they

had for witnesses they wanted to call, but they were unwilling to do so. Ms. Spurge would have testified that Peizer was not telling the truth. Judge Wood found Peizer credible and concluded Michael had obstructed justice. There was no evidence, other than this testimony, that he ever did.

Mr. Peizer also testified that at a later time, he was looking through his files for documents responsive to a government subpoena. He testified that Michael Milken opened an empty drawer and said words to the effect of "You cannot provide what you do not have." Peizer did testify he did not necessarily assume Michael Milken was telling him to throw out documents, and in fact he indicated he did not throw out documents.

We did demonstrate that Mr. Peizer was not credible in any event. We showed the court that Mr. Peizer produced a sheet of paper to the prosecutor that he said had Michael Milken's handwriting on it that did relate to the relationship with David Solomon. As it turned out, the handwriting referred to was not Michael Milken's. Mr. Peizer further claimed that moments after the announcement on November 14, 1986, of the Boesky plea agreement with the government, he was sitting next to Michael Milken on the trading floor. He testified that Michael was on the phone as he read the news, started to almost stutter, got off the phone, and immediately got up and quickly walked toward his brother Lowell's office. Before Michael reached Lowell's office, Lowell came rushing out of his office; the two of them met and then turned and quickly went into Lowell's office and shut the door. In fact, this very dramatic meeting of the two brothers at this crucial moment never happened. Lowell had been ill and was not even in the office at that time, as shown by evidence presented to the court. We also showed that Mr. Peizer signed an affidavit stating he had complied with the Drexel subpoena when in fact he had withheld a responsive document as a future bargaining chip with the prosecutors. Judge Wood's ruling about our evidence impugning Peizer's credibility was as follows:

> [His] demeanor and manner of response convinced the Court that if [this employee] misidentified handwriting as that of Michael Milken, it was an innocent mistake; that his placing an encounter between Michael Milken and Lowell Milken at "soon after" the announcement of Boesky's cooperation, which I will assume was incorrect, was an innocent mistake in recalling how much time elapsed between the two events; and that his previously having sworn to having made complete document production when he had withheld one document is explained as having occurred before [he] made the decision to disclose wrongdoing that implicated his boss, Michael Milken, and himself.

Mr. Peizer did not make an "innocent mistake."

Another immunized government witness, Jim Dahl, stated that on Sunday, November 16, 1986, two days after the subpoenas had been issued to Michael Milken and Drexel in November 1986, Michael asked him to come into the office and said to him while in the men's room with water running something to the effect that since subpoenas had not been issued, whatever he needed to do, he should do. In fact, subpoenas had been issued. Mr. Dahl testified that he did not interpret these alleged statements as asking him to destroy documents, he never had further discussions with Michael Milken on the subject, and he never destroyed documents. Nevertheless, Judge Wood found "Michael Milken directed [Mr. Dahl] to come into the office 'for the sole purpose of signaling to him the advisability of removing or destroying documents.'"

Other than this obstruction finding, the Fatico findings concluded that the government had failed to prove its three allegations of criminal conduct against Michael Milken. The court went to great lengths to find that Michael Milken had attempted to obstruct justice even though the prosecutors did not list obstruction as one of the allegations they were seeking to prove and it was never proved that any document had been destroyed.

We attacked the credibility of witnesses, but we also made the decision that Michael himself would not testify. Judge Wood in her first high-profile case seemed sensitive to the media. The media had been a resource for the government for over four years. Arthur was concerned that

> Other than this obstruction finding, the Fatico findings concluded that the government had failed to prove its three allegations of criminal conduct against Michael Milken.

if Michael testified and Judge Wood did not believe Michael, she would say he perjured himself and use that as a reason to impose a draconian sentence. It seems unfair that it is so risky for a defendant to testify to defend himself. Jay Regan had initially received a longer sentence for taking the witness stand and testifying in the Princeton/Newport case.

Despite the risks of Michael testifying, I did advocate for Michael to take the risk. For four years, everyone other than Michael Milken had been defining Michael Milken. For four years, everyone was defining Michael's business except Michael. There was no more compelling advocate for Michael or his business than Michael himself. I understood the risks, but I had confidence in Michael. As I explained to Michael and Arthur, I believed this judge was about to make the most important decision affecting Michael Milken's life, and everything she knew about Michael Milken came from someone other than Michael Milken. I also argued to Arthur that Michael was probably the smartest client he'd ever represented and certainly could be thoroughly prepared for his testimony. No matter what he was asked by the prosecutors—or the judge—he would be prepared to answer forthrightly and convincingly.

My thoughts about Michael's testifying were also influenced by Judge Wood's reaction when she heard Michael was not going to testify. Before court one morning, I was discussing this issue with Arthur. At the end of the proceedings that day, as the attorneys and the judge were reviewing certain procedural matters or motions, Arthur addressed the issue:

> There's one other matter, Your Honor, but I don't think you want me to take the time of taking it up now, which is the issue with respect to the defendant himself—he doesn't have immunity—and what the ground rules would be at the end of the proceeding if I wanted to call him. It's a complicated question. It would obviously take more than the time that Your Honor has now to discuss it.

Judge Wood replied,

> I have roughly twenty minutes. Maybe you can lay out for me part of the problems.

Though I was not aware Arthur would bring this up at this time, it was clear he had Judge Wood's attention, and she wanted to discuss the issue at that moment. Arthur raised the fact that if Michael took the stand, he would be testifying without immunity. He would be exposed, since the government would be free in their cross-examination to go beyond the five transactions he'd pleaded to and also the three transactions selected for the Fatico hearing. Judge Wood said she thought he did have immunity for all his activities relating to Drexel or his business or investments while he was employed by Drexel. Arthur responded that he did not have that immunity until he was sentenced, and he did not have immunity from the possibility of individual states' actions. Also, since it would be possible for Michael to withdraw his plea if the government breached the plea agreement, there was a further reason that Michael would not have immunity.

Judge Wood asked,

> Has this [withdrawal of plea due to government breach] ever happened in your experience?

Mr. Liman replied,

> Your Honor, there are so many things in this case that have happened that are not in the experience. ... I can't be put in a position of having someone testify without immunity when the whole structure of this agreement ... was that it wasn't effective immediately.

Judge Wood again brought up the subject shortly thereafter:

> Mr. Carroll, was your understanding correct that even if the Government were to give Mr. Milken what is known as use immunity with respect to his testimony, that it would not bind states or other agencies?

Carroll said it would create problems that would infect a future attempt by a state to prosecute Mr. Milken. Judge Wood's response was as follows:

> I understand the assertion of the privilege with respect to the six counts as to which Mr. Milken pled guilty, that is, he should not be required to reveal the details of wrongdoing on the stand in this forum. With respect to the unadmitted conduct, it was my belief that the defendant took the position that there was no wrong-doing, and under the applicable law it seems to me we could go question by question.

Mr. Liman responded that he understood from the government that they wanted to have freedom to cross-examine on more than the three transactions introduced by the government at the hearing. Judge Wood stated,

> I may not let them do that. We can structure it appro-priately … I think we can separate transactions into at least three categories. One are the six [counts] as to which Mr. Milken pled guilty, and I never intended in this Fatico Hearing to have a trial on those six. I could understand why the Government may want to bring that out by way of background or otherwise, but I think Mr. Milken's interests are much stronger, his countervailing interest in not testifying on the six … The second category would be the three transactions that are the primary subject of testimony here, and then another category would be other alleys that we went down. To make it manageable you might want to limit it to those three. [speaking to John Carroll] I will leave

> it to you to discuss it with Mr. Liman. You don't have to
> react right now. It seems to me we should at least explore
> the question whether a defendant can testify in his own
> Fatico Hearing if he wishes to.

Consistent with his strategy throughout the investigation, Michael deferred to the advice of our legal team. The decision to avoid the risk of testifying, especially after receiving advice not to, was the risk averse thing to do.

After the obstruction finding, the court's findings addressed the allegations of the three transactions: Regarding the Storer Communications transaction, in 1985 Kohlberg Kravis Roberts & Co. (KKR) acquired Storer Communications in what at the time was the largest leveraged buyout ever effected. Drexel structured the transaction and raised $1.465 billion on behalf of KKR, which included different types of securities, including $261 million of a pay-in-kind preferred stock ("PIK Preferred") and $5 million through selling limited partnership interests in a KKR-controlled partnership. The partnership held warrants to purchase 32 percent of the common stock of the new company. KKR could decide if and when to exercise the warrants, in which event the limited partners would have to contribute additional funds for the exercise.

The $261 million PIK Preferred was the lowest, or most junior, tier of the financing and the most risky and difficult to market. Michael Milken discussed this preferred with Fred Joseph, the CEO of Drexel, who indicated that though Drexel was committing to raise the other $1.2 billion of the financing, Drexel did not want to be obligated to purchase the PIK Preferred if it could not otherwise be sold. KKR needed assurance with respect to the total financing in order to have the acquisition approved by Storer Communications' board of directors.

In discussions between Fred Joseph and Michael Milken, Michael offered to personally commit to the purchase of the PIK Preferred in order to complete the transaction. It was not unusual for Michael to assist Drexel financially in transactions, and Fred Joseph agreed Michael would also be able to purchase the interests in the limited partnership that would own the warrants. Fred Joseph testified to these facts at the Fatico hearing. The transaction went forward based upon these commitments.

A Drexel customer purchased 20 percent of the PIK Preferred together with limited partnership interests, and Michael Milken and his associates in the High Yield Department committed to purchase the other 80 percent of the PIK Preferred. The government argued that KKR made the equity available to Drexel to induce third-party purchasers to purchase securities and that by Michael having purchased it, he somehow committed a fraud. We had argued it was in Drexel's discretion to use the equity as Drexel saw fit. There would have been no transaction had Mr. Milken and partnerships he was involved with not committed to this purchase. The court agreed in its findings:

> I find the partnerships agreed to purchase the preferred and for whatever risk such a purchase entailed. Michael Milken received the approval of Fred Joseph before purchasing the preferred for the partnership; indeed, Joseph expressed his satisfaction that the partnerships were willing to make the purchase that Drexel was unwilling to risk.

The government next contended that Drexel should have disclosed in the prospectus the fact that these partnerships were purchasing the equity, though Fred Joseph testified that Drexel's policy did not require disclosing these purchases by employee-related partnerships.

The judge held, "The court is not willing to enhance Milken's sentence based on Drexel's having followed such a policy, in the absence of any evidence that Milken had a role in formulating that policy."

The government next alleged Milken should have told KKR that most of the equity warrants were being purchased by these partnerships. A representative of KKR testified at the hearing that KKR would have gone ahead with the transaction whether it knew Milken or associates were going to purchase most of the warrants. KKR just wanted to get the deal done. The representative of KKR did testify that he "might" have negotiated Drexel's fee differently if it knew about this purchase of equity but admitted that was speculation. Judge Wood did find as follows:

> Milken deliberately failed to disclose to KKR the fact that Milken and his family and associates were keeping most of the warrants themselves. … I will take this non-disclosure into account in assessing Milken's character.

There was no finding that anyone was damaged by the "nondisclosure," and it certainly was not a crime. Judge Wood did not refer to this finding at sentencing.

Again, with respect to Storer, the government further alleged that when limited partnership interests were repurchased by Drexel from a client, Milken handpicked individuals who were able to purchase these interests—many of whom were fund managers of Drexel clients who'd bought securities in Storer. The defense argued there was nothing illegal or improper about fund managers purchasing these interests. Each institution the fund manager worked for bought Storer preferred based on the merits of the transaction before it was known these interests might be available. It was very difficult to assess the value of these partnership interests at the time, though they turned out to be very valuable. One of the witnesses for the government stated he believed this investment would either be a "strikeout or a home run." The government alleged that since these managers worked for institutions that had bought preferred stock in the transaction, they were given an illegal gratuity. The court found that whether these individuals violated their obligations to their principals was not something Michael Milken would have been aware of or was responsible for.

> As has been the case with several other Government allegations during this hearing, the record contains little direct evidence linking Milken to wrongdoing in connection with the sale of partnership interest to fiduciaries of Drexel clients and customers. In fact, only one witness testified that he spoke with Milken regarding this investment, and that witness had been immunized during the Fatico Hearing for the purpose of testifying at the hearing.

The government therefore alleged multiple violations with respect to the Storer transaction, and Judge Wood found for Michael on all of them. She only found he should have told KKR that he was purchasing certain securities—a purchase encouraged and approved by Drexel management.

The next finding discussed the Wickes transaction, where it was alleged there was a manipulation of the price of Wickes common stock on April 23, 1986. Wickes had a preferred stock outstanding that was convertible into common stock. Under the terms of the preferred stock, Wickes could retire the preferred stock or force its holders to convert into common stock if the Wickes common stock closed at or above a certain price on twenty out of thirty consecutive days. Since the preferred paid a high dividend, it was in Wickes's interest to be able to retire the preferred or force conversion into common stock, which would end Wickes's obligation to pay a dividend. The stock had closed at or above the price for nineteen of twenty-nine days. An immunized employee of Drexel and an immunized employee of the Boesky organization both testified at the Fatico hearing that they spoke together on that thirtieth day, and as a result, the Boesky organization purchased 1.9 million shares of Wickes common stock in the last half hour of the trading day. The stock did close at the designated price that day, so Wickes could call the preferred. These two witnesses each testified that they had no discussions with Michael Milken about this purchase of Wickes stock. A third witness, also a Drexel employee who was immunized solely to testify at the Fatico hearing, testified that Michael Milken told him to take notice of Wickes stock that day but said nothing else. Judge Wood commented that this recently immunized witness had twice previously lied under oath in both SEC and grand jury testimony and found this witness not credible. Judge Wood found that there was a lack of credible evidence of Michael Milken's involvement in this Wickes transaction.

The last transaction, Caesar's World, was the only allegation of insider trading. The securities involved in this transaction were bonds, not common stock. The allegation was that Michael Milken received material nonpublic information about Caesar's World prior to June 29, 1983, and that based on that information, he traded Caesar's World bonds for his own account as well as for Drexel's account on that day.

This transaction had been the subject of an SEC investigation in 1985. After taking extensive testimony, the SEC decided not to bring any action at that time.

There had been a meeting between Drexel and Caesar's World on June 29, 1983. Based upon the evidence presented, Judge Wood found that Michael Milken surely did not possess any material nonpublic information prior to the June 29, 1983, meeting between Drexel and Caesar's World officials. The June 29 meeting was the first meeting between Drexel and Caesar's World and was only an exploratory meeting. Judge Wood found the following:

> By the end of the meeting, the probability of Caesar's World doing ... a particular transaction was not high enough for information gained at that meeting to be material. ... Michael Milken thus did not receive material nonpublic information at the June 29th meeting. ... I am unable to find that Michael Milken traded on material nonpublic information.

The investigation had started as an insider trading investigation involving Ivan Boesky and ended with the only allegation of insider trading involving neither Ivan Boesky nor a stock.

As I read the court's Fatico findings before the sentencing hearing in November 1990, it was clear we had won, that the government failed on each of the transactions it had handpicked. The government picked presumably its best cases to prove Michael had committed crimes beyond his plea. They never called Ivan Boesky as a witness and never referred to or played any of the Boesky tape. They also never called as witnesses Seth Mooradian or Charles Thurnher, both government witnesses, who kept the records about the transactions that the government alleged led to the $5.3 million fee. The government had access to the three individuals who allegedly were the three individuals with the most knowledge about the $5.3 million fee. They chose to call none of these persons as witnesses.

Having finished reading the court's Fatico findings, I could have been somewhat optimistic about the length of Michael's sentence. Not only did the findings show that the government had failed to connect

Michael to any other wrongdoing, but Judge Wood had previously acknowledged many of Michael's positive qualities, especially surrounding his work in the community prior to the government's investigation. *The sentence should be nonconsecutive and less than five years*, I believed and/or hoped. Yet Judge Wood found wrongdoing from the "background" information on obstruction. After reading these findings hours before sentencing, I had no idea what the sentence would be, but I was concerned.

That Wednesday, November 21, 1990, was a mild day in New York City. It was also the day before what would have been an uneventful and happy Thanksgiving. I would have otherwise been home in Los Angeles with my wife and three children, but there I was in the United States courthouse for the Southern District of New York as my childhood friend, Michael Milken, was about to be sentenced. Four years of the most intensive securities law investigation to that date was about to culminate before United States District Judge Kimba Wood.

I had spent every day of those four years working to prove Michael was innocent of the charges against him and making sure the system treated him fairly. The only preparation I had when the investigation started was a value system that taught me loyalty and to do what is right and ethical and live each day with integrity no matter what the circumstances. Whatever my efforts were, Michael was about to be sentenced.

Bob Litt, an attorney with the firm of Williams & Connolly, and I visited Michael in his hotel room at the Carlyle Hotel the night before sentencing. As we left his room, Bob remarked to me how concerned he was about what the sentence would be. Bob was a former Assistant US Attorney for the Southern District of New York and had previously worked under US Attorney Rudolph Giuliani. Bob indicated it was highly unusual that after a plea, the defendant and the government in a white-collar case would submit sentencing memoranda with such diametrically opposed views about what happened. Judge Wood was an inexperienced judge. Her background was not criminal law. Bob was concerned that under the circumstances, Judge Wood could side with the government, ignore the statement that the government would not request consecutive sentences, and issue a sentence that could be as much as ten years. I found this prospect quite chilling.

Now here we were that morning in the hallway of the courthouse outside Judge Wood's chambers reviewing the Fatico findings, which we'd just received. Members of Judge Wood's family exited her chambers smiling, joking with one another, and taking pictures. When we went into the courtroom, there was a special area for the members of Judge Wood's family to sit. This heightened my concern about what was about to happen. The courtroom was packed, with a large section reserved for members of the media. There were hundreds, if not thousands of people outside the courthouse. As Judge Wood took the bench, my fear increased. I remember thinking, *This must be like the atmosphere in ancient Rome when crowds gathered to watch gladiators.* This was going to be the most important moment at that time in Judge Wood's career and in

> **There were hundreds, if not thousands of people outside the courthouse. As Judge Wood took the bench, my fear increased. I remember thinking,** *This must be like the atmosphere in ancient Rome when crowds gathered to watch gladiators.*

Michael Milken's life, and they had really never met. Michael's family was there to support him. Why was Judge Wood's family there? How many sentencing hearings have they ever attended before or since?

The hearing began. Jess Fardella spoke on behalf of the government and gave his presentation, and Arthur Liman made his presentation on behalf of Michael. Judge Wood then began to speak.

I was sitting behind Paul, Weiss partners Arthur Liman and Marty Flumenbaum, who were at the counsel's table. Steve Kaufman was sitting next to me, which mirrored the seating arrangements during the Fatico hearings and other court appearances. The Paul, Weiss attorneys felt strongly that it was not in Michael's best interest for me, a close associate, to make official appearances before the court. I understood and accepted that advice.

Sitting in the first several rows behind us were Mike's family, including his wife, Lori; his mother, Ferne; and his brother, Lowell. My wife, Ellen, one of Lori's closest friends since college, was also present, as were other friends and supporters.

I can still recall the anxiety I felt as Judge Wood began to speak:

> Sentencing practice dictates that before imposing sentence, the Court makes findings as to any undisputed facts to be taken into account in sentencing. …
>
> Before I summarize those findings, I want to note the purpose of making the findings and the limit of those findings.
>
> The law is clear that a sentencing judge should consider all of the defendant's conduct in sentencing, not just the conduct to which he pled guilty. This sometimes works to a defendant's advantage where, for example, the rest of his conduct has been exemplary. One of the contentions of the defendant here was just

that, that his other conduct has been exemplary and should result in a lenient sentence. ...

I chose to hold a Fatico hearing in this case for two principal reasons. First, unlike a white-collar criminal who pled guilty to one count of criminal conduct, the sentence for which is typically limited to a narrow range of 0 to 3 or 0 to 5 years, Defendant here pled guilty to six counts carrying an unusually wide range of possible prison sentence from 0 to 28 years, and, second, there was a stark contrast between the defense version of the defendant's conduct and the Government version. ...

It is unusual for a judge to be presented with both such a wide range of possible sentences and such a stark contrast between the defendant's version and the Government's version of the defendant's conduct.

At this point, Bob Litt's concern became my concern. Judge Wood continued,

The evidence offered at the Fatico hearing established neither the Government's version of Defendant's conduct nor Defendant's own version. It established that Defendant engaged in the additional misconduct of attempting to obstruct justice and obstructing justice ...

Judge Wood asked the government to present evidence from its intensive four-year investigation of any other misconduct Michael had engaged in other than the technical violations of regulations he had pleaded to. The government did not identify obstruction of justice as one of the types of conduct it would show. It put on witnesses with respect to the alleged misconduct it was trying to show, who stated they had received "signals" from Michael that they should destroy documents, though they never did so and Michael never did so. Judge Wood seemed unusually interested in this testimony during the Fatico hearing.

And Michael had not testified at the Fatico hearing.

Judge Wood addressed Michael:

> You are being sentenced for six counts of criminal activity spanning approximately three years in participation with several other people involving several different transactions that violated securities laws, tax laws, and other laws.
>
> You have attempted to mitigate these crimes by claiming they represented no more than overzealous service to your clients, that they involved mere technicalities, and that they did not represent the core of how you did business. ...
>
> It has also been argued that your violations were technical ones to be distinguished from accumulating profits through insider trading and that your conduct is not really criminal or that it is only barely criminal.
>
> These arguments fail to take into account the fact that you may have committed only subtle crimes not because you were not disposed to any criminal behavior but because you were willing to commit only crimes that were unlikely to be detected. ...
>
> In this regard, your post November 14, 1986, comments to other employees about subpoenas are of the same character as the six admitted offenses. You did not order employees to destroy or remove documents, but you communicated the advisability of their doing

so in subtle terms that preserved some deniability on your part. …

Let me turn then to the purposes of sentencing and their application here. As was pointed out, purposes are generally thought to be individual deterrence, general deterrence, punishment or just desserts, retribution, and rehabilitation. …

I have given considerable thought to whether a sentence of lengthy community service would be an adequate penalty here. It would have the advantages of permitting you to work productively with others which I believe you could do well rather than having you be warehoused in a prison. Nevertheless, I believe that a prison term is required for the purposes of general deterrence; that is, the need to deter others from violating the law and the possibility that the sentence given in one case will prevent others from violating the law.

I turn now to the sentence that is appropriate.

In deciding how long a prison term is appropriate and how much community service is appropriate, I have taken into account that long before your current legal problems you took a significant amount of your own personal time to serve the community by working with disadvantaged children rather, for example, than using all your personal time to acquire possessions. You also successfully encouraged your colleagues at work to do the same.

I have also taken into account the emotional support that you have provided to your family, neighbors, coworkers, and the fact that many colleagues and competitors found you to be forthright, honorable, and honest in your dealing with them over the years.

You also committed crimes that are hard to detect and crimes that are hard to detect warrant greater punishment in order to be effective in deterring others from committing them.

I made my own independent evaluation of the conduct of and sentences given to Mr. Boesky, Mr. Levine, and others based on my reading of their presentence reports and the transcripts of sentencing arguments and I arrived at my own conclusion as to the appropriate proportionality among them.

Mr. Milken, please rise.

You are unquestionably a man of talent and industry and you have consistently shown a dedication to those less fortunate than you. It is my hope that the rest of your life will fulfill the promise shown early in your career.

However, for the reasons stated earlier, I sentence you to a total of 10 years in prison consisting of two years each on counts 2 through 6 to be served consecutively, and I also sentence you to three years of probation on count 1. A special condition of your probation is that you serve full time community service, 1800 hours per year for each of the three years, in a program to be determined by the court.

I advise you that you have a right to appeal this sentence.

You may be seated at this point.

I assume that the defendant may surrender to the facility designated by the Bureau of Prisons.

I was in a complete state of shock. She had done exactly what we had negotiated so long and hard with the US Attorney's Office to avoid. She'd imposed a sentence of greater than five years. She'd imposed consecutive sentences on five of the six counts—because of the obstruction and because his crimes were not blatant—using a form of reasoning that I still do not understand.

Arthur Liman and Steve Kaufman both lamented to me that Judge Wood's decision negated the advice the attorneys had given Michael about the most important decision in his life, advice based upon their best judgment resulting from years of experience. All the rules changed or were ignored in the process. Four years and one week after the government announced that Ivan Boesky had pleaded guilty to only one count, Mike was going to prison with a sentence four times the length of the Boesky sentence. How could this have happened? How did we get there?

> I was in a complete state of shock. She had done exactly what we had negotiated so long and hard with the US Attorney's Office to avoid. She'd imposed a sentence of greater than five years.

Mike had pleaded to engaging in five transactions as technical violations of securities regulations that had never been the subject of prior criminal prosecution. The government claimed he was guilty of far worse but failed to prove it when given the chance. Judge Wood agreed that Mike's works in the community and support of friends and colleagues were extraordinary. Michael was guilty of wrongdoing in five of the hundreds of thousands of transactions he was involved in and was subjected to probably the most draconian sentence ever imposed in a white-collar case involving violations of securities laws: ten years' imprisonment plus three years of full-time community service at eighteen hundred hours a year.

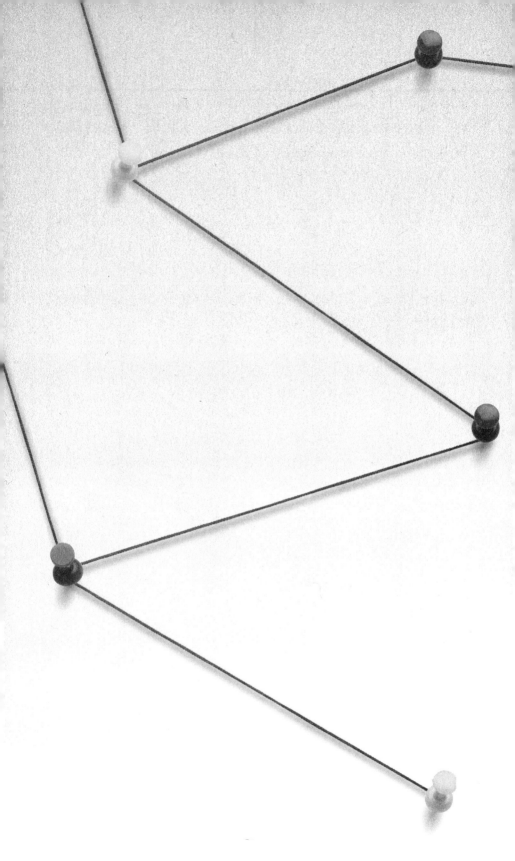

CHAPTER 13

Postsentencing

We were all stunned. Lowell came up to me and asked me what the sentence was. Since we all believed there would not be consecutive sentences, he was asking whether the sentence was two years or ten years. Michael, sitting between his Paul, Weiss lawyers, Marty Flumenbaum and Arthur Liman, asked them what the sentence was. It was ten years plus three years of eighteen hundred hours of community service a year. It was a shock. No one had ever heard of a ten-year sentence or, for that matter, an eighteen-hundred-hour-a-year community service sentence in a securities case, and certainly not both.

We had planned to leave from the courthouse and go directly to the airport to fly back to Los Angeles. The jury room behind the courtroom was made available to us to meet before and after the hearing. We went directly there after the hearing to avoid being confronted by media or anyone else. Lori joined Mike in the jury room, and I waited outside in the hall with Arthur, Steve Kaufman, and a few others. It is hard to describe the next ten to twenty minutes. It seemed like forever.

You could hear Michael's and Lori's grief-filled cries clearly out in the hallway. They were shocked, devastated, and distraught. They'd never considered the possibility of a ten-year sentence, otherwise there would have been no plea. After a few minutes, Judge Wood walked by us as she was leaving. She looked at me and politely said, "Hello, Mr. Sandler." I just stared at her, being too angry and devastated myself to do anything but stare and nod. I recall Judge Wood looking subdued and stunned herself as she clearly heard the cries.

Jan McGaff, the head of security for Drexel in Los Angeles, who had organized the logistics for our entering and exiting the courthouse with the US marshals, told me he was concerned that Michael would start hyperventilating. I went into the jury room to try to calm Mike and Lori and make sure they were okay. I cannot remember what I said, but we all eventually regained our composure sufficiently to leave. At that moment, neither Michael nor Lori had any idea how long he would be away, but

> You could hear Michael's and Lori's grief-filled cries clearly out in the hallway. They were shocked, devastated, and distraught. They'd never considered the possibility of a ten-year sentence.

it was considerably longer than the couple of years they'd expected and already dreaded. The federal marshals, who could not have been more professional and considerate, arranged for us to leave through the garage to avoid the media and crowds outside.

As we left the courthouse, I could not help but think, *What more could I have done? What did I miss?* Throughout this entire process, Mike and I would question our legal team about numerous matters but would always defer to them. This was clearly an area where we had no experience and they did. Out of fairness to the legal team, no one had ever seen a case like this where experience did not seem to make a difference. As Arthur Liman said in his memoirs, "Never had I felt that I so badly let a client down." I had never seen a lawyer give more of himself to a client than Arthur did to Michael, but here we were.

I also second-guessed myself and the decision for Michael not to take the stand and testify in his own defense at the Fatico hearing. Should I have been more forceful? How would I have felt had Michael testified and still received a ten-year sentence? I know that the advice not to testify was sound legal advice. And I certainly will never know if it was the correct decision. On November 21, 1990, Michael Milken had not testified and now had a ten-year sentence.

I also decided that going forward I would take a more active role in the process to get Michael's sentence reduced. Up to that time I had taken a background seat, especially on the issue of dealing with the prosecutors between the time of the plea and the filing of the sentencing memorandum. Our legal team was adamant that it was not in Michael's interest for me to take a more active role. Since I was a close friend who also worked with Michael, the prosecutors would not deem me credible, which would diminish the effectiveness of our legal team and put me at risk. Michael and I agreed that they were the experts. There was no question that the team was correct and had given the correct advice initially. But by the time of sentencing, I had developed my own relationship with the prosecutors and was known to Judge Wood and decided to start being more assertive.

Needless to say, the ride home was unpleasant. We tried to watch movies and engage in small talk, but Mike and Lori were too distraught by the decision, and both had a difficult time maintaining their composure. We had always assumed Mike would get a prison sentence and would go to a minimum-security federal prison camp. In the federal system there are maximum-security, medium-security, and minimum-security prisons. Regardless of what the media sometimes refers to as "country club prisons," that is an absurd moniker. They are all prisons. You are at the mercy of the guards and the prison officials to determine your schedules, your job, your everything. If you get sick, you only have access to doctors or medications that the Bureau of Prisons provides, if and when it provides them. That said, in a minimum-security federal prison camp, you are not in a cell and are in a safer environment.

At the end of the sentencing hearing, the following discussion took place between Arthur Liman and Judge Wood:

> Mr. Liman: Your Honor does not have the power to designate a facility, but Your Honor has the power to make a request and we would like to submit a proposed request for designation early next week. We have talked to the Government about that.
>
> The court: Yes. There is no reason for me not to honor your request to make that recommendation.

Michael asked me on the way home whether I thought he would still be eligible for a federal prison camp. In spite of everything, I was comfortable that the type of facility would be a federal prison camp. What turned out to be unusual was that the Bureau of Prisons did not accept the judge's specific recommendation. We had requested that Michael serve his sentence at the federal prison camp located at Nellis Air Force Base in Las Vegas. Las Vegas was very easy to get to from Los Angeles. Mike and Lori had many friends in Las Vegas. Judge Wood agreed and recommended Nellis Air Force Base. It is rare for the judge's recommendation not to be followed, but in this case, like almost everything else that had happened, the Bureau of Prisons deviated from its normal practice and assigned Mike to the federal prison camp in Pleasanton, California, a relatively new facility called FCI Dublin. Assistant US Attorney John Carroll stated to me, after interviewing Mike at the Pleasanton facility, that this was the worst such facility he had seen. He even commented that it even seemed to him that Michael could not get a break in the process.

The day after sentencing was Thanksgiving. I called Lowell that morning, and we decided to drive out to Boron, California, to see what the federal prison camp there looked like. There was no real reason to do that other than to spend some quiet time together, discussing the past four years and starting to plan for what we needed to do going forward. Over the next couple of days, I could not stop thinking about the sentence. In our sentencing memorandum, we had listed ninety criminal prosecutions in the Southern District of New York for securities fraud from 1980 to the date of the sentence. The sentences ranged from a few days to a couple of years—with most sentences being less than a year or probation. Sometimes probation included as much as forty hours a month of community service. Michael Milken's sentence was not only

> Michael Milken's sentence was not only ten years in prison but included three years' probation and approximately forty hours a week of community service. I believe there has never been a sentence like that before or since in a securities regulation white-collar case.

ten years in prison but included three years' probation and approximately forty hours a week of community service. I believe there has never been a sentence like that before or since in a securities regulation white-collar case.

John Carroll agreed to a March 4, 1991, surrender date.

I reviewed our options to reduce the sentence with Arthur. We did have the right to appeal the sentence, and Arthur had made a record before Judge Wood to support an appeal. We filed a notice of appeal and prepared an appellate brief arguing both that the Fatico process had deprived Michael of his due process rights and that the prosecutors had violated the plea agreement. At Fatico, the prosecution was given the opportunity to prove anything it chose, but Michael was not given the opportunity to prove what his business and life were all about, though the hearing was about his character. In addition to the appeal, we also had the option of filing a motion for reduction of sentence under Rule 35 of the Federal Rules asking the judge to reduce the sentence.

A ten-year sentence would require Mike to spend approximately six and a half years in prison. It is devastating enough to spend a month in prison, but when you plead, believing you would spend two to three years at the most in prison, the thought of adding four years to that number is horrifying, especially when your children are between nine and seventeen years old.

At sentencing, Mr. Liman asked the court to agree that the sentence would be imposed pursuant to the statute that allowed a parole board to decide when it would consider the possibility of parole. The judge responded, "That will be done, and I will also be filling out a form that deals with parole, which the defendant will have access to." Parole was a third option for getting Michael an early release. We had the right to pursue all three options.

One week after sentencing, on November 28, 1990, we were back in court at the request of Judge Wood. She stated,

I have checked with a number of people, including the Chairman of the United States Parole Commission. ... We have to deal nonetheless with whether Mr. Milken is in category 5 or category 6.[2] That's a determination for the Parole Commission, but it seems to me that this group now has more information than the Parole Commission is likely to have. ... My understanding is that the allocation between criminal fine and criminal penalty does not matter to the Parole Commission. What does matter is a totally separate point, and that is whether fees, such as the Fischbach fee, should be included in calculating the severity of the offense for parole release purposes—and I have had views on that all along. I still have views. ... I think it might be useful for us, as a practical matter, to move on to see whether we can reach some consensus ... as to the amount of money that should be viewed for parole guideline release purposes. ... The guidelines are clearest in dealing with tax fraud—tax evasion. Section 501 says that "if the amount of tax evaded or evasion attempted is more than a million dollars, you grade as category six. If it's between two hundred thousand, but not more than a million, you grade as category five."

Now, as we know, Mr. Milken gained no money whatever from his involvement in the Solomon tax

---

2   Under parole guidelines in effect at the time, category five means someone is eligible for parole after serving twenty-four to thirty-six months, and category six is forty to fifty-two months. The economic effect of the crime determines the category.

fraud ... so it seemed to me that at our level here in the Southern District of New York we got to try to figure out what's appropriate so that it's that that goes to the Parole Commission, and Ms. Bracken agrees. ... I thought it might be helpful, since we know more about what happened, to come up with the Court's recommendation, and certainly Ms. Bracken might want some guidance here.

Mr. Liman made it clear to the judge that the plea was to aiding and abetting a false filing, not tax evasion, especially since Solomon deferred tax by taking the loss but eventually paid tax. And there was no allegation that Michael did not pay his taxes. The government agreed that calculations of Solomon's tax situation would be made available to Mr. Liman so that we, too, could weigh in on what the amounts were. Jess Fardella, on behalf of the government, suggested that consideration of this be deferred until the Parole Commission met. Judge Wood's response was as follows:

There is a problem going in. The Parole Commission needs to grade Mr. Milken's offense severity, they have to do it for a number of their own purposes. Plus, I think it's important for Mr. Milken to know what he is facing. They may never have dealt with anything like this before, and I think may be open to considering some of that money unless there is a contrary recommendation, so I think that that needs to be thought through. In other words, they intended to take into account dollars that were taken from a victim, dollars acquired from no conduct other than completely wrongful conduct. Here we have dollars acquired from hybrid conduct—

> the wrongful conduct may have been one motivation of many for a transaction that had occurred and much of the Drexel conduct may have been perfectly appropriate investment banking conduct—I don't think the Parole Commission ever had this in mind.

We were exactly seven days after sentencing, and Judge Wood had us back in court and was strongly advocating for Michael to be eligible for release from prison through parole long before the time the ten-year sentence suggested. She also showed sensitivity to what Michael was now going through and to the fact that what he'd pleaded to did not result in profits to him.

At the end of the hearing, Judge Wood stated, "May I see counsel briefly in the robing room? Thank you; we're adjourned."

As the prosecutors and Messrs. Liman and Flumenbaum from Paul, Weiss started moving toward the robing room, I followed. Whatever would happen to Michael Milken going forward, I was going to play a direct role.

What transpired next was quite unexpected. We all sat in the robing room with Judge Wood. As she began to talk, there was a knock at the door. Her clerk answered the door and came back and said the media was requesting to have a representative present at the meeting. As was usually the case, a number of reporters had been in the courtroom. Judge Wood paused for at most two seconds and said, "No, this will be a private discussion with the lawyers." Judge Wood had always been very deferential to the media. But Judge Wood made it very clear that reporters were not going to be invited into this off-the-record meeting. I was pleasantly surprised.

Judge Wood then looked at John Carroll and Jess Fardella and told them they had done an outstanding job at the Fatico hearing. Nevertheless, she said they were unable to show any further wrongdoing by Mr. Milken. "The evidence just was not there." She made it clear she felt it was time to stop the fighting and to work together to come to a fair resolution of the economic effect of what Mr. Milken had pleaded to, which could be provided to the Parole Commission. It was also clear that she believed the number was less than $1 million. Though she had given the ten-year sentence, she intended that Michael Milken should actually serve considerably less time. I do not know if this is what Judge Wood had intended when she handed down the sentence or if she was affected by what had happened immediately after the sentencing when I saw her in the corridor. It might have been both.

In any event, Mike's freedom and future were at stake. The demeanor of the Judge Wood I saw that day was different from that of the Judge Wood who only a week earlier had said, "For reasons stated earlier, I sentence you to a total of ten years in prison." I felt as we left court that day that Michael would serve less than the ten-year sentence. He still faced too many years in prison.

Arthur Liman consulted with Professor Laurence Tribe, a well-respected expert on constitutional law at Harvard Law School, regarding the appeal. Professor Tribe believed there was a strong basis for appealing the sentencing proceedings. The notice of appeal had been filed, and the appellate brief filing date was set. That filing date was the week before Michael was to begin serving his sentence. The draft of the brief was well written and presented the arguments very strongly. I believed in the arguments. The problem was that the brief was extremely critical of both Judge Wood and the prosecutors. Up to this point, fighting with the prosecutors or the judge had not been a winning strategy, especially when there were other options.

I discussed this issue with Bob Litt at Williams & Connolly and Brad Karp at Paul, Weiss, who was working on the brief. They were also concerned that pursuing the appeal would reduce the chances of being successful with a Rule 35 motion. The Rule 35 motion would be filed with Judge Wood, and the prosecutors would have an opportunity to object. Even if the appeal was successful, the result could be resentencing by Judge Wood. I was concerned that if we were not successful on the appeal, Michael would be in a worse position, having attacked both the prosecutors and the judge—especially now that Judge Wood was supporting an early release through parole.

I was advised by Bob Litt and Brad Karp that we could withdraw the appeal without prejudice. Since we had filed the notice of appeal, we had perfected our right to appeal. By withdrawing the appeal without prejudice, we could come back later and again pursue the appeal if we felt it was necessary. We would need to tell the appellate court that we were withdrawing the appeal at that time because we intended to pursue the Rule 35 motion and did not want to take up the court's time if that motion was successful.

Arthur and Lawrence Tribe felt this was a mistake. They were concerned the court of appeals would conclude that the appeal was not serious if it depended on an unsuccessful Rule 35 motion. I understood and appreciated that argument. I had a phone call with Arthur and Larry Tribe. I asked Larry what he thought our chance of success was on the appeal. He said it was a very good appeal and that we probably had close to a 50 percent chance of being successful, which was a very strong appeal. Of course, I'd believed we had almost no chance of getting a ten-year sentence, so I did not like the fifty-fifty odds. I believed pursuing an early parole and a Rule 35 motion to Judge Wood provided the best chances for Michael to get an early release, and so I advised Michael.

Larry and Arthur also spoke with Michael. Michael was about to leave for prison in a few days and was torn about what to do. He was very upset about everything that had transpired since he'd pleaded. He did not disagree with my concerns, but he also heard what Arthur Liman and Larry Tribe were saying. Michael asked his parole officer, Michaela Bracken, what she thought. Ms. Bracken said she really could not advise him other than to say she would listen to the person whom he felt was influenced only by what was in Michael's best interest. Michael knew we all cared about his best interests, but that was all I cared about. Mike agreed we should withdraw the appeal without prejudice at this time. I felt very comfortable with the decision.

On March 3, 1991, it was time for Mike to report to prison. The reporting date had been set as March 4, 1991—a Monday. Since this date was public, Mike and I were concerned that there would be media present. Our consultant on prison and parole matters, Herb Hoelter, suggested Mike report a day early. The Bureau of Prisons agreed that Mike could report the evening of March 3.

> On March 3, 1991, it was time for Mike to report to prison.

I met Mike and Lori at their home, and we went to the airport together for the hour flight. Mike and I talked about the fact that as a lawyer, I was not restricted in the number of times I could visit with him to discuss legal matters. I would consult with the officials at the prison camp to make arrangements to visit as often as twice a week. Mike, Lori, and I engaged in a lot of small talk on the short flight, and I tried to let Mike and Lori speak alone. We landed, got into the rental car, and drove to Pleasanton. Prison officials were waiting for us, and fortunately there were no members of the media present. Mike had received very specific instructions about what he was allowed to bring with him, and he'd packed accordingly. For example, he could wear a baseball cap, but not one with any insignia or logo on it. He could have a watch, but not one with a calculator or a computer.

Mike got out of the car, said goodbye to the two of us, and went with the prison officials. Lori and I sat in the car for a while as we watched him enter the building and could see him through a window. I turned to Lori and said, "I guess we should go."

She turned to me and said, "I want to go back in there and get him." To this day I feel the emotion of that moment.

We drove sadly out of Dublin camp and flew home, talking about what had happened and what the next couple of years might be like. We would both visit Dublin camp many times. Lori had been amazing through all of this. She was the same grounded, selfless, caring human being I'd met when I was twelve years old. And she is that same person today. Mike and Lori were high school sweethearts, and their relationship only grew stronger. She would get through this, and she would make sure that Michael and their children would too. I was glad I could be with Michael and Lori that evening.

I told John Carroll and Jess Fardella that they should be required to do what I did that Sunday evening when I took Michael to prison. It would expose young prosecutors to the fact that the people they were investigating were human beings with families.

Judge Wood scheduled a number of hearings in order to provide some guidance or assistance to the Parole Commission. After a series of submissions, Judge Wood issued her conclusions on the amounts involved to present to the Parole Commission:

> With respect to the calculation of Mr. Milken's offense severity category … it is the Parole Commission that decides whether Mr. Milken will be given an offense severity category of five or six. And it's for the Court only to state to the Parole Commission on Form AO235

whether it agrees with the calculation made by the probation officer, Ms. Bracken.

In a sentencing such as this in which a defendant is not sentenced to real time and in which the Parole Commission will be applying its own rules in deciding when to release a defendant, a sentencing judge usually begins by formulating a view as to how much real time a defendant should serve, and then reviews the Parole Commission practices and procedures to ascertain how likely it is that application of Parole Commission practices and procedures will result in a defendant serving the real time that the judge had in mind.

If a judge thinks a defendant should serve less time than the parole release guidelines would mandate, the judge can sentence a defendant to a sentence low enough to trump the parole release guidelines. This happened, for example, with the sentences of Ivan Boesky, Dennis Levine, Marty Siegel, and Robert Freeman ... although they each caused losses of over one million dollars, and thus fit within offense severity category six, with presumptive release dates of forty months, they had each been sentenced to less than forty months. Because under the federal parole system every well-behaved defendant is given one-third time off for good behavior, each of them served roughly two-thirds of their sentences, which was substantially less time than application of the parole release guidelines would have mandated. Thus, Ivan Boesky served twenty-four and one-third months.

Unlike those cases, this is a case where the real time that the Court believed the defendant should serve coincided with a number of months within the parole release guidelines. Specifically, the Court believed that a period of thirty-six to forty months' incarceration fit the crimes and the offender, based on the evidence before the Court, and was in proportion to the sentence given to defendant's coconspirator, Ivan Boesky, by Judge Lasker.

The Court gave a sentence that permits, but does not require, incarceration for longer than thirty-six to forty months, to allow the Parole Commission to take into account any important new evidence bearing on Defendant's character that might surface in the Government's continuing investigation in the near term and also effect general deterrence.

One purpose I had in mind in deciding to file a Form AO235 was to explain to the Parole Commission the factors that went into the sentencing and to avoid the distortion of the sentence that could result if I did not file the form, specifically the possibility of overreliance on dollar amounts …

Because the real time to be served that I had in mind fit the top end of category five and the bottom end of category six, I was satisfied that either categorization would permit the period of incarceration I had in mind.

Judge Wood was clear in indicating that she considered the Parole Commission a partner in her sentencing process. I found that unfair. Michael deserved to be sentenced by the judge overseeing his case based upon the evidence and arguments presented to that judge at the time of sentencing. That had been the case with Levine, Boesky, Siegel, and Freeman. I could not understand why a Parole Commission would have so much discretion and be able to take into consideration "any important new evidence bearing on the defendant's character." What new evidence? Michael had pleaded. Hundreds of pages of sentencing memoranda were filed. There had been a Fatico hearing. Judge Wood found that the government had failed to prove Michael was involved in any wrongdoing other than what he'd pleaded to.

In any event, Judge Wood was extremely active in the parole process to make sure that Michael Milken's parole release date was within the time she intended. Judge Wood went through each of the counts that Michael had pleaded to with respect to the economic effect.

> On Fischbach, my view is not enough is known yet to quantify a loss, if one occurred …
>
> I am skeptical that the entire amount of the fee for legitimate investment banking services should be viewed as the product of wrongdoing. I thus quantify the loss as zero …
>
> With respect to MCA, the Court finds that the Government has failed to establish that Defendant's wrongdoing resulted in any shareholder loss. …
>
> With respect to Helmrich and Payne … the Government had made no attempt to quantify any market impact and the Court thus has no basis for doing so.

With respect to Finsbury and the trade adjustments within the bid and ask of the market, Judge Wood stated to John Carroll,

> It seems to me particularly inappropriate for a Court or for the Parole Commission to speculate in a matter having criminal consequences and I wanted to give you an opportunity to respond to my reading of this.

Mr. Carroll responded,

> Your Honor, I don't think I can tell you anything that
> would give you a greater basis to quantify.

The court replied,

> Thank you. All right, I'll simply rely on Defendant's
> position there.

Our position on this was that the only adjustments the government identified amounted to $318,082. It will never be known whether these particular trades would have been done at the same or different prices, but since Michael had pleaded to this wrongdoing, we calculated the adjustments to total $318,082.

That left the Solomon tax trades. Judge Wood indicated she would take into account taxes paid by Drexel as well as taxes paid on future gains by Solomon:

> I agree with the Defendant that loss from this tax fraud
> should be viewed as zero.
>
> Finally, I note that there is no dispute between the
> parties concerning whether the money allocated to the
> restitution fund and a fine should be considered as part
> of any "loss" or "market impact"—the Government
> has agreed with Defendant that Defendant's agreement
> to pay large amounts as fines and for any restitution
> found to be due should not be used against Defendant
> in any way.

So the court found an economic effect to be $318,082. Judge Wood did file her Form AO235, Report on Committed Offender, showing a severity rating of five with the range of time to be served being twenty-four to thirty-six months. Judge Wood even filed an addendum to the AO235 that included the conclusions she had previously announced in court:

> In an eight-day Fatico Hearing, the Government presented evidence of unadjudicated offenses (selected by the Government) to the Court. The Court found that the Government failed to carry its burden to establish the offenses by a preponderance of the evidence except for the obstruction of justice findings and the finding of failure to disclose to a client the fact that the defendant and associates were buying certain warrants issued by Storer Communications. Unless new evidence emerges between now and any relevant parole proceeding, the Court believes that the remaining unadjudicated conduct is unlikely to be established by a preponderance of the evidence. … The Court imposed a ten-year sentence because it (1) permits the defendant to be released after serving thirty-six to forty months, (2) promotes general deterrence, and (3) gives the Parole Commission the flexibility to incarcerate Mr. Milken for an appropriate period of time if information developed in the ongoing investigation should cause a Parole Commission to conclude that the information before the Court was inadequate to assess to Defendant's wrongdoing …

Judge Wood was respecting what she said in that meeting in her robing room after the hearing on November 28, where she told the prosecutors they had done a good job but that they clearly did not have the evidence to establish the unadjudicated conduct.

The addendum continues,

An important factor in the Court's concluding that between thirty-six and forty months' time served is sufficient for general deterrence is that Defendant is unusual in his devotion of his own time and energy to working productively with disadvantaged members of society. The Court and the Probation Officer conducted a time-consuming inquiry into Defendant's character as reflected in his pre-1986 volunteer work with disadvantaged, inner-city children as reflected in his dealings with coworkers, neighbors, and families. That inquiry resulted in the Probation Officer and the Court concluding that Defendant has a genuine commitment to spending substantial amounts of his own time and resources to improving society by helping disadvantaged children which commitment predated his current legal problems and is likely to result in substantial benefit to the disadvantaged in the future. … Because it is so rare to encounter this personal devotion to community service among Defendants, it is the Court's view that (1) nothing would be lost in general deterrence in crediting this behavior by releasing Defendant after he has served between thirty-six and forty months and (2) such release date will send the appropriate message to others that the offender's entire character, not just the offense behavior, is taken into account in sentencing.

Judge Wood also addressed the amount of money Michael had agreed to pay to a restitution fund, stating,

WITNESS TO A PROSECUTION

> The Government represented to the Court that the large
> size of the restitution fund "was not set as any sort of
> specific quantification of victim damages or losses."

From that painful moment on November 21, 1990, when Judge Wood announced the sentence, she in effect advocated for Michael. She explained that her intent was that Michael not actually serve a ten-year sentence but serve no more than thirty-six to forty months. She found the economic effect of Mike's crimes was $318,082. She explained to the Parole Commission that Michael's crimes were what he'd pleaded to and nothing else.

> **From that painful moment on November 21, 1990, when Judge Wood announced the sentence, she in effect advocated for Michael.**

Unfortunately, the prosecutors made their own filing with the Parole Commission, indicating they thought the amounts were over $1 million. Arthur, Steve Kaufman, and I had a meeting with the prosecutors. I explained that I felt betrayed, since I had encouraged Michael to reach the plea agreement with the belief that was the best way for him to move on with his life. The prosecutors had encouraged that belief. I certainly did not expect them to continue the fight after the plea and the sentencing. They stated to me that I should not expect Michael to get any special treatment. I said that I only wished for Michael to receive the same treatment any other defendant would get. They acknowledged they had never before submitted information to a Parole Commission that could result in a defendant serving more time. Now we could only hope that the Parole Commission would listen to Judge Wood.

CHAPTER 14

Prison and Parole

From November 21, 1990, when Mike was sentenced until March 3, 1991, when Mike reported to the federal prison camp at Pleasanton, Michael's focus was (1) spending time with family, (2) beginning to meet with the prosecutors and SEC as required under the plea agreement, (3) preparing for an onslaught of civil suits by class action attorneys, and (4) trying to learn about life as an inmate under the control and jurisdiction of the Bureau of Prisons.

As we were addressing all these issues, Michael and Lori went to see the movie *Reversal of Fortune* about the efforts of Alan Dershowitz (played by Ron Silver) to get the murder conviction of Claus von Bulow overturned. Seeing the success Alan Dershowitz had as depicted in the movie, Lori asked if we could meet with Mr. Dershowitz and ask if he had any different thoughts about what we were doing, in the hope of achieving a better result.

Arthur Liman knew Professor Dershowitz and arranged a meeting in New York for Mike and Lori, Arthur, and me with Alan Dershowitz in early 1991. Professor Dershowitz admitted that he had been affected by the reporting on the case and had a somewhat negative view of Michael until he'd read more thoroughly and had a chance to actually meet Michael. Alan agreed to work with us and try to assist in any way he could.

He brought in two other lawyers to help review and analyze the case: Harvey Silverglate and Andrew Good from Boston. All three of them held very negative views about prosecutors and how they abused their power. They felt that Michael's sentence was outrageous. Their job was to review the case, working with Paul, Weiss, and independently of Paul, Weiss at the same time. They were to bring a "fresh set of eyes" to the matter and advise on anything they thought we should do going forward.

Harvey Silverglate and Andrew Good completed their analysis in the spring of 1991, after Michael began serving his sentence. Alan, Harvey, Andrew, and I met with Michael at Pleasanton. During that meeting, Harvey and Andrew expressed their belief that the prosecutors had violated the plea agreement and that Judge Wood had made serious mistakes in holding the Fatico hearing and in the sentencing. They also believed that Michael had been treated differently than any defendants in white-collar cases.

They had several comments about the case being handled in a risk-averse manner and blamed Michael in part for that. They felt our defense strategy should have been more aggressive and that the biggest mistake was not proceeding with the appeal and taking the prosecutors and the judge to task. Since Michael's cooperation was not going to help the prosecutors make cases against others, it was Messrs. Silverglate's and Good's view that the Rule 35 motion to reduce the sentence would not be successful. Though I may have been a loyal friend, I was not a criminal defense lawyer, and Mike had made a mistake by taking my advice over such respected and experienced lawyers as Arthur Liman and Lawrence Tribe.

I developed a good relationship with Messrs. Dershowitz, Silverglate, and Good. I understood where they were coming from. They had been asked to look at the case with fresh eyes and advise whether we should be doing anything different. Though hearing these opinions was not easy, I was also sure we had made the right decision regarding the appeal, and I was not about to defer to others when I disagreed with them. I may not have had any criminal defense experience before this case, but I had now lived this case for almost five years and spent hours with John Carroll and Jess Fardella as well as hours in court with Judge Wood. I had no doubt that Mike's best chance for an early release was to work with the prosecutors and the court, especially after Judge Wood had expressed her views about parole. I, too, was upset with the conduct of the prosecutors and the decision of the judge, but fighting them had not been a successful strategy once the decision was made to plead. Harvey and Andy did what they were asked to do. And I was going to continue to do what I believed I had to do. During this entire process, I never lost sight of what I knew and what I did not know.

Mike started his agreed-upon meetings with lawyers from the SEC and the US Attorney's Office, sometimes together but most often separately, soon after sentencing. The US Attorney's Office had made it known to us they would like help from Michael in their investigation of Columbia Savings & Loan and its CEO, Thomas Spiegel. Tom Spiegel was confident he had done nothing wrong and was going to defend himself. Michael did not have any information that would help the prosecutors. At one point, Reid Figel, the Assistant US Attorney working on that Columbia case, explained to me exactly how he thought Michael could help him. Implicit in this conversation was the fact that the US Attorney's Office would help Michael during a Rule 35 motion for reduction of sentence if he could in fact provide assistance in the Columbia matter. I came to know Reid Figel during this period. I would describe Reid somewhat as a zealot in his belief that Michael, Columbia Savings & Loan CEO Thomas Spiegel, and others had violated the law. Mr. Figel would never want a witness to be untruthful, but he certainly let me know exactly what Michael could say to help him and how he could help Michael. Though the US Attorney's Office for the Southern District of New York extensively investigated Columbia Savings and Spiegel, it never brought any charges against Columbia Savings or Mr. Spiegel.

This ability to suggest to witnesses how they could help the government was a weapon prosecutors had at their disposal. If I approached a witness and told him what I believed happened and told him I could help him if he would testify that way, I would be indicted for obstruction of justice. The prosecutor can tell the witness not to lie, but if the witness can tell the prosecutor what the prosecutor wants to hear, the witness can be rewarded.

Though it was hard to find humor at the time, we had one meeting with the representatives from the SEC that I, in retrospect, found humorous. SEC lawyers and Michael met in Los Angeles early in 1991. We decided to meet in a conference room at my father's law offices in Century City, California. The meeting went all day. Members from the US Attorney's Office were also present. Because we worked through lunch, we ordered from a local delicatessen and had sandwiches brought in. One of the attorneys for the SEC came up to me and handed me some money. When I asked what it was for, he told me he was reimbursing me for the lunch. I told him that wasn't necessary, but he insisted, saying that under their rules they needed to reimburse for lunch. The representatives from the US Attorney's Office apparently were subject to different rules. Then at the end of the day, the same attorney from the SEC handed me his parking ticket and asked if we validated. I shook my head as we validated his parking ticket and saved the SEC the cost of parking but not the cost of lunch.

As if being in prison with an uncertain sentence, Drexel going bankrupt, and the onslaught of class action civil suits were not enough, James Stewart, the main reporter for the *Wall Street Journal*, published a book in 1991 about these investigations with a special emphasis on the Milken/Drexel investigation. It was, as expected, a personal attack on Michael based upon speculation, innuendo, and falsehoods—a mean-spirited and dishonest portrayal of Michael Milken. It was excerpted in the *Wall Street Journal* in October 1991, which just added to Michael's frustration and distress.

Michael's adjustment to being at a federal prison camp was not easy. A prisoner's schedule is set for him: when he gets up, when he goes to sleep, when he eats, what he eats, when he works, and what his job is as well as who he can talk to and when. If he gets sick, he will only have access to a doctor when a doctor visits. Mike was allowed to communicate with people by telephone, but only by making collect calls from a prison phone all inmates had access to that

> **Michael's adjustment to being at a federal prison camp was not easy.**

was available only at designated times. Calls were monitored. Calls with lawyers are not supposed to be monitored. Michael was allowed to have visitors who were precleared on designated visitors' days. Visitors' days were on Sundays for several hours and one evening during the week.

I was able to visit with Michael more often because there was an exception to the visiting rules for meetings with attorneys. I would still need to call an officer at the Bureau of Prisons and arrange for each visit. When I was not otherwise traveling to New York to continue working with the Paul, Weiss team, I would visit with Michael for two to three hours a couple of days during the week to review everything from the civil suits being filed, to the strategy to get Michael out of prison, through the parole process and the Rule 35 process. And it was a rare day when Michael was not able to call me. I knew exactly what Michael was feeling and thinking the whole time. It was painful.

Lori Milken kept a diary during this period and wrote several accounts about experiences during the investigation. The following is based on what she calls "Seder at Pleasanton 3/21/91," approximately three weeks after Michael reported to the federal facility, and provides a glimpse into the conditions Michael was living under.

> I knew exactly what Michael was feeling and thinking the whole time. It was painful.

Lori arrived at the guard desk Friday afternoon at around four thirty. Lori was with her eldest son, Gregory, who would be graduating from high school in a few months. "His father will miss the ceremony where his son will receive more awards than any other student in the class of 140." Their youngest daughter, Bari, and Michael's mother, Ferne, were also with them.

Gregory, Lori, and Ferne signed in, but Bari did not have to sign in since she was under twelve, or at least that had been the rule for the first few visits. Purses had to be see-through plastic, since visitors were restricted as to what they could bring with them. They were not allowed to bring in food or more than twenty dollars. Lori had been used to bringing a deck of cards and the kids' homework, which Mike liked to go over. On this particular visit, Lori brought a grocery bag. It was the Jewish holiday of Passover, and they were bringing the Haggadahs, or prayer books, for Passover; matzo; hard boiled eggs;

and a few other traditional Passover foods. The guard said they were not allowed to bring any of this in. When they explained it was for a religious service, the guard called for the officer in charge, and she said they could not bring it in. This officer in charge then left, and the guard told the family they could not bring in the homework or the cards that they had been allowed to bring in on prior occasions. "Banning the homework permanently would be very hard on Michael, much harder than his current employment of cleaning toilets and mopping floors. The kids' homework has become his greatest connection to them. School and homework occupy most of their waking hours." The kids were upset about not being permitted to do the Passover service.

The family then went outside to a picnic area, and Michael joined them as Bari came over to give her dad a hug. Next they were told Bari must also sign in. Ferne told Mike she was concerned about how he looked. He explained that his two roommates, including the person in the lower bunk, both snored. There was a window right next to his head that allowed cold air to blow in, so he had been getting very little sleep. Ferne asked him about the food at the camp and whether he was able to maintain a low-fat diet as prescribed by his doctor. He indicated that based on the food they got, that was really impossible. He did not want to starve.

They all then went inside to a visiting area and located a table that had two Passover prayer books and some matzo on it, though not the prayer books or matzo Lori had brought. Then, another inmate, Matt, came in and took one of the prayer books, saying it was his. Michael picked up the second one. Obviously someone had brought in prayer books and food. So the family had started the Passover service when the phone on the guard's desk rang, and the guard told Matt there were some trays of food for him over in the other building that needed to be picked up.

Michael volunteered to go with Matt and to help him carry the trays back. While Michael was away, the guard came over to Lori and told her their visit had to be terminated. "Whenever any inmate leaves from here, the visit is terminated, and Milken knows that." Lori reminded him that Michael had merely gone to help the other inmate get a tray of food. Again, she asked to speak to the supervisor or officer in charge. When the supervisor appeared, Michael returned carrying trays with the other inmate. The supervisor asked Michael what he thought he was doing with the trays. Mike responded that he would put them away for later. The supervisor then turned to Lori and said they could in fact finish their visit. The family started the service again. After another few minutes, the guard called Michael over. Michael returned and said they were going to write an incident report on him. Then a different supervisor came in and told Michael that the report would not be filed.

It was a few minutes before eight o'clock when the guard then informed them the five-hour visit was over. Michael explained to the guard that his family had arrived at four thirty and that it was now eight o'clock—it had only been three and a half hours. The guard replied, "Four o'clock, five o'clock, six o'clock, seven o'clock, and eight o'clock—that's five hours." Mike was not going to convince him otherwise. Michael told Lori that from now on they should come a few minutes after the hour and leave a few minutes before the hour so the hours don't get counted in fractions. As Lori writes, "That's what I love about him. No anger or frustration. His brain nimbly devises an alternative or a different way around a problem." The family said goodbye to Michael and told him they would see him next week. As they left, the guard returned their grocery bag with the prayer books, deck of cards, and food. Bari was distraught as she went to hug her dad.

This is an example of the capriciousness and conditions faced every day by an inmate, especially a high-profile inmate, in the prison system.

Mike's initial jobs were doing maintenance work and tutoring inmates for their graduate equivalency exams (GED). The maintenance work included cleaning bathrooms, washing dishes, and mopping floors. He was a model prisoner. He never complained to me about having to do this work. He also had an incredible success rate as a tutor. Almost every inmate he tutored passed the GED exam. Normally the passing rate is far less than 50 percent.

Michael's initial parole hearing was set for June 1991, three months after he reported. During my visits during the first couple of months, we prepared for the parole hearing. Our consultant, Herbert Hoelter, who was an expert with respect to both the Bureau of Prisons and the parole process, was extremely knowledgeable and helpful. Herb, too, connected with Michael and became committed to him. As I think back, everyone from the lawyers who worked on the case to our economic consultants, Andy Rosenfield and Daniel Fischel; our media consultants led by Kenneth Lerer; and our prison consultant, Herb Hoelter, all believed in Michael Milken.

Herb Hoelter visited Michael with me at Pleasanton on a number of occasions to get prepared for the parole hearing. He knew the questions they would be asking and what issues they would focus on.

> This is an example of the capriciousness and conditions faced every day by an inmate, especially a high-profile inmate, in the prison system.

Prior to the hearing, the parole hearing officers had a chance to review the submission from Judge Wood; the report from the probation officer, Michaela Bracken; the report from the prosecutors; and a submission I made on Michael's behalf.

We believed there were two main issues we had to emphasize to the Parole Commission: (1) the economic effect of everything Michael had pleaded to, since, as Judge Wood made clear, the amount of money would directly affect Michael's release date; and (2) the obstruction charge, since Michael vehemently denied its validity, and we did not want this to affect the decision of the Parole Commission.

Judge Wood's submission to the Parole Commission concluded that the offense should be a category five and that the dollars involved totaled $318,082. In her Form A0235, she also discussed her belief that there should be some proportionality between the sentence served by Ivan Boesky and that to be served by Michael:

> The Court believes it's fair to assume that had Mr. Boesky not cooperated (and had he thus not been permitted to plead guilty to only one count of conspiracy to file a false statement), that Mr. Boesky would have served at least two to three times as long as he served, or longer; he actually served twenty-four months and eleven days, and thus, absent cooperation, he might have actually served approximately four and a half to six years or more. The Court believes that Defendant should serve less time than Mr. Boesky would have been expected to serve absent Mr. Boesky's cooperation, because although their crimes are similar in important respects, Mr. Milken devoted substantial time and energy to helping poor children before his legal problems surfaced. These considerations led the Court to conclude that Defendant

should actually serve approximately three to three and a third years in order for there to be the appropriate proportionality between the two sentences.

In a footnote, Judge Wood also addressed the argument that Michael's crimes were less serious than those committed by Boesky:

> The Court believes that any advantage Mr. Milken gains over Mr. Boesky in that comparison is offset by the fact that Mr. Milken attempted to obstruct justice, and obstructed justice, after he became aware of the investigation.

After I read this, I called John Carroll and asked him if, in fact, Boesky had obstructed justice. I would have been shocked had he not destroyed documents before he agreed to cooperate. John confirmed Boesky had in fact destroyed documents. I brought this to Judge Wood's attention, and she immediately sent a letter to the chief of staff at the United States Parole Commission on June 21, 1991, prior to Michael's parole hearing in which she stated the following:

> It has been brought to my attention by counsel for Michael Milken, Richard Sandler, that footnote 1 on page 2 of the AO235 I sent to you regarding Mr. Milken contains a mistake of fact. Mr. Sandler has confirmed with one of the prosecutors, John Carroll, that before Mr. Boesky began cooperating, he obstructed justice by destroying documents and instructing one or more of his employees to destroy documents. In view of these circumstances, which were unknown to me when I filed the AO235, I was wrong ... given that both defendants obstructed justice, there would be no offset to

any advantage Mr. Milken would obtain if his crime comparison argument were accepted.

In preparing for the hearing, we submitted a memorandum that focused on the computation of the dollars involved and on obstruction. In order to bolster our obstruction defense, Arthur Liman retained the services of a respected lie detector expert who had often been used by the government to administer lie detector tests. This individual gave the test to Michael while in prison, going through every scenario of the obstruction charges. According to this test, Michael was truthful in denying obstruction or attempted obstruction.

Since the government felt compelled to file its own statement on the economic effect of what Michael had pleaded to with the Parole Commission, making the same arguments the judge had already rejected, I went into detail in my submission of the calculation of economic effect for every offense. For example, the government was contending that the fee Drexel earned in its Fischbach financing should be included in making the computation of economic effect. Judge Wood had specifically rejected the government's argument, as had the probation officer. The court and the probation officer both found that any fees earned by Drexel in connection with the Fischbach transaction were the result of legitimate investment banking services rendered by Drexel and were unrelated to the offense Michael Milken had pleaded to.

The other two offenses the government contended provided additional economic impact were Finsbury, where Judge Wood found the $318,082, and the Solomon tax trades, where Judge Wood found the number to be zero. In Finsbury, the government contended that there were additional amounts that Milken had not sought reimbursement for but would have. This is total speculation and contrary to the allocution and the plea. At the hearing on February 19, 1991, Judge Wood stated,

> It seems to me particularly inappropriate for a Court
> or for the Parole Commission to speculate in a manner
> having criminal consequences.

I also asked the Parole Commission to take into account in whatever decision it reached the fact that once Michael was released, he still faced substantial restrictions on his liberty, since he was required to perform three years of community service of eighteen hundred hours a year. The United States Sentencing Commission Alternative to Imprisonment Project issued a report a few months before our hearing entitled *The Federal Offender: A Program of Intermediate Punishments* in which it calculated that for community service, every twelve hours of work is equivalent of a day of imprisonment. Applying that formula to the community service sentence Michael Milken faced would be equivalent to adding fifteen months to his sentence. I argued that Ivan Boesky personally had made millions of dollars from his crimes. Dennis Levine had made millions from his crimes. Martin Siegel had received at least $800,000 in cash for information he'd sold. They served twenty-four months, eighteen months, and one and two-third months in prison, respectively. Michael Milken made nothing from his crimes, which were found to have an economic effect of $318,082, and he would serve the equivalent of another fifteen months after his release.

Finally, I pointed out to the Parole Commission that although Michael had been at Pleasanton for only a few months, his prison progress report stated that he was "an excellent employee that is not afraid of menial labor" with an excellent rapport with both peers and staff and "is seen as a mature, intelligent, and congenial inmate who has made an excellent adjustment to his incarceration."

The hearing took place on July 2, 1991, two days before Michael's forty-fifth birthday, at the prison. Two officers from the Parole Commission attended, along with Michael Milken, Lori Milken, and me as a personal representative, not as a lawyer.

The parole officer explained they would be interviewing "Mr. Milken" and that toward the end of the hearing they would give Lori and me an opportunity to make a brief statement. Then we would step out of the room while they deliberated. When we came back, they would inform us what their recommendation would be. Their recommendation normally goes to a parole commissioner, who makes the final decision. Because of the publicity in this case, they would probably recommend the case be classified as "original jurisdiction," meaning the matter would go to Washington for a decision by the national commissioners rather than a single commissioner. This process usually takes three to six weeks. The hearing officer reminded me that I was there as a representative and not as an attorney and that they had gone through all the material very carefully, so there was no need for me to go into it again in any detail.

The parole officer next explained that they had received a letter dated June 28, 1991, from the probation officer, Michaela Bracken, as an addition to the presentence report to clarify that there was no relationship between the amounts paid by Mr. Milken as a result of his plea and the actual dollar amount that could be assigned to the offenses for which he was being sentenced. The letter explained that after sentencing, Judge Wood recognized there was likely to be misunderstandings in this regard due to the complexity and unusual nature of the offenses. For that reason she'd held a series of hearings to determine the amounts involved in the conduct for which Mr. Milken was sentenced. Further, as stated in Ms. Bracken's letter, all the parties had agreed that the amounts paid as fines, penalties, and a restitution fund should not be considered part of any loss and used against Mr. Milken in any way.

As the hearing started, the parole officer asked Michael why he would have been involved in something like this, since he was very successful and this all appears to be "miniscule compared to the way you were rewarded for what you did at Wall Street."

Michael, for the first time, personally spoke on his own behalf:

I have asked myself that question every night for over five years, maybe six years now. … And I have been wrestling with that. We're really talking about specific instances, a few of them that occurred with two individuals, you know, during my fifteen- to twenty-year career. And I think it was somewhat a weakness in my personality that occurred, and you know it's hard to sleep at night for the last four years because I think first—my first feeling is that I didn't think it would hurt anybody. The only one who could get hurt in these instances was myself. I was taking the risk and I didn't see anyone else getting hurt. Second, my own department had grown and I personally, you know, it's not an excuse at all but, you know, I just didn't have time, I didn't contemplate what I—when I told these people I would help them out or accommodate them I just don't think I spent that time thinking about the ramifications. … And I understand that that's not an excuse, but I had a lot of things on my mind. Third, I think and I say a failing in my character to a degree that I always felt I could help everybody. … I always felt I could solve problems and I spent a lot of time with my probation officer discussing this with her. … And I think people were complaining, I wanted to get on to the next thing, someone else wanted my attention, and after a number of complaints it was just easier at that time to say okay, I'll make it up to you. I think that these types of activities I understand are wrong, but they had never been criminally prosecuted and I didn't understand them to be criminal at the time.

He was then asked what compelled him to do things with Boesky and Solomon that he really had not done before.

Well, in the case of these two individuals, Mr. Boesky—I think everyone thought until that day in 1986 that he was an upstanding member of the community. I mean I wasn't alone. I was first introduced to Mr. Boesky by the senior manager of my firm. He was a customer of the firm, not of my department or myself. ... And at the time he was considered to be a very prestigious person. No one knew ... he had conducted insider trading or had paid people money in bags for information.

In the case of Solomon, I had a different relationship with him that I had covered him personally and had talked to him a great deal in the early and mid-'70s and in the late '70s someone else started covering Mr. Solomon. I would like to say in the case of Mr. Solomon we're talking about thousands and thousands of transactions. We're not talking about a way of doing business. And the same thing with Mr. Boesky. You did many transactions. So obviously these decisions have destroyed my life, destroyed my family, negated fifteen to seventeen years of hard work.

At this point Michael had to stop to compose himself as he broke down with emotion. The parole officer stated that it is not uncommon for him to talk to individuals who would not do anything to hurt their family, but doing something for someone else has the result of hurting their family. Mike composed himself and continued:

> I think my point I would make to you is that these activities were not the way my business was conducted before, during, or after. They aren't the standards that I conducted my life on. I received no benefits. It didn't enhance my business. ... I did not give people inside information. Mr. Boesky called me constantly asking me for this information, and I put him off, I never gave him, I never sold a client out.

The parole hearing officer then indicated he had reviewed my letter of June 28, 1991, indicating why the plea with respect to the Fischbach transaction was a disclosure matter and had nothing to do with the financing that Drexel did and therefore the fee Drexel received had nothing to do with wrongful conduct. He stated,

> I have carefully reviewed Mr. Sandler's recent letter regarding the offensive area and we're going to drop where we talked about a fraudulent takeover of a business in excess of one million dollars. That will be removed from the offensive area.

At this point he indicated that with respect to the Finsbury transaction, which is where Judge Wood had come up with the $318,082 number, they had come up with $544,239. That was the amount that the prosecutors speculated would have still been due from these adjusted trades. The parole officer also noted that he felt the count related to aiding and abetting Solomon's income tax filing had an economic effect of $477,791. He totally dismissed not only all of our arguments but also Judge Wood's decision on these matters. The sum of $477,791 and $544,239 is $1,021,000. I said to myself as I was sitting there, *What a coincidence! This amount is just $21,000 over the $1 million threshold to make this a category six rather than a category five offense.*

It was clear they wanted the category to be a category six so the Parole Commission would not be criticized for being lenient with Michael Milken.

The parole officer then gave Michael a chance to comment further on the Finsbury and the Solomon matters. Michael explained the transactions very much as he had in his allocution. He explained Finsbury. Mr. Solomon at first agreed to reimburse Mr. Milken's department through a legitimate soft-dollar arrangement called "designations." When designations did not amount to enough to recoup the fee, Solomon agreed to make the adjustments to trades, all within the bid and ask of the market. Michael stated,

> The only thing that was wrong in this case was that on these trades amounting to approximately $300,000, it was not disclosed to the client that these adjustments were made. An adjustment or sales credit or designation in itself there is nothing illegal about. I personally have never been involved with the disclosure process and I have never managed money, but as head of the department I think I accept the responsibility that I should have made sure that this was on the confirmations since I knew it was being done.

With respect to the tax transactions, Michael made it clear he always paid his own taxes. He also emphasized that Solomon bought these securities and that he did not have to sell them back to Drexel. The transaction was not a sham or improper transaction.

This was the transaction Judge Stanton in the Rosenthal case found was not even a crime.

Michael was next asked about the obstruction. Mike became even more animated:

> The obstruction issue, of everything we've talked about today, is by far the hardest, sir, since it didn't happen. And I know what the findings were. I have made mistakes, I know I have made mistakes. I have accepted those mistakes, I have accepted responsibility for the mistakes. You know, I lie in bed for the damage that it has done, that these were things that I know I did. I also know, sir, I didn't do this. I did not obstruct justice.

The hearing officer asked Michael if he gave any kind of signals to try to convince associates they should do certain things and not provide documents to the government. Michael responded as follows:

> We're talking about two or three instances here that occurred almost five years ago. And I don't, cannot say to you what they interpreted. I know what I was doing. And I have asked my lawyers what I can do to right this. I spoke to my lawyers, and they told me that there was this person that could give me a lie detector test who the government, US Attorney used and would be a very credible person. They came four to six weeks ago here and gave me a lie detector test, which I passed. ... Sir, I didn't even know this ledger existed. I could not have asked the person not to turn it in. In addition to that, I sat in the evidentiary hearings and both the witnesses said in their testimony that they did not interpret anything I said to tell them to destroy documents or to obstruct justice.

Michael was also asked about his responsibilities at Pleasanton. He explained that he was originally assigned to be an orderly at the detention center and to help another person, since they felt it was a two-person job. Then the other person got transferred, and at this point Michael was the sole orderly for the morning, afternoon, and evening. He also requested to be able to tutor inmates in mathematics and other subjects, which he had been doing. He helped organize a family day where they set up a booth for all the children at which he created math games for the children and things that the parents and inmates could work on with their children together.

It then came time for Lori and me to speak. I went first. July 2, 1991, was also the first time I had spoken in any proceeding on Michael's behalf:

> It's an unusual position for me. I have represented him [Michael] since the beginning of this case, November of 1986, four and a half years ago, and I am probably here as much as a friend as a lawyer. I have never had such a close relationship with a client and I have never had such a strong belief in any position as I believe in the position that I set forth in my submission to you, which I appreciate the fact that you have reviewed. I have known Mr. Milken thirty-five some years, I know Lori, I know the children. I know what kind of individual he is and what kind of character and values he has, and the kind of values he has instilled in those children. As a result of that, I know how difficult this four and a half years has been. I have lived through it with him. I know the anguish, and I know the remorse, and I know what it has done to the family. Today, I hope in having the opportunity to talk directly, we will

be able to separate a little bit the symbol from the man and the myth from the reality. I think this case has been surrounded with so much rhetoric, that very few people even know what's involved here or what it is Mr. Milken did. I know that Judge Wood when she first got the case made a statement one day on the public record how this case was going into uncharted waters, meaning that she'd read the indictment and seen the allegations of activities that had not been criminalized—not that that excuses them, but she knew that there were a lot of complexities and complications. After the sentencing and after even the lengthy sentencing hearings, I think she felt that there were misunderstandings and misconceptions about Mr. Milken and what he did. She held a rather extraordinary proceeding, from what I've been told, and that was these postsentencing hearings for the sole reason of trying to, in a very respectful way, assist the Parole Commission in its independent task of having to make an evaluation. … And she came to a conclusion—and I believe using the same preponderance of evidence standard that you have to use, though I know you have to make your own evaluation—that there was $318,000 involved. …

The Judge in the 235 Form also talks about what an unusual individual Michael is as a defendant because of the commitment and devotion he has given to the community, to his family, and to his friends. Having known him for such a long time, I at least was glad to see that this had been recognized and thankful that the Court asked the Probation Department to conduct an independent investigation as to when did Mr. Milken start this commitment to the people that the Judge refers to as the neediest and most disadvantaged children in this country. And the Probation Officer and the Judge concluded, which they concluded because it's true, that this activity began long before Mr. Milken's investigation started.

Lastly, on the obstruction issue, I have with me, and I will give you, the results of the polygraph test if you like them. Again, it's two pages.

Mr. Milken was so upset about obstruction his lawyers asked him if he would submit to one. I was there after the investigation started. This is also a very difficult area for me because I know Mr. Milken and his character. I was with him almost every minute for those first couple of weeks after the investigation started. I am convinced there was never an attempt to obstruct justice. … [W]hatever decision you come to today, Mr. Milken will be punished and a deterrent message will be sent to the financial community beyond that that has affected any other case that has gone on during these Wall Street investigations. … He will still be separated for the next two years from his wife and children and from the kids that he is devoted so much to. He will miss graduations as he missed several weeks ago when his son graduated from high school. He will miss birthdays, he will miss anniversaries, he will miss events in these children's lives that can never be made up.

I concluded as follows:

I want to say that we're really not asking for any favors, and I'm really not asking for any leniency. What I am pleading for is a just and fair result and I thank you for listening to me.

A few weeks prior to this hearing, I attended the graduation of Michael's oldest son, Gregory, from high school, at which he received extensive honors. It was heartbreaking that his father was not there.

Next, Lori spoke very briefly on behalf of her husband:

Like Mr. Sandler, I have known Michael since he was 12 years old, so I feel I know him better than anyone around and I can attest to his character, and I am in total agreement with the assessment of Mr. Sandler that Michael tries to be everything to everybody. He felt that he has always been a person who could do ten things at one time, and he always thought he could find solutions to everything. In addition, he's a nonconfrontational person. It is very difficult for him to be in a confrontational mode, so if somebody ever came to him with a problem he would always try to work it out with that person. I don't know if you're aware of this, he never fired anybody from Drexel the entire time he was ever there, and he could never fire anyone any time. So this is a part of his character that does exist. Thus far, the separation from his family has been extremely difficult on him and us and especially on his daughter.

The hearing closed with Michael making one last statement:

[I] was wrong. I have to live with that the rest of my life. I think the penalties outside of incarceration are so enormous for someone who has a reputation that he has lost that no one would live through.

Michael began to sob.

We were then asked to step out of the room. We waited outside the room as we consoled one another. When we came back, the parole officers said they were going to recommend the case be referred for original jurisdiction based on media attention. They were going to make a recommendation to the parole commissioners who would be deciding the case. The recommendation would be that the offenses be a category six based on their numbers for the Finsbury nondisclosure adjustments and the tax matter. They then stated that in spite of the polygraph, they would consider obstruction an aggregating factor and recommend a parole date at the midpoint of the guidelines. Since the guidelines were forty to fifty-two months, they were recommending a date at forty-six months, which would have been December 30, 1993. We were reminded there were appeal rights if Michael was not satisfied with the decision when it came down from the commission.

I left that day feeling that at least Michael finally had had a chance to make his case but frustrated by the fact that the parole officer seemed to have concluded it would be a category six no matter what the facts were. They totally ignored the judge's findings and the probation officer's report from Michaela Bracken. Still, where Mike had faced about seventy-eight months in prison before the hearing, he now faced forty-six months. It was an improvement—but still hardly the message we were hoping for.

We now had to wait for the final decision by the Parole Commission in Washington before deciding on an appeal. In early August, Michael received a notice of action from the regional office of the Parole Commission in California informing him that his case had been designated as original jurisdiction. On August 12, 1991, I sent a letter to the chief of staff at the United States Parole Commission in Chevy Chase, Maryland, which emphasized the two main issues: the calculation of the amounts involved and obstruction.

On August 20, 1991, Michael received notice from the Parole Commission that it had decided on a release eligibility date of forty-four months total time served. Michael had gained another valuable two months, but there was no reason not to appeal this decision.

On September 10, 1991, Judge Wood went to the trouble of sending a letter to the chairman of the National Commissioners of the United States Parole Commission stating she understood the commission had determined that a forty-four-month term was appropriate for Michael Milken and that it was likely this determination would be appealed:

> I am writing to ask the Commission, in the event of such an appeal, to look closely at the community service rendered by Mr. Milken for many years prior to his current legal difficulties in deciding whether a lesser period of incarceration is appropriate. It is the quality and duration of his service to the community ... that led me to conclude that a sentence exceeding forty months would be unnecessarily severe. I made my determination fully aware of the nature of his crimes, and his obstruction of justice. If the Commission's choice of forty-four rather than forty months reflects a concern with the acts of obstruction of justice, I would like to communicate to the Commission that in my view what is revealed about his character in the obstruction of justice deserves to be balanced by what is revealed about his character in his unusual service to the community prior to wrongdoing. I think that both consideration of fairness to Mr.

Milken and the importance of signaling the value of such contributions to the community suggest that Mr. Milken's community service should weigh heavily in your determination, and should lead to no more than a forty-month term of incarceration.

Everything Judge Wood had continued to do from the date she announced her sentence on November 21, 1990, recognized the nature of what he'd pleaded to, of who he was, and of what could be expected of him in the future. Even at forty months plus three years of full-time community service, Michael's sentence greatly exceeded the sentence of anyone ever convicted of violations of securities regulations.

On December 18, 1991, Michael received the notice of action on appeal from the United States Parole Commission. The notice provided as follows:

Decision dated August 20, 1991, modified. Reasons for the decision affirmed. Reopen and advance presumptive parole date of October 30, 1994, and continue to a presumptive parole after the service of forty months on June 30, 1994. Although the Commission disagrees with your argument for a category five offense severity rating, it accepts that mitigating circumstances recommended to it by the sentencing court as warranting a decision at the bottom of the applicable guideline range of forty to fifty-two months.

Though the Parole Commission was not going to budge on this being a category six, it did follow the judge's recommendation on our appeal, and we gained another four valuable months. Michael's reaction? "We're definitely going in the right direction."

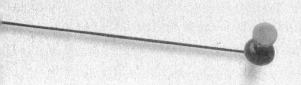

CHAPTER 15

Civil Settlements

As soon as the original indictment was issued, the class action lawyers started to circle, much like vultures. My experience with these firms was not positive. They were very good at identifying a vulnerable target with significant assets and then using the legal process to extract as much money as possible, often through a court-approved settlement. The lawyers I dealt with really knew nothing about Drexel's business or high yield bonds. What they knew was there was a wealthy defendant who was accused of violating the law, had pleaded guilty, and was an attractive target for a class action suit.

We were contesting over one hundred civil suits. Probably the most notable lawsuit was not a class action. In January 1991, the Federation Deposit Insurance Corporation and Resolution Trust Corporation, an entity formed to oversee the resolution of problems in the savings and loan industry, filed a complaint against Michael Milken and twenty-seven other individuals, including me, claiming $6 billion in damages. These government agencies hired the prestigious law firm of Cravath, Swaine & Moore to represent them. The savings and loan industry was having serious financial issues, due mainly to poor government regulation and unwise real estate loans and investments. It had become commonplace at this time for Drexel

Burnham, Michael Milken, and high yield securities to be blamed for all financial problems.

Our legal teams and economic consultants did an analysis of all of Drexel's savings and loan clients. The result was that high yield securities owned by these institutions proved to be the best investments those institutions had made. History has further shown that Drexel and Michael Milken had nothing to do with the savings and loan crisis and that high yield securities were the best or second-best investments these institutions had made, along with credit card loans. Even Reid Figel, the Assistant US Attorney in the Southern District who was investigating savings and loans, told me he would not, and could not, make the allegations that were in this lawsuit. Even the representative of Resolution Trust Corporation assigned to oversee this litigation told me Michael Milken was not at all responsible for the savings and loan problems.

> History has further shown that Drexel and Michael Milken had nothing to do with the savings and loan crisis and that high yield securities were the best or second-best investments these institutions had made.

Probably the most well-known securities law class action law firm at the time was Milberg, Weiss, Bershad, Hynes & Lerach. Two of the most visible attorneys at that firm were Melvyn Weiss and William Lerach. It was Melvyn Weiss who headed the suits against Michael, together with Thomas Barr and David Boies at Cravath, Swaine & Moore.

The most important person I dealt with in respect to addressing these lawsuits was not a lawyer. He was Judge Milton Pollack, a senior judge on the District Court for the Southern District of New York. Judge Pollack had been assigned the original SEC case against Michael and Drexel. Judge Pollack was considered a pro-government and pro-SEC judge. In the few appearances we made before Judge Pollack before Michael settled with the SEC, it was clear that Judge Pollack sided with the SEC. At the same time, Judge Pollack was very smart and knew how to use his powers as a federal judge to secure a result he favored. As much as one dreaded having Judge Pollack against you, it was a huge benefit to have Judge Pollack on your side.

Judge Pollack let all the relevant parties know he was interested in trying to resolve all the Milken-related civil cases. Within the federal court system, the Judicial Panel on Multidistrict Litigation exists to help manage lawsuits filed in multiple jurisdictions. Judge Pollack sat on that panel. Since he was on the panel and such a senior judge, he was in the best position to try to settle all these cases filed in jurisdictions throughout the country. Judge Pollack viewed the possibility of settling all these cases as the capstone of an esteemed career. We benefited from his experience as he used his talents and authority to do just that.

Mel Weiss called Arthur Liman and asked for a meeting with Arthur and me some time in 1991. We met in Arthur's office in New York. Mr. Weiss was very conciliatory and said he would like to help Michael get all these lawsuits behind him and even help Michael reduce his sentence. He further stated I might have known more about his partner William Lerach but assured me that he was easier to work with and get along with than Mr. Lerach. I knew very little about either one of them, but I found it unusual that in his first meeting with me, the lawyer who was trying to make money from Michael's misfortune would tell me he wanted to help Michael, who he was suing, as he was telling me he was the "good cop" and his partner was the "bad cop." Ironically, in later years both Mr. Weiss and Mr. Lerach went to prison for improperly soliciting clients for their class action suits.

Arthur Liman had asked his partner Mark Belnick to lead the team defending the civil suits. We were invited to a meeting with the lawyers from Cravath, Swaine & Moore—principally Thomas Barr and David Boise—along with Melvyn Weiss and several of the other class action lawyers to discuss the idea of the settlement. Cravath was an established Wall Street firm that had represented clients in many Drexel transactions in the past. It had taken this case with an agreement with the government to charge a discounted hourly rate with an understanding that if it received a large-enough judgment or settlement, its rates would be increased. This arrangement received criticism at the time from members of Congress.

Mr. Barr led the meeting and made it clear that all the lawyers present were interested in a "fair" resolution. They were willing to leave Michael with a significant net worth, although it was clear they wanted to decide what "fair" and "significant" meant. It was difficult for me to listen to all this, since I knew if we wanted to spend the time and resources, we should win every one of these cases. At the same time, I knew that the process could take another decade, and there were always the risks. For Michael's and others' health and families' sake (including my own), we needed to try to resolve these suits and move on with our lives. As our discussions progressed, it was clear that the most important person in this process was Judge Milton Pollack, not any of the lawyers.

Stephen Kaufman had become integral to our legal team. He had a good relationship with Judge Pollack. Judge Pollack requested a meeting with attorney Steve Kaufman and me in his chambers to discuss the idea of a global settlement. Judge Pollack was very direct in telling me that if he undertook the task of trying to get the litigation settled, he would require a significant additional settlement payment from Michael Milken. In exchange, he would give Michael peace with respect to all the civil suits, both federal and state, though he was a federal judge. This would have been the largest and most complex multicase, multijurisdictional settlement ever. Judge Pollack wanted this.

Judge Pollack told me he would undertake this task and put his credibility on the line if Michael was willing and able to agree to pay an additional significant settlement amount. I expressed to Judge Pollack that the $400 million disgorgement fund Michael had created as part of the SEC settlement was already a significant amount. Judge Pollack said it would take $1.3 billion to settle everything. Since there were a number of other defendants besides Michael Milken, and there was insurance coverage that might cover some of the claims for former Drexel employees, Judge Pollack computed $400 million to come from the SEC disgorgement fund; $300 million to come from all the other defendants; $100 million to come from insurance coverage; and an additional $500 million would have to come from Michael Milken. Judge Pollack said he would certainly understand if Michael could not do this, but without this sum, he would not be able to use his good offices to settle the cases. But if Michael was willing to do this, Judge Pollack would get all lawsuits, state and federal, settled.

As I left the judge's chambers that day, I had mixed emotions. On the one hand, when I had been in his courtroom for hearings in the *SEC v. Milken* case, Judge Pollack could not have been more arbitrary and negative toward Michael. He was true to his reputation for being almost tyrannical in favoring the government or SEC against Michael Milken. Yet on this particular day he was almost paternal as he explained he would settle the cases and give Michael peace if he was willing to pay the amount. Once again I would have to explain to Michael that though we all believed the $400 million SEC disgorgement fund would be more than enough to settle these suits, this case was sui generis and he would need to pay over double that amount if he wanted to settle. Since Judge Wood found the total economic effect of everything he'd pleaded to was $318,082, he would be paying almost three thousand times this much to settle what we believed were baseless claims. It seemed so arbitrary and unfair, but fairness never made an appearance in the case. Seeing justice was done in either the criminal or civil cases was not going to happen. It was all about the government and the plaintiff lawyers extracting as much money as possible

Legal teams were already in place defending these lawsuits. Paul, Weiss had its team. The investment partnerships made up of former Drexel associates named in the lawsuits had retained Dan Murdoch at the firm of Donovan, Leisure, Newton & Irvine. A number of the individuals named in the lawsuits had their own lawyers. And everyone understood the risks and complexities.

There would be a settlement only if Michael Milken was willing to pay the large additional amount. Michael and Lowell concluded that as distasteful as it was, if they could settle, it was time to move on. Michael proved that he meant what he said to Arthur Liman and Edward Bennett Williams back in November 1986 when he indicated he'd started with nothing and that if he could get peace, money would not be an issue. He was confident that he could continue to invest successfully based upon his ability to research companies, industries, credit, and capital structures. The various partnerships and their members also were willing to pay the $300 million, especially since the partnerships had significant assets in them that we valued to be in excess of $300 million. Peter Ackerman, who had been a principal in the High Yield and Convertible Bond Department and had a significant share of these partnerships, took a leadership position and convinced others that this "global settlement" should be pursued.

I told Michael that Judge Pollack had told me that if Michael helped resolve these cases and clean up the federal court docket, Judge Pollack would consider it the highest form of "cooperation." He did not say he would advocate for Michael with Judge Wood if Michael settled, but I was told Judge Wood greatly respected Judge Pollack, and the clear message to me was that the settlement certainly would not hurt Michael's chances of success in the Rule 35 motion to reduce sentence. It was impossible to put a value on being released from Pleasanton early as well as ending this painful ordeal. Also, part of the settlement included

> If the saying "the devil is in the details" ever applied, it certainly applied to this situation.

the fact that all the settling parties would emphatically deny any wrongdoing or liability. I informed Judge Pollack that we accepted the terms.

If the saying "the devil is in the details" ever applied, it certainly applied to this situation as we went through the details of what the settlement would look like. With respect to the $300 million, we tried to get the plaintiff attorneys to accept the partnership interests in lieu of payment. We provided them a valuation. Likewise, we tried to get the plaintiffs to accept Michael's partnership interests as sole security for his contribution. We had a meeting with the lawyers' group and Judge Pollack on a Sunday in January 1992 in New York at which a former Drexel employee, Joe Harch, who had his own money management firm, provided a detailed analysis of the partnerships to show that there was sufficient value. Judge Pollack told me he believed the value was there and that we could negotiate a settlement on behalf of Michael where he could use his partnership interests as sole security for his obligation.

In February of 1992, Judge Pollack, who spent most of his winters in Houston, "invited" the participants in the settlement discussions to Houston to finally resolve all remaining issues. When I arrived in Houston, Judge Pollack told me that Michael could not use his partnership interests as sole security and would have to be personally liable. He was apologetic, but he said I would have to accept that. I was confident that the value of the partnerships was still sufficient. I told Judge Pollack that since Michael was at Pleasanton, I needed to get his consent, which could take a day or so since I needed to wait for him to call. Judge Pollack sternly and impatiently told me he would not accept that explanation and that I had to make the decision. I felt very uncomfortable agreeing to any change without letting Michael know about it, but I also knew I had no choice.

When we were asked to come to Houston, I felt it was essential that Steve Kaufman be there. I had come to rely upon Steve for his wise judgment in dealing with Judge Pollack, and it was clear Judge Pollack respected Steve. Steve was in Hawaii at the time celebrating his sixtieth birthday. I called Steve to alert him to this meeting. Without hesitation, he agreed to leave his birthday celebration and meet me in Houston for two days and then return to Hawaii. I will never forget that. As it turned out, it was important he was there.

The morning after I agreed to the change in terms without being able to consult with Michael, I went back to the offices we were using in Houston so we could finalize the global settlement. Steve Kaufman was there with Arthur Liman. We went into a conference room, and they told me another issue had come up. Tom Barr of Cravath was now insisting that Michael Milken also agree to put up additional security to his partnership interests if at any time those interests appeared to be worth less than his obligations under the settlement. We had agreed that Michael would give a full recourse note covering his total obligation and would be liable for it whether partnership interests were sufficient. I was not ready to agree to anything else on behalf of my friend and client. I said, "No! No! No!" Enough was enough.

When Arthur and Steve said I should seriously consider it, I finally cracked from the pressures of the previous five years. I started screaming that I would not agree to another term and threw all the papers on the table in front of me onto the floor. I picked up a bottle of Perrier water and, though not intending to break it, hit it against the table, and it shattered. And I stormed out of the room, shouting at the top of my lungs. I have never before or since "lost it" like that, but for five and a half years of this process, I was the recipient of everyone else's frustrations. In a vacuum, this one issue certainly did not justify my reaction, but after five years, I had finally reached my breaking point. I took a walk around the block, basically reliving the past five years. I gathered myself and came back. I apologized to Arthur and Steve. By now they were dear friends. I think they understood, but they both looked stunned.

We then went upstairs to meet with the lawyer teams and Judge Pollack. Tom Barr explained why he needed this additional security. Steve Kaufman argued why it was not needed and why it was not a fair request. Tom Barr then interrupted Steve. Mild-mannered Steve Kaufman looked at Tom Barr and said, "Tom, you're a fine lawyer. But there comes a time to stop talking and to just to listen. Now is the time to listen."

The room fell silent as Steve continued with his argument. The result? Michael did not have to post any additional security whether the partnership interests were sufficient or not. All terms of the global settlement had been agreed to as we left Houston. I was grateful Steve Kaufman was there.

As I boarded the plane to come home on a Friday, I was satisfied with the global settlement and was hopeful it would help the Rule 35 motion. Nevertheless, I was still shaking from those two days.

Michael Milken had agreed to pay $900 million toward a $1.3 billion settlement of civil suits we were convinced had no merit whatsoever. This was a business decision. What was the value of being freed from more years of litigation, distraction, and the extraordinary pain this investigation and everything that came with it caused? More importantly, what was the value of an early release from prison? Michael was paying over twenty-eight hundred times the amount found by Judge Wood to be involved in his wrongdoing to put all of this behind him.

I was back in my office the next day, a Saturday. Michael was able to call me, and I explained to him what had happened. At first he was not happy the terms had been changed, but he heard the emotion in my voice and knew the change really was not that important. It was time to look forward. And at that moment, he still faced another two years of incarceration—plus three years of full-time community service.

My focus was now on the Rule 35 process so Michael could be released from custody, begin his community service, and get this nightmare over with as soon as possible.

CHAPTER 16

Motion to Reduce Sentence

I put all my efforts into the Rule 35 motion. I discussed with Steve Kaufman the issue of who should lead the Rule 35 process. Due to my familiarity with the case and with Michael, I suggested I take the lead on the Rule 35. Neither Arthur Liman nor Steve disagreed.

Our motion to reduce Michael's sentence was filed with Judge Wood in October 1991, seven months after Michael had reported to prison camp. We did not expect to get a decision for some time, but it was shortly after the parole hearing and it was the appropriate time to file. In the motion, we reviewed the background of the sentencing and the fact that Judge Wood had indicated the "real time" Mr. Milken should serve should be between thirty-six and forty months. We discussed the fact that the actual length of the ten-year sentence and the continued notoriety of the case made Michael's incarceration particularly burdensome. He started out as an orderly in prison emptying wastebaskets, cleaning toilets, and mopping floors. As his supervisors put it, "Mr. Milken [is] an excellent employee ... not afraid of menial labor." Though it would have been normal for a person in Mr. Milken's position to be eligible for a clerical position after a few months, Michael remained an orderly for over six months and was told by an official at the prison that his assignments were to protect the Bureau of Prisons from any adverse publicity.

He also tutored prison inmates seeking high school equivalency diplomas. He attended classes with the inmates and met with them individually to review their work. Several evenings a week he held open sessions, teaching inmates math games and puzzles they could use when their children visited. One inmate even described Milken as "an exceptional teacher who will go out of his way to help all interested in the opportunity to learn; he will even wake people up at five a.m. to achieve their goals."

Our motion also disclosed that Michael had been named in over one hundred lawsuits, many involving securities he had never even heard of. Being incarcerated certainly prejudiced him in preparing a defense. We discussed the parole process. There was no evidence of additional wrongdoing or damages, nor would there ever be. Based upon the court's submission to the Parole Commission, parole should have resulted in the maximum of twenty-four to thirty-six months. As of the time of this filing of the motion, the parole decision was on appeal and the global settlement had not been completed.

We further pointed out to the court that under Bureau of Prison regulations, an inmate who has been granted community custody status is eligible for furloughs

> He started out as an orderly in prison emptying wastebaskets, cleaning toilets, and mopping floors. As his supervisors put it, "Mr. Milken [is] an excellent employee ... not afraid of menial labor."

under certain situations. Such status is not granted until an inmate release date is twenty-four months or less.

We discussed in detail Michael's extensive postsentencing cooperation. We acknowledged that Michael's recollection of events differed from that of other witnesses, but the prosecutors agreed that these differences cannot—and need not—be resolved for purpose of deciding this particular motion. They even confirmed that such cooperation resulted in at least one substantial ongoing criminal investigation, though it did not involve any activities by Milken or Drexel.

I filed a forty-three-page affidavit with the Rule 35 motion detailing Michael's cooperation. I participated in every session with representatives of the government and helped coordinate the scheduling of each session as well as providing the government with requested information. As of October 1991, Michael had met with the government on twenty-nine different occasions in sessions lasting from four to six hours. He had spent approximately 152 hours in these sessions and over 250 hours preparing for the sessions by reviewing documents and records, some of which were supplied by the government.

There were times when the government would question Michael about inconsistency between Milken's recollection and perceptions and those of other witnesses. And there were times when Michael questioned positions taken by the government respecting certain transactions or their understanding. I pointed out that at the first meeting with the prosecutors, they told Mr. Milken the parties could be just as strong friends as they had been adversaries. He was told the measure of his cooperation would not necessarily be based on cases the government chose to bring. He would be expected to do as he agreed and to tell what he knew and remembered.

After extensive interviews, Michael was asked to testify under oath in connection with the government's case against Alan Rosenthal related to Finsbury. The act of testifying in the Alan Rosenthal trial was very difficult for Michael. Alan Rosenthal was a close personal friend as well as a colleague in the High Yield and Convertible Bond Department at Drexel. After Michael testified, both Alan Rosenthal and his attorney, Peter Fleming, told me how much they admired and appreciated Michael and how he'd testified.

My affidavit also stated that Michael was questioned extensively about the relationship between Drexel and Columbia Savings. The prosecutors had told us at the beginning of the cooperation meetings that they hoped Michael could help them in their investigation of Columbia Savings, and he could not. Michael explained that neither Drexel nor Columbia ever owned a beneficial interest in any securities on the books of the other organization, contrary to the government's assertion.

The prosecutors accepted my affidavit as an accurate description of what went on in cooperation.

The motion also argued that under the law, the decision to bring a case is a matter of prosecutorial discretion, beyond the control of a defendant or the court. Therefore, a sentence reduction should not be based on how the government chooses to exercise its discretion but rather on what the effort was from the defendant to be forthright and cooperative. Mr. Milken's meetings with the government included eleven Assistant US Attorneys (nine from the Southern District of New York), two United States postal inspectors, three FBI agents, and twenty-six members of the staff of the SEC's enforcement division.

Judge Wood had indicated a number of times there should be proportionality between the Milken sentence and the Boesky sentence. We again reminded the court that Boesky's crimes included insider trading, secret offshore bank accounts, and payments made in suitcases of cash. When the court had indicated that Michael should serve thirty-six to forty months, she had assumed Michael had obstructed justice and Boesky had not, which was not accurate. We argued this should be an additional consideration in further reducing the sentence.

We brought to the court's attention that since the time of Michael's plea, the Second Circuit Court of Appeals had reversed white-collar convictions in other securities cases brought by the Giuliani office. Two of them were *United States v. Mulheren* and *United States v. Regan* (the Princeton/Newport case), and both arose out of the Boesky/ Drexel investigation and involved many of the same legal issues that would have arisen had Michael gone to trial.

In the Mulheren case, the Second Circuit reversed the conviction of John Mulheren based on allegations that he purchased a certain stock for the purpose of raising the stock's price as a favor to Ivan Boesky. The government's principal witness was Ivan Boesky. It was the only time the government used him as a witness. Though the court of appeals stated it had misgivings about the government's expansive view of "manipulation," the court never reached a conclusion on that issue, since it ruled that no rational trier of fact could have found that Mulheren intended to commit a manipulation based solely on a conversation in which he was told by Boesky, "It would be great if the stock traded" at a specific price. Had Michael Milken gone to trial, the same ambiguities and uncertainties about cryptic conversations would have permeated the government's case, and the same defenses would have been asserted.

In *United States v. Regan*, the court of appeals reversed the convictions on conspiracy, tax fraud, mail and wire fraud, false records and reports, and RICO charges and concluded that "proof of guilt in such cases must be predicated upon voluntarily intentional violations of a known legal duty" (937 F.2d at 827 [1991]). It also stated that with respect to mail and wire fraud charges, the government bears "an even more onerous burden proving beyond a reasonable doubt that the defendant was guilty of a conscious knowing intent to defraud."

How would this reasoning have applied to the Finsbury count that Michael pleaded to as a mail fraud for nondisclosure on confirmations of trade adjustments to pay commissions? We pointed out to Judge Wood that the government's case against Michael would have turned in large part on complex provisions of federal securities and tax laws. The very securities law charges that the court of appeals reversed in Princeton/Newport were part of the government's indictment against Michael Milken.

The Second Circuit had also reversed the conviction of James Sherwin in *United States v. GAF Corp.*, another Boesky-related case, where a jury convicted the defendant of a stock manipulation and which conviction was later reversed. The prosecutors decided not to retry the case.

The reason we brought these cases to the court's attention was to show that Michael's case was triable and that he should receive credit for not contesting charges in what would have been among the most complicated and protracted trials ever.

After these reversals, people asked me whether Michael was sorry he did not go to trial. I have never looked back on the decision to plead, nor has Michael. I learned that if the government is truly out to secure a conviction against you, it is willing to spare no resource in doing so. Michael Milken was an individual who, at the time, the government was committed to convict. His case was therefore different from other cases at the time. In all the cases reversed on appeal, the government decided not to retry the defendants. It is not a coincidence that all these decisions not to retry the case occurred after Michael pleaded. I am sure the government would never have stopped prosecuting Michael Milken as long as it believed it could "convict" him. The US Attorney's Office for the Southern District of New York had invested too much to ever acknowledge it was wrong. It was a real-life *True Believer*.

Edward Bennett Williams, who had better judgment and instincts than any trial lawyer I had ever met, was concerned from day one that the combination of an ambitious and unscrupulous prosecutor, securities laws that were vague and subject to different interpretations, and a target with Michael Milken's notoriety and wealth would make it extremely difficult to win at trial. Michael made the right choice for himself and his family.

The Rule 35 motion for reduction of sentence concluded as follows:

> We respectfully request that the Court reduce Mr. Milken's sentence so the actual period of his incarceration be substantially less than the thirty-six to forty months originally contemplated by the Court. Such a result would enable Mr. Milken, who throughout his life has exhibited qualities of community involvement that are singular in a businessman, to resume a productive role in society at the earliest possible time.

At the time we filed the motion, discussions were proceeding with respect to the global settlement of the civil cases. We did not expect a decision on the motion for many months. John Carroll became head of the fraud unit in the US Attorney's Office during this time. He agreed to our timing on this motion and further agreed that the government would affirm certain benefits of Michael's cooperation, would not dispute Michael's record at prison, and would not dispute the description of the cooperation set forth in my affidavit. John

Carroll was willing to proceed solely on those parts of the record we could agree upon and not ask the court to resolve the parts of the record we did not agree upon.

On behalf of the New York US Attorney's Office, he filed a response to the Rule 35 motion for reduction of sentence that stated,

> While we do not dispute the recitation of Mr. Milken's statements contained in the Affidavit of Richard Sandler he has filed in support of Mr. Milken's motion. In the Government's view, Mr. Milken has not provided substantial assistance in the investigation or prosecution of another person who has committed an offense. While Mr. Milken has devoted substantial time and energy to the process and certain of his disclosures have resulted in the commencement of criminal and SEC investigations, his cooperation has not resulted in any indictments or convictions. … In contrast to the cooperation offered by Ivan F. Boesky, Boyd Jefferies, Martin Siegel, and Dennis Levine, Mr. Milken's cooperation has not been timely, nor has it been nearly as productive measured by its materiality to the investigation and prosecution of other persons. In the Government's view, therefore, Mr. Milken's cooperation has been of limited value to criminal investigation.

I did not find anything in John Carroll's affidavit surprising or troubling, and there was nothing in it that asked the court not to reduce the sentence. Judge Wood had already confirmed that the government was not able to prove that Michael was involved in any conduct beyond that to which he'd pleaded. It was very important that this response did not continue to accuse Michael of any wrongdoing.

We filed a supplement to the Rule 35 motion in March 1992. At that point in time we had agreed to all the terms of the global settlement. We argued that this settlement was extensive cooperation with the federal court system. Pat Hynes, a partner from the Milberg, Weiss firm, wrote a letter to Judge Wood supporting the reduction in sentence due to the global settlement. I will never know whether Judge Pollack ever spoke to Judge Wood about the original sentence or the motion for a reduction of sentence, but based upon the hours that I spent with him, I believe he did both.

In this supplement to the Rule 35 motion, we also brought to the court's attention the fact that the SEC had recently settled with over one hundred banks and investment firms that had engaged in disclosure and trading violations in the treasury securities markets that compromised the integrity of those markets. These settlements included fines of between $5,000 and $100,000 with no other sanctions or criminal proceedings being brought. This was an incredible contrast to how the government treated Michael Milken for far less serious infractions.

In March 1992, Michael's expected release date was July of 1994, in twenty-eight months. Since we had an understanding with John Carroll that the Rule 35 motion could be decided based upon the uncontested facts, we did not plan on any further filings in the effort to obtain a sentence reduction and an earlier release date. We expected the court to either set a date for a hearing or to just rule on the motion. But then the SEC decided to get involved in a criminal proceeding.

I met with one of the SEC attorneys, James Coffman, around this time in Pleasanton, California, the night before he and I were to meet with Michael. Mr. Coffman told me about an investigation of a former colleague of Michael's. Coffman told me the SEC had a gap in its evidence that if Michael could fill would result in the SEC writing a very positive letter to the court in support of the Rule 35 motion. The problem was that Michael was not aware of any wrongdoing by this individual and could not fill in this "gap." So on June 22, 1992, the SEC wrote a letter to Judge Wood signed by William McLucas, the director of the enforcement division. It stated,

> In contrast to Milken's willingness to attribute knowledge of his admitted wrongdoing to certain of his superiors, he has provided little information of value to the SEC's preexisting investigations of his former customers and associates in his High Yield Bond Department. … Milken has offered his analysis of what he perceived to be questionable trading and sales practices in the securities industry generally. Often the examples he has cited involve alleged practices of former competitors and in some cases, the alleged conduct of those who have cooperated with the government's prosecution of him. The Commission has commenced several investigations and inquiries based, in part, on this information. … Milken has been least helpful regarding matters as to which he could be most helpful.

When I read this letter, I became angry. The SEC was interjecting itself into a criminal matter and trying to adversely affect our motion. We had an understanding with the US Attorneys' Office, and in a criminal matter the government is represented by the US Attorney, not the SEC. This letter was also inaccurate.

Two days later, I sent a letter to Judge Wood—with copies to John Carroll and William McLucas—and filed a supplemental affidavit to my previous affidavit citing in detail instances of Mike's cooperation that were inconsistent with the statements made in the SEC's June 22 letter:

I understand that in a criminal case, the United States Attorney's Office represents the United States Government; and that its evaluation of a defendant's cooperation is binding on the Government—or at least takes precedence over the report of another agency. In this case, the SEC has decided to submit its own letter regarding Mr. Milken's cooperation. ... Having been present at every session at which the representatives of the SEC or United States Attorney met with Mr. Milken and having had direct contact with members of the SEC staff regarding scheduling matters and information requests, I feel compelled to make yet one more submission to Your Honor to address the unfounded and unfair accusations and conclusions set forth in the SEC letter.

Mr. Milken has made a sincere effort to cooperate with the SEC. It is clear, however, from the SEC's letter that he could not overcome the deep-seated and biased attitudes that the SEC developed before it ever spoke to him. This bias makes it impossible for the SEC to give Mr. Milken credit for his cooperation, unless he admits to all the allegations set forth in the SEC complaint, and whatever other theories and suspicions the SEC subscribes to. The SEC seems to forget that it agreed to settle its case against Michael Milken without an admission or denial of liability. The SEC knew at the time that Mr. Milken and many other witnesses whom it had interviewed denied most of the allegations in the SEC complaint.

Mr. Milken has now met with the SEC on twenty-four separate occasions for over one hundred hours. He

WITNESS TO A PROSECUTION

has candidly answered all of the SEC's questions. ... The SEC is as parsimonious in crediting Mr. Milken for the admitted assistance he has provided as it is generous in making unwarranted accusations that he must know wrongdoing that he has not disclosed. ... SEC is trying to prevent Mr. Milken from obtaining relief from his present circumstances, unless it gets further vindication for all the unproven and unsubstantiated claims it has made over the years. Mr. McLucas, who did not actively participate in the sessions, has been misinformed about Mr. Milken's cooperation on this matter. That almost all the meetings with the SEC, one or more of either Mr. Kaufman, Mr. Liman, or Mr. Robert Litt was present with me. Each of us encouraged the SEC and the United States Attorney to push Mr. Milken as far as possible when they believed he was capable of providing additional or different information, and urged them to refresh Mr. Milken's recollection whenever appropriate. I cannot recall the SEC's ever confronting Mr. Milken on any subject with a single alleged inconsistency between witnesses or documentary evidence. Messrs. Liman, Kaufman, and Litt have confirmed to me that they share my recollection. ...

An SEC staff attorney recommended that an Assistant United States Attorney from Jacksonville, Florida, meet with Mr. Milken due to his "unique insights" and understanding of the markets. It would seem only fair that the SEC share such opinions with the Court. ... Attorneys I have spoken to cannot remember another case in which the SEC has submitted a letter to the Court on sentencing—certainly not on a Rule 35 motion.

I concluded as follows:

> In our prior submissions, we have agreed with the United States Attorney that a hearing is not necessary based upon the undisputed record of Mr. Milken's cooperation. If, however, the Court concludes that it needs to reconcile the disputes between the SEC's letter and this letter, I would respectfully request a hearing on the matter. The SEC's view of Mr. Milken's activities, which was formed before the SEC ever interviewed Mr. Milken, is so sharply disputed that it would not seem to be subject to resolution on this motion.

After receiving my letter, Judge Wood immediately contacted all the attorneys and asked us to appear in her courtroom the next day, June 25, 1992, at 3:30 p.m. Arthur Liman was in Switzerland at the time. I appeared in court together with Steve Kaufman and Brad Karp from Paul, Weiss, Rifkin, Wharton & Garrison.

William McLucas appeared for the SEC, and John Carroll and Nelson Cunningham appeared for the US Attorney's Office. Judge Wood opened the hearing by asking Messrs. Carroll, Cunningham, and McLucas whether it was the government's view that Mr. Milken should be credited for his cooperation and assistance with respect to the case he'd testified in at the request of the US Attorney's Office but no other credit, or if it was their view he should not even receive full credit for that case because of lack of full disclosure to the SEC or with respect to the US Attorney. John Carroll responded as follows:

That larger picture includes Mr. Milken's effort at cooperating with our office and efforts at cooperating with the SEC. In some sense we came to Mr. Milken's cooperation with certain expectations. Those expectations were borne of four years of investigation looking at piles of records, piles of facts, looking at statements of numerous witnesses. And I would tell the Court that our expectations were not borne out. That does not mean that Mr. Milken wasn't helpful in some situations, he was helpful in some situations. I think on a couple of them he was helpful in ways that were probably of more assistance to the SEC than to our office. There are issues of candor, as we've said to Your Honor in our submissions and as SEC said to Your Honor in its submissions. Those issues are brutally hard to evaluate. If you evaluate candor by reference to our expectations and the SEC's expectations, I think you would score Mr. Milken not that high on the candor scale. If you evaluate candor by whether the Government is going to call Mr. Milken a liar or a perjurer, I wouldn't do that, Your Honor. I certainly can't do that.

Judge Wood continued,

You say there is a lack of candor here, but it doesn't rise to lying or perjury; is that what you said?

Mr. Carroll replied,

Your Honor, I wouldn't call someone a perjurer unless I could prove them a perjurer. As we do not begin to have the evidence here that would cause the Government to walk into the grand jury and charge someone with perjury. ... There is not clear-cut proof of who is truthfully recalling the past and who is not.

The court replied,

When you say expectations, though, I don't know how realistic they were or what they were based on. If you want me to subtract some value from his assistance because of lack of candor, what am I going to rely on for that?

Mr. Carroll continued,

But we do recognize, Your Honor, that coming to some final determination of candor on all these issues is a swamp, and it's a swamp that we do not wish to invite Your Honor to get down into. We think that this now five-year-old case could be ten years old before we ever finish evaluating all those issues. For that reason, Your Honor, we have made every effort to try to just evaluate what the facts are where Mr. Milken is net plus on the facts.

Mr. McLucas spoke next:

We are in one hundred percent agreement with the United States and with Mr. Carroll's remarks on the issue of Mr. Milken's cooperation.

The court continued,

I have one last question for Mr. Carroll. The wording of some—well, some of the wording in one of your letters to me—made me wonder whether you contest this preguideline proposition that a defendant's cooperation need not result in the criminal prosecution of another person in order both to be useful to law enforcement and to warrant leniency.

Mr. Carroll responded,

Your Honor, I think that Mr. Milken is entitled to credit for cooperation he gives to the SEC for example or in another context. If I was confusing on that I hope I am not now.

Judge Wood then addressed Mr. Kaufman and me:

I know that Mr. Sandler's letter suggests a hearing. And I guess I'm just wondering what level of deference you think I ought to give to the prosecutor. And after that I will ask you what would I hear at a hearing and what standard would I use to guide me.

I responded as follows:

To address the last point, Your Honor, about the request for a hearing, our goal—and I think Mr. Carroll and Mr. Cunningham's goal, and probably the SEC's goal, or at least our goal because we are the parties in this case—has been to give the Court as complete a picture of what happened since sentencing, because I think it's postsentencing events that we are focusing on. And obviously one of the focuses of those events—and, of course, we have submitted to this Court respectfully more than just cooperation, but the focus is always on cooperation.

Judge Wood stated,

Oh, I don't mean by focusing today on cooperation to suggest that I'm not going to consider all of the other points that were made. There are some very good points.

I responded,

I know my personal goal—and in talking to Mr. Carroll, about his goal, too, and I have heard nothing different from that—was to try to reach some kind of consensus. I think we have had a long history in this case, and it has gone on for a long time, and I think the inability to reach consensus has not served anyone well in the past, and we have tried to reach consensus over the period, and I thought we had reached a consensus, at least on certain cooperation issues, some acknowledged by Mr. Carroll. Then we have the issue which I think Your Honor—one of many other issues, which is cooperation with the Courts, which I think you've gotten a full submission from us and I think a letter from Patricia Hynes with respect to the civil settlements, the Global Settlements of those cases. I really had hoped that at least up until Monday there would be no need for anyone to suggest a hearing because there seemed to be an agreement on what was done. There may be different interpretations on the value or what it would have been. I think it was clear to the Court and to everyone else at the time of sentencing that there was a wide gap between what some of the expectations were of wrongdoing and our view of what the facts were with respect to those wrongdoings.

I sincerely believe that Mr. Milken had answered all questions in all candor based upon his best recollections to date.

Judge Wood then commented on how the courts defer to prosecutors unless a defendant makes a claim of subjective bad faith by the government and indicated she would listen to a claim of bad faith or invidious discrimination. She went on,

And I don't think you are making those claims, although your response to the SEC suggested that you might be claiming subjective bad faith on their part. And I wonder if you wanted me to have a hearing—which I hope you don't, but I'm not precluding it—on whether the SEC acted subjectively in bad faith.

I responded,

I'm not suggesting that we have a hearing on subjective bad faith. The only situation in which I would even envision it is if the Court were to credit statements in the SEC letter that I have addressed based upon my own personal knowledge.

The court replied,

You see, that gets me into the role of being a dispute resolver, which I don't think I am, but I am open to hearing from you if you think I should be here. I think I should do what judges traditionally do, which is rely on the prosecutor. What it means is I will credit Mr.

Milken for everything that the Government says he should be credited for.

I continued,

I think that he should be credited with the undisputed record. And I think it would include the tremendous time and effort he has discussed—that he spent discussing industry practices.

The court responded,

I think I have an answer. I think you have answered it. That is, you have said I should look at what is not in dispute and give him credit for that. It's not in dispute that he spent a lot of hours with you. How valuable those hours were in terms of law enforcement seems to me is a question as to which you and the Government do not agree.

I pointed out that in our submission, we cited cases where the court felt a defendant should get credit for his efforts, even if the government disagreed as to the value of the cooperation.

The court replied, "There just haven't been cases anywhere near as complex as this."

And I said, "I am sure of that."

Mr. Kaufman reminded the court that the government's expectations may have been great going in, to which Judge Wood replied, "I don't care at all what their expectation was. It could have been unrealistic."

The hearing ended with the agreement by all that the court would take into account that which had been agreed upon between the parties and ignore everything else. There would not be a hearing. I left the court believing the strategy of not proceeding with the appeal and working with Mr. Carroll rather than against him proved to be the right strategy. I also heard Judge Wood say the government's expectations "could have been unrealistic," that the arguments in our motion beyond cooperating would be considered to include "some very good points," and she was hoping I did not insist on a hearing. I took these comments together with her prior comments that she did not believe the government could prove anything beyond the five transactions pleaded as a positive indication she was thinking about reducing the sentence.

By this time Mike had been at Pleasanton for sixteen months. He, too, was very upset with the SEC letter in addition to books that had been written and other personal attacks, and he had told me he would welcome a hearing to call the SEC to task and deal with the lies. When he received the transcript of the hearing, he called me and was upset that I did not insist on the hearing to attack the SEC. I explained that I was in court listening to what the judge said, hearing her tone, and watching her closely. It was clear she did not want a hearing; she's said, "I hope you don't" want a hearing. I left court strongly believing she was planning to reduce the sentence further. I suggested that he call Alan Dershowitz about the advisability of a hearing. A couple of days later, early on Sunday morning, my phone rang, and it was Professor Dershowitz, who also had Mike on the line. We discussed the hearing we'd had in court, and Alan said that having read the transcript and talked to me, he, too, was comfortable with how the hearing went and what the resolution was. I understood better than anyone Michael's frustration. He was the one in prison; he was the person who was vilified in books and articles and by the SEC.

William McLucas, who appeared for the SEC at the hearing, was a guest at the class I taught at Stanford Law School in February of 2020, almost thirty years later. I asked him whether in his eight years as an SEC director he had ever seen the SEC submit a letter on a motion to reduce sentence as it had in the Milken case. His reply was as follows:

> No, never did. … I honestly, as I sit here, I don't remember how it came about. When a motion for reduction was filed, I think there was a sense that the Commission ought to weigh in some way, shape, or form if we think that the motion for reduction is really not appropriate.

So now we were waiting for the decision. Though Mike had told me and others he wanted to address all the lies from books, articles, and the government even if so doing resulted in his sentence not being reduced, I did not buy it for a second. I visited with Michael once or twice a week and spoke to him every day. I knew how difficult it was for him, how difficult it was for Lori and the family, and how badly he wanted to be home. I also knew the best result for my friend was to obtain as early a release from Pleasanton as possible.

I was hoping Judge Wood would reduce the ten-year sentence to between three and four years, meaning at worst that Michael would be released from Bureau of Prisons custody between March and October 1993, where the parole release date at the time was July 1994.

> I knew how difficult it was for him, how difficult it was for Lori and the family, and how badly he wanted to be home.

I was on a vacation with my family and Lowell's family in Hawaii on August 6, 1992, when early in the morning (Hawaii time being six hours earlier than New York), the phone rang. It was Arthur Liman. Judge Wood had issued her opinion. He read to me the last two paragraphs of the fourteen-page opinion:

> The Court grants the defendant's Rule 35 motion for sentence reduction. Before the decision on this motion, the defendant was expected to be released after serving thirty-six months (assuming he would receive four months credit for teaching in prison, which the Parole Commission would otherwise give him were the Court not giving him credit for that service). The Court reduces defendant's sentence such that he will serve a total of twenty-four months in prison, twelve months less than the thirty-six months he would otherwise serve. Because he has already served seventeen months in prison, he will be released in seven months. A reduction of the defendant's sentence to thirty-three months and twenty-six days will cause the defendant actually to serve a total of twenty-four months. The Court makes no change in the remainder of the defendant's sentence, which includes three years of full-time community service to commence when he is released from prison.

I was ecstatic! Judge Wood had reduced the sentence by more than the reduction of sentence I was hoping for. It was almost five years and nine months since this nightmare began on November 14, 1986, and we finally got a positive result. The sentence was actually less than the sentence Ivan Boesky received.

I immediately called Lori. Neither of us could contain our emotions. She asked, "Can I tell Michael, or do you want to do it?"

I told her by all means she should inform Michael. What I did not realize was how long it would be before I actually spoke to Michael myself. Since the day I went with him to FCI Dublin, I had probably spoken to Michael an average of twice a day every day. Though he could only make collect calls and only at certain times a day, he seemed able to find me at all times no matter where I was. There were no iPhones in those days, so he had to call me collect on a landline. Since I was in Hawaii, he would call me through the office, which would call the hotel. For several days, every time he called I was out of the room. Finally, after several days, we did speak, and I could hear a sound in his voice that I had not heard for almost six years. He was calm. He was grateful. He was happy.

When I returned to California the following week, I went to visit Michael. We were going over some important issues regarding the global settlement and were about fifteen minutes from the time our meeting had to end. All visits had to end at a specific time. We were always conscious of the time and would make sure we ended the meetings a few minutes early. On this particular day, Mike suddenly said, "We can continue to discuss this another time." I was a little stunned, since we had another fifteen minutes. He was sitting across the table from me as he continued, "Since you have to leave in a few minutes, there is something I want you to know. If the book *Den of Thieves* were to be made into a movie and was nominated for the Academy Award for Best Picture, and won, that would mean as much to me as a single grain of sand on the beach compared to my getting out of here." I knew how upset he was about that book and was not sure where he was going with this comment. At that point, he stood up, looked me directly in the eye, and reached his hand across the table to shake my hand as he said two words with tears in his eyes: "Thank you."

Every time I had left Pleasanton from March 3, 1991, the day when Michael reported, I'd left with a sinking feeling of sadness that I had to leave him there. That day, for the first time, I left feeling his time there was almost over. He was positive for the first time in over six years.

We knew that Bureau of Prison practice is to release individuals up to six months in advance of the release to what is called a "halfway house." This would be a facility under the jurisdiction of the Bureau of Prisons in the community in which the individual lives. Once released to a halfway house, an individual can go home for meals, can go to work, and eventually can sleep at home and report in to the bureau every day. Though I had contacted the bureau to see if it was possible for Michael to be home for Thanksgiving, he was finally released, unannounced, early Sunday morning, January 3, 1993. He called to tell me he was at the halfway house and could come home for the day. I was so excited as I went to pick him up to bring him home to surprise his family. As I drove Mike into the driveway of his house, I thought about our drive out of that same driveway on that other Sunday, twenty-two months earlier. Happy New Year!

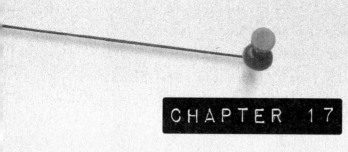

CHAPTER 17

Postrelease Government Investigations

Judge Wood approved Michael's request to fulfill his community service with the D.A.R.E. PLUS Program, an after-school program that was an extension of D.A.R.E. established by the Los Angeles Police Department to work with young people in the community with an emphasis on drug education (Drug Abuse Resistance Education). Michael's previous philanthropic work introduced him to D.A.R.E. and the deputy police chief from the Los Angeles Police Department who was in charge of D.A.R.E., Glenn Levant. Chief Levant wanted to expand D.A.R.E. to develop an after-school program. Judge Wood approved Michael's community service, as Michael had helped initiate D.A.R.E. PLUS as an after-school program for students to provide classes such as cooking, art, school tutoring, and working with exotic animals. Mike's probation officer in Los Angeles, Donald Bizar, monitored Mike's community service.

Michael threw himself into his community service the way he did everything else. He often would open an after-school center by bringing celebrities to the opening. At one of the schools, Mike's surprise guest was Michael Jackson. Mike also would recruit friends of his to teach in the after-school program classes. My wife, Ellen, and her friend Lynn Bider taught a cooking class for a number of years and enjoyed doing so.

I wish this story ended with Mike's being reunited with his family, doing his community service, and moving on with his life. Unfortunately, fate and the Securities and Exchange Commission could not let that happen.

Soon after he was home, Michael went to see his doctor for a physical for the first time in over two years. A couple of weeks before Michael's release, Stephen Ross, who was the CEO of Time Warner and Warner Communications and a very close friend of Michael's, had died from complications relating to prostate cancer. Michael learned there was a test called a PSA (prostate-specific antigen) to assist in early detection of prostate cancer and asked his doctor to give him a PSA test. The doctor told him it was really unnecessary, since Mike had no symptoms and at forty-six years old, it was highly unlikely that he had prostate cancer. Mike insisted on having the test, since it was only a blood test. The test came back with an elevated PSA, an indication he should be tested further. He then went to see a urologist, Dr. Stuart Holden, and learned that in fact he had an aggressive form of prostate cancer. I am convinced that Mike's stress level during the preceding six years contributed to

> I wish this story ended with Mike's being reunited with his family, doing his community service, and moving on with his life. Unfortunately, fate and the Securities and Exchange Commission could not let that happen.

what was a very unusual diagnosis for someone his age. Dr. Holden assured me that was a distinct possibility.

Dr. Holden suggested to Mike that they attend an upcoming medical conference on prostate cancer at MD Anderson Cancer Center in Houston. At that point in time, prostate cancer was not receiving the attention or the funding other cancers and diseases were receiving, and treatment options were limited. It was February 1993, and Michael was still subject to the jurisdiction of the Bureau of Prisons until March 1. That meant he could not travel without permission. I called officials at the Bureau of Prisons for permission for Michael to go to Houston and was told the bureau would deny the permission but was willing to take Michael back into custody and have him admitted to a Bureau of Prison hospital. That was not an option.

I contacted Judge Wood and made an appointment to meet her and Mike's probation officer, Michaela Bracken, in her chambers. I brought a letter from Dr. Holden. Judge Wood called Dr. Holden during our meeting. She was very understanding and sympathetic to the situation. She called the head of the Bureau of Prisons to ask that Michael be allowed to attend the conference in Houston, and permission was granted. Again, Judge Wood used her discretion and position with great sensitivity to Michael's situation.

It is somewhat ironic that within weeks of the time Michael was released from Pleasanton, Judge Wood had her own taste of unfair media scrutiny. President William Clinton became the fortieth president of the United States on January 20, 1993. He made it clear he would nominate a woman as his attorney general. He first nominated Zoe Baird, a respected lawyer. Ms. Baird withdrew her name from consideration when she disclosed the fact that she and her husband had hired an illegal alien to work in their home. They had not paid social security taxes for this individual, which violated the law and for which they paid a fine.

President Clinton then nominated Judge Wood to be the attorney general. The publicity Judge Wood had received from the Milken case probably contributed to this nomination. It turned out that Judge Wood, too, had hired an illegal alien to be the nanny for her children. Unlike Ms. Baird, Judge Wood had not violated any laws in effect at that time, since she did make required social security payments. Still, when this fact about the nanny became known to the White House, Judge Wood withdrew her name from nomination. It was reported that the White House was embarrassed that the president had nominated two candidates who had to withdraw for related reasons. News accounts suggested that Judge Wood had not been forthright when her name was first put into nomination, resulting in her being asked to withdraw her name. Judge Wood strongly denied such a suggestion. But as I'd learned early on, it is very hard to chase lies with the truth.

At the medical conference in Houston, Mike again had to digest bad news when one of the doctors presented statistics that indicated his form and stage of cancer gave him a life expectancy of nine to fifteen months, even though he then had no symptoms. After getting over the shock of this news, Mike again did what he always does. He went to work to solve a problem. He formed the Prostate Cancer Foundation. Since Michael and Lowell had engaged in philanthropic efforts to advance cancer research for years, Michael picked up his philanthropic work in this area by forming a new foundation to attack a disease that was receiving very little attention. Through treatment and lifestyle, he defied the statistics. From 1993 to the present, the Prostate Cancer Foundation has been remarkable in leveraging government funding and changing the science in this area, as hundreds of researchers and projects have been funded and have resulted in new treatments and drugs saving millions of lives.

Michael diligently devoted his eighteen hundred hours a year to D.A.R.E. PLUS. He also interacted with former customers and clients who would call him to seek his advice regarding their businesses. A number of them wanted to retain Michael as a consultant. At the time Mike agreed to settle with the government, Arthur Liman was very clear on what he could or could not do. He could not be involved in the securities business in any manner whatsoever. His bar order from the SEC said he could not "be associated with" a broker dealer or an investment advisor. That meant he could not be in the business of buying or selling securities for the account of others or providing investment advice to others for a fee with respect to purchasing or selling securities. He could consult with businesses about industries and the economy.

I prepared two consulting agreements with companies that sought Michael's advice. These agreements stated very clearly exactly what Mike was being retained to do and the activities he would not get involved in, such as consulting on the structure of a security, valuation of a company, or the purchase or sale of a security. He consulted on two transactions where he introduced the parties and advised the parties to consider a business combination because of the synergies of their various businesses. One of Mike's talents was seeing the future. Wayne Gretzky, the great hall of fame hockey player, used to say he would not skate to where the puck was but to where he thought it was going. Part of Michael Milken's genius was to think about where a business or an industry was going and what it would look like in the future.

In one transaction, he introduced Rupert Murdoch and News Corp to New World, controlled by Ronald Perelman. Both Rupert

Murdoch and Ronald Perelman had been clients of Drexel. News Corp and its Fox network had acquired the rights to broadcast NFL football games. New World owned television stations. A business combination would allow Fox to expand its affiliates. The result was a $2 billion transaction.

In another transaction, Michael introduced News Corp to MCI Communications, another company Michael had financed at Drexel. Mike advised MCI to expand its communications network by acquiring more content to distribute. At the same time, News Corp had content and was always looking for further distribution sources. MCI and News Corp entered into a partnership involving another $2 billion in investments.

As a result of these two transactions, Michael earned fees of $42 million, approximately 1 percent of the value of the transactions. The fact that Michael was involved in these transactions was mentioned in a *Wall Street Journal* article. Soon after the article appeared, I received a call from Jim Coffman at the SEC inquiring about the transactions to make sure Michael was not violating his SEC bar order. I assured him I was working closely with Mike, and he definitely was not violating his order. I immediately consulted with an outstanding securities lawyer, Richard Phillips, from the K&L Gates firm. Mr. Phillips advised that I voluntarily send documents to Mr. Coffman and cooperate in this informal inquiry. When I heard nothing for a couple of months, I called Mr. Coffman to tell him I was going on vacation and wanted to know if I should keep this matter on my "radar screen." He responded that I could remove it from my "radar screen."

Soon after the *Wall Street Journal* article appeared, Mike received a call from Ted Turner at Turner Broadcasting, who told Mike that if he was consulting for others, Ted wanted Mike to also consult for Turner Broadcasting. So again I prepared an agreement after conversations with Turner's lawyers, being very specific as to what Mike could or could not do. Shortly after this agreement was signed, Ted Turner received a call from Time Warner about the possibility of Time Warner acquiring Turner. Michael had long-standing relationships with the executives of Time Warner, with John Malone of Tele-Communications Inc., the nation's largest cable company at the time and a significant shareholder in Turner, and of course with Ted Turner. Michael was invaluable to this transaction as the person who could credibly speak with each of the principals about the benefits of the merger. Each company had its own investment bankers involved in the transaction, which should have eliminated any suggestion that Michael would act in any manner as a broker dealer or investment advisor.

There was a meeting at an airport in Colorado attended by Ted Turner; John Malone; Gerald Levin, the then CEO of Time Warner; Michael Milken; and others. I attended that meeting just to witness for myself the role Michael was playing. He was in no way acting inconsistently with the SEC order. Turner was merged into Time Warner in a transaction valued at over $7 billion. The fee paid to Michael was $50 million, less than 1 percent. When Mike's involvement in this transaction was reported in a number of newspapers, Mr. Coffman called me

> When Mike's involvement in this transaction was reported in a number of newspapers, Mr. Coffman called me again—this time to tell me the SEC was going to open a formal investigation and issue subpoenas.

again—this time to tell me the SEC was going to open a formal investigation and issue subpoenas.

I immediately contacted Dick Phillips and my old friends Ted Wells, who had represented Jay Regan in the Princeton/Newport case, and Steve Kaufman to strategize on this new SEC investigation. Dick Phillips had spent many years at the SEC and had relationships throughout the industry. Clearly the SEC was never going to leave Michael Milken alone. There was no way he was violating his order or any securities laws.

The Turner/Time Warner transaction was announced in September of 1995. Michael was completing his community service, and probation was due to end on March 1, 1996. I felt I should communicate with the US Attorney's Office about this SEC investigation. They would learn of it in any event, and it could have an effect on Mike's probation. I called Reid Figel, who at that time was heading the fraud unit at the US Attorney's Office for the Southern District of New York. He was in San Francisco at a conference, and I flew up to meet with him to review with him exactly what the SEC was looking at and why I was sure that Michael had done nothing remotely violating his order.

As a result of this new SEC investigation, the US Attorney's Office would not consent to Michael's probation ending on March 1, 1996. I reached an agreement with Mr. Figel to ask Judge Wood to extend the probation period for ninety days while relieving Michael of most conditions of probation. Judge Wood agreed to our understanding. I wrote a letter to the court on February 28, 1996, reminding Judge Wood that nine years had passed since the investigation had started and over five years since Mr. Milken was sentenced. I also pointed out that Michael had completed over fifty-five hundred hours of meaningful community service, more than required. I set forth for the court why Mike had not violated the SEC settlement and why I was frustrated:

> In 1990, I, as well as others, discussed with Mr. Milken what the Consent Decree meant so that he'd have a clear understanding of what the future restrictions would be on his activities. Since then, we have had many discussions about the fact that he had no interest in being in the securities business, and wanted to make sure he never again got into a position where the Securities and Exchange Commission could question the legitimacy of his activities. I have consulted continuously during this period with a securities law expert, Richard Phillips, an attorney with the firm of Kirkpatrick and Lockhart [K&L Gates]. I wanted to make sure that we understood clearly what Mr. Milken was permitted to do as a consultant in businesses before he began any such activity. ... I consulted with Mr. Milken and others who work with him almost daily to make sure that our goal of staying clear of any questions was always achieved. Both Mr. Phillips and I remain convinced that Mr. Milken is well within the boundaries of permissible activities.

My letter closed with a proposal Mr. Figel agreed not to oppose: (1) the probation would be extended for ninety days as unsupervised probation, (2) the standard conditions of his probation would be modified to eliminate all of the intrusive provisions regarding travel, reporting obligations, and other restrictions that Michael's probation officer had agreed to, and (3) the required community service was completed and was no longer a condition of probation.

The SEC investigation dragged on and on as we continually extended the probation period. After a couple of months, I received an "emergency" message from attorney Tom Newkirk at the SEC on a Friday afternoon when I was away from the office. When I called him, he informed me the commission had decided to bring an action against Michael Milken for violating the terms of his consent order and violating the securities law. It seemed Mr. Newkirk took pleasure in calling me on a Friday afternoon to inform me of the decision. The SEC's institutional bias against Michael Milken was not going to end.

I could not believe we were back in defense mode. Fortunately, this time the government could not produce witnesses incentivized to suggest Michael had done anything wrong. We started to prepare a submission to the SEC with opinions from four experts on the securities laws, including a former head of the SEC Division of Trading and Markets that regulates broker dealers, a law professor who wrote the casebook on broker dealers, and two other former SEC officials. Dick Phillips recommended we go to four different experts so we would hopefully have two or maybe three definitive opinions that under the facts as presented, the expert would have advised Michael he could do exactly what he did. It turned out that all four experts gave us such opinions, which we submitted to the SEC.

Dick Phillips, Steve Kaufman, Ted Wells, and I then met at the SEC in meetings in which Tom Newkirk and Bill McLucas were present. The SEC indicated it would settle the matter if Mike would give back twice the total fees he'd received as a disgorgement plus a penalty. There was no chance he would pay a penalty, since that could be interpreted as admitting a violation of probation. And he had done nothing wrong.

While the SEC was investigating this matter, I learned the US Attorney's Office for the Southern District of New York had started investigating whether Michael really had complied with the terms of his probation and had spent the number of hours required on his community service. Michael's probation officer, Mr. Bizar, told me he was being pressured by representatives from the US Attorney's Office in questioning whether Mike had completed all the required hours of community service. Mr. Bizar had written to Michael:

> During the three years of supervised probation you completed over fifty-four hundred hours of community service work. Your massive six-volume summary of the D.A.R.E. and D.A.R.E. PLUS program was deserving of a PhD thesis. You displayed a creative and resourceful ability to research current nationwide after-school programs, evaluate which activities work, developed new options, and planned, budgeted, recruited, trained, and motivated teachers and volunteers. For this creative and exceptional community service work I commend you highly.

That put an end to that US Attorney inquiry.

The SEC next informed us they were prepared to file an action alleging that Michael had violated his order with respect to the News Corp/New World and News Corp/MCI transactions, but not the Turner/Time Warner transaction, even though the SEC only began its formal investigation after Michael's involvement in the Time Warner transaction became public. They had taken the depositions of all the principals and all the individuals who had worked on the transactions and knew the weakness of their case.

We had another meeting at the SEC where Mr. McLucas indicated that the SEC would settle if Michael would pay the SEC the amount of the fees from the two transactions other than the Turner/

Time Warner transaction, with no penalty, and sign a consent decree without admitting or denying liability. In addition, the SEC would not allege any intentional wrongdoing on Michael's part. Dick Phillips informed me that it was almost unheard of for the SEC to settle a case and not allege intentional wrongdoing, let alone not insist on a penalty. Since this settlement would end the probation period and finally close the book on this eleven-and-a-half-year investigation, we reluctantly agreed to it. The parties reported to the court that the matter had been resolved.

Mark Pomerantz, then chief of the Criminal Division in the Southern District of the US Attorney's Office, wrote a letter to Judge Wood dated February 26, 1998, that I had not expected:

> We write to advise the Court of the United States Attorney's Office for the Southern District of New York, has determined not to recommend the initiation of violation of probation proceedings against Michael R. Milken.
>
> The decision not to recommend the initiation of probation violation proceedings is based on several factors including: The nature of Milken's consulting activities while on probation and the conflicting evidence regarding those activities; the problem that's presented by seeking criminal penalties and the absence of controlling regulatory authority and judicial precedent construing the term securities "broker" in this context; evidence that Milken relied on the advice of counsel that his consulting activities did not violate the Exchange Act or the Consent Order and the lack of evidence establishing that Milken attempted personally to mislead the Court. …. After the most careful consideration, however, we have concluded that the initiation

of probation violation proceeding in this matter is not warranted by the existing evidence and by law.

During the process, we voluntarily brought Michael to meet with Mr. Pomerantz and Mr. Figel. Michael's forthright answers to their questions made all the difference. It made me think more about what might have happened had Michael testified at the Fatico hearing.

We issued a press release that was agreed to in advance by the SEC:

> The SEC does not allege that Mr. Milken willfully violated the Order or the securities laws and Mr. Milken is not paying any fine or penalty. Mr. Milken received legal advice before engaging in any consulting activities. However, Mr. Milken is battling prostate cancer and has decided not to contest the SEC allegations to determine who is right and who is wrong. Therefore, without admitting such allegations, or denying them, and without any findings of wrongdoing, Mr. Milken is returning the fees that he received with respect to the two transactions that are the subject of this action.

The investigation and prosecution of Michael Milken that began November 14, 1986, finally ended on March 1, 1998.

Unfortunately, the SEC still could not move on. A few years later, a former Drexel employee, who was an investment advisor in Florida, relocated to Los Angeles. He was doing consulting work for some of Michael's investments. When the SEC found out that he was working in the same building that Michael Milken worked in, it started an investigation to see if Michael was somehow involved in this person's investment advisory business. Again, Dick Phillips got involved. This is how Dick Phillips described this matter years later at Stanford Law School in 2012:

There's an enforcement investigation. The case originated in the Miami office of the SEC. They subpoena
Mike. In LA from the Miami office, I walk into the
room, and I've been doing that now for thirty, forty
years. I have never seen an SEC examination of a witness
with eight—count them—eight attorneys from the
Miami office, flying all the way out to California to
take the testimony of one person. I criticized the way
the SEC works. Sometimes, their investigations take a
year, if a day, because they often put one lawyer, just
out of law school two years, on an investigation. They
understaff these investigations. And this one has eight
people in it. Why? 'Cause it's Mike Milken, only reason
and the testimony is taken. There is nothing there.
And they never bring a case not only against us, but
the broker dealer who did have some technical violations from their inspection in Miami. It was the most
amazing thing I've ever seen, how once you become a
cause célèbre, at a regulatory agency—and I don't think
the SEC is unique. I think any regulatory agency—
you become one of the great cases, you never, can feel
that you're secure from further inquiry. I've never seen
anything like this.

The well-known author Michael Lewis wrote a column for
Bloomberg in 1998 titled "Time to Free Michael Milken and Let
Mike Be Mike."

If you had a choice of hearing the views of a Nobel
prize–winning economist or Michael Milken, which
one would you choose? ... People who did business with

Milken before he went to jail still want to do business with Milken now that he's out. Of all the financiers in America, Milken is still the most highly valued by the people who know financiers. ... Milken is the only one who is forbidden from practice of finance ... A man more or less restructures American capital markets so that capital moves more freely from those who have it to those who need it. And the man who helped to make it all happen is sentenced to ten years in jail and considered evil for the rest of his life. Is that fair?

There are two things worth saying about the Milken story. ... The first is that everything important that Milken did was either perfectly legal, or might as well have been. ... The people who were upset by Milken were upset by the way he unsettled corporate life.

The second salient fact about Milken's career is that the worst deals—the LBOs that destroyed large companies—were done not by him, but by his cheap imitators. ... The continued harassment of Michael Milken seems more than a little unfair.

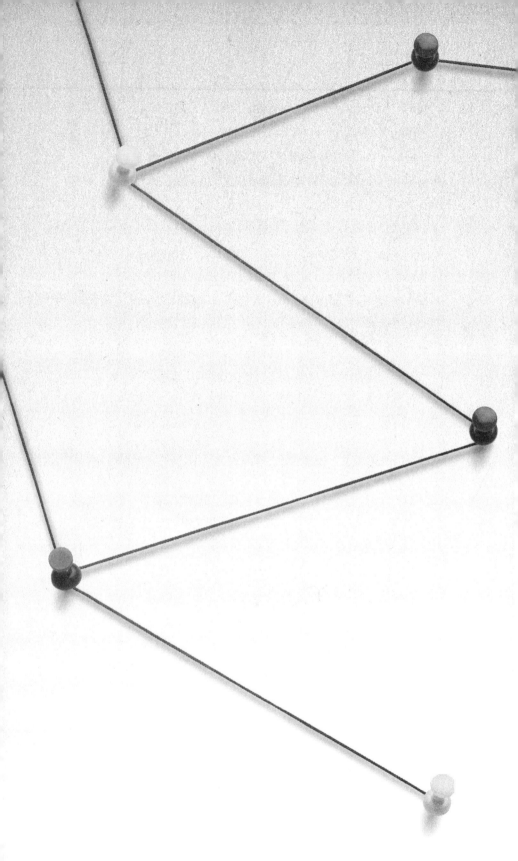

CHAPTER 18

Pardon

When the investigation began in 1986, Ronald Reagan was president of the United States; when Michael pleaded, George H. W. Bush was president; and when Michael completed his sentence, William J. Clinton was president. No matter how unfair we thought it was, Michael was a convicted felon—as Michael and I discussed the night before he agreed to plead. The only official acknowledgment Michael could hope for about this process and his true contributions to society would be a presidential pardon. President Clinton's term was ending in January 2001, and presidents often granted pardons at the end of their terms, especially when they involved high-profile individuals. Michael and I decided to request a pardon.

The research that I had done clearly showed Michael met every qualification to receive a pardon. So in 2000, I met with Ron Burkle, a friend, who then also had a close relationship with President Clinton. I was looking for guidance as to the most appropriate process to request a pardon. The pardon decision is solely within the discretion of the President, but the Justice Department does have a pardon attorney and a process one can go through to apply for a pardon. If one does apply to the Justice Department, the pardon attorney then makes a recommendation to the President based on specified criteria.

Ron spoke to someone at the White House and told me we needed to go through the Justice Department process and submit an application to the pardon attorney. I proceeded with the petition to the Department of Justice and provided a copy to Ron. The pardon petition included an explanation of what Michael had pleaded to. It emphasized the plea did not involve the kinds of activities the media had been writing about, such as insider trading, and had nothing to do with the underlying soundness and integrity of the capital markets in which Michael specialized. It emphasized that Michael accepted responsibility for his actions and had served his sentence. The petition detailed Mike's extensive philanthropic history, both before and after his plea, as support for a pardon.

Of course, once the petition was filed, news articles began to appear and different writers expressed their "opinions" on whether Michael should receive a pardon. When contacted by the media, we declined to even acknowledge the petition. So now it was up to President Clinton.

Even Rudolph Giuliani, the prosecutor who was responsible for spearheading a very public racketeering investigation against Michael and Lowell, was quoted in the *Wall Street Journal* as saying he believed Michael Milken was entitled to a pardon. This statement by Mr. Giuliani probably was the result of a lunch Michael attended with Mr. Giuliani after Mr. Giuliani had been diagnosed with prostate cancer. A mutual friend arranged the lunch. Michael did not hesitate to attend the lunch and help Mr. Giuliani in his battle with prostate cancer. Michael always tried to solve people's problems—even the person who'd tried to destroy his life.

President Clinton's last weekend in office was spent at Camp David. Mike and I had also discussed the pardon petition with Haim Saban, another friend who also was friendly with President Clinton.

Both Ron Burkle and Haim Saban were with the president in Camp David that weekend. They both told me after that weekend that the president had said the pardon "looked good" but the SEC was against it, and President Clinton wanted "to talk to some people on Wall Street."

I went to Washington, DC, right before the inauguration of President Bush on January 20, 2001, in case there were any last-minute questions that might come up. I could not sleep that night knowing the decision on the pardon would be made the next day. Ron Burkle called me at four o'clock on the morning of January 20 and told me that the president had called him and told him he was sorry, but he had a lot of pressure from the SEC and the Treasury Department and he would not grant the pardon. He liked Michael and hoped he could get a pardon in the future. Another punch to the stomach.

All this was confirmed by President Clinton in his book *My Life*:

> Although I would later be criticized for some of the pardons I granted, I was more concerned by a few I didn't grant. For example, I thought Michael Milken had a persuasive case, because of the good work he had done on prostate cancer after his release from prison, but Treasury and the Securities and Exchange Commission were adamantly against my pardoning him, saying it would send the wrong signal at a time when they were trying to enforce high standards in the financial industry.

The *New York Post* ran a story by Niles Lathem on February 1, 2001, "Wall St. Scuttled Milken's Pardon":

> The opponents of the pardon included Citigroup's influential Robert Rubin, a former treasury secretary

in the Clinton administration, and Evercore Partners chairman Roger Altman, a former deputy treasury secretary, sources said.

The article compares the denial of the pardon to Michael Milken with the controversial granting of a pardon to Marc Rich.

> Milken faced prosecution, pled, and served his sentence where Rich fled the country in 1983 rather than face an indictment and continued to operate a business from foreign soil. Milken's lawyers went through the established procedures filing a petition with the Justice Department. Rich's lawyer, former White House aide Jack Quinn, bypassed the Justice Department and quietly slipped his petition directly to the White House. The debate over Milken's pardon was reported in the news media which gave opponents the opportunity to mobilize against it where Rich's petition was not. … Richard Sandler, Milken's lawyer, said he learned from the department on the night before George W. Bush's inauguration that Milken's name was not on the list of 140 last-minute pardons. "All I was told was there were certain people who were very much against it. It was disappointing," Sandler told *The Post*.

Michael was still a symbol—judged not by who he is or what he did but by what others had done and the perception fostered by the government and the media. Michael really felt he would receive a much-deserved pardon from President Clinton. Michael was extremely disappointed. Again he got up, dusted himself off, and went about trying to make a positive difference in the world—without bitterness and with a positive attitude. I, too, was very disappointed. We had done everything openly and appropriately to secure a much-deserved pardon.

Eight years later, when President George W. Bush was at the end of his second term, we decided to make another attempt to secure a pardon. Michael's record of philanthropy and giving back to society had continued and was even more impressive. Though I believed it was mostly unfortunate circumstances that had resulted in our failure to receive the pardon from President Clinton, I wanted to try to reduce the risks with President Bush. We were willing to file a petition again with the Office of the Pardon Attorney, but this time I felt we should retain counsel that was known in Washington and hopefully respected by the Bush administration. I was introduced to Fred

> Michael really felt he would receive a much-deserved pardon from President Clinton. Michael was extremely disappointed.

Fielding, a much-respected Washington lawyer. I had a preliminary meeting with Mr. Fielding in Washington. We agreed we would both think about it and talk again in the next couple of weeks. Mr. Fielding called me a week later to tell me that he had been offered the position of White House counsel and was taking the position. Apparently I was introduced to the right person at the wrong time.

Fortunately I met Theodore Olson of the Gibson, Dunn law firm. Ted Olson had been the attorney who argued the *Bush v. Gore* case in the United States Supreme Court on behalf of President Bush with respect to the controversial presidential election of 2000. Ted was an impressive and very thoughtful attorney. After doing his own research, he believed Michael deserved a pardon and agreed to represent him. He even told me that he had decided not to represent anyone else seeking a pardon so that he could be most effective. Mr. Olson prepared a draft petition. We provided letters of support from individuals from different walks of life who knew Michael and could speak to his outstanding character and contributions to society. These letters came from everyone from heads of companies to educators to doctors and friends. There was even a letter from the president's father, President George H. W. Bush, in which he stated,

> Though I have met Michael Milken, I do not know him well. However, I do feel that his life, now built largely around helping others, has been exemplary since his conviction. Those who know him well speak glowingly of him; and as one who has proudly seen what he has done in the battle against cancer, I join them in my admiration of Michael Milken.

Rudy Giuliani even wrote a letter saying Michael fulfilled every criterion for receiving a pardon. Mike and I also had a friend in Los Angeles, Brad Freeman, who very much admired Michael and was a close personal friend of President Bush. Brad was at the White House shortly before the end of President Bush's term and told me he'd mentioned to President Bush he would like to have a private word with him. President Bush's response was that he would be happy to talk to Brad about any subject "other than pardons." Before I heard this, I'd believed this time Mike would receive the much-deserved pardon. Now I was concerned that once again the stars were aligned against us.

As it turned out, Vice President Cheney had asked President Bush to pardon Scooter Libby. Scooter Libby had been an assistant to the vice president for national security affairs and chief of staff to the vice president. Mr. Libby resigned when he was indicted by a federal grand jury concerning an investigation into a leak of the identity of an officer of the Central Intelligence Agency. He was subsequently convicted of one count of obstruction of justice, two counts of perjury, and one count of making false statements. President Bush commuted Libby's prison sentence but left the conviction intact. Vice President Cheney had asked President Bush to grant Mr. Libby a full pardon, but President Bush refused to do so.

President Bush was not generous in granting pardons, either as governor of Texas or as president. President Bush's term ended with neither a pardon for Scooter Libby nor for Michael Milken. Despite the fact that we went through the Justice Department process, deserved the pardon, and had support of the president's father and the former US Attorney, we were denied.

Though Michael was turned down by presidents Clinton and Bush, in later years both President Clinton and President Bush appeared with Michael Milken at the Milken Institute Global Conference in Los Angeles. They were both extremely complimentary of Michael and what he has accomplished.

A number of people supportive of Michael contacted me during President Barack Obama's administration, offering to help us try to get a pardon. I thought it was highly unlikely President Obama would grant a pardon to a high-profile person who had been highly successful on Wall Street and had been convicted of securities violations. President Obama often derided persons on "Wall Street" who were wealthy. It had been so painful to go through the process the prior two times. I did not want to do it again unless I thought there was a higher likelihood the president would grant the pardon.

The two candidates who ran for president to succeed President Obama were Hillary Clinton and Donald Trump. Hillary Clinton's husband had appeared at the Milken conference and had spoken very favorably about Michael. A number of Mrs. Clinton's major supporters and friends were also very close to Michael. With respect to Donald Trump, the Prostate Cancer Foundation had held a fundraising event for a number of years at the Mar-a-Lago Resort in Florida at which President Trump had participated. President Trump and Michael also had a number of close friends in common. For these reasons, I believed it was far more likely that either Mrs. Clinton or President Trump might favorably consider a pardon, especially now that so many years had passed.

It is unfortunate I felt we needed to have a relationship with the president for Mike to be granted a pardon. Michael Milken had been so mischaracterized for so many years that unless there was someone who could make the case to the president directly, the president would be advised against granting a pardon, as had already happened two times.

President Trump showed from early on in his presidency he was not reticent to grant pardons, even controversial ones. I spoke to a number of friends who were close to the president, including Nelson Peltz, Ted Virtue, and Steven Mnuchin. Mike knew President Trump, but they did not have a close relationship. Michael never financed Donald Trump in business nor was Michael a contributor to political campaigns.

I explored the possibility of the pardon with a number of people and was willing, once again, to file a petition with the pardon attorney if that would help. I prepared a summary of Michael's philanthropic activities that discussed four areas:

1. Medical Research: The Milken Family Foundation, founded in 1982 by Michael and Lowell when they were both still in their thirties, early on focused on

cancer and epilepsy research. Michael helped sponsor the first National Cancer Summit in 1995; was cosponsor of the 1998 Cancer March on Washington involving a half million Americans; focused on government and industry medical research and developed the Young Investigator Program advancing the careers of over five hundred leading medical researchers; founded the Prostate Cancer Foundation and the Melanoma Research Association, which have led to FDA-approved drug treatments that did not exist before and that improved and saved millions of lives.

2. Education: The Milken Educator Award Program has honored nearly three thousand exemplary K-12 educators in every state and the District of Columbia, including awards of $25,000 each; the Milken Scholars Program created opportunities for close to five hundred future leaders who came from low-income families and had a 99 percent graduation rate from colleges such as Harvard, Stanford, Yale, Berkeley, and Penn State.

3. Veterans: Michael has instituted programs for veterans, including a partnership between the Prostate Cancer Foundation and the Department of Veteran Affairs.

4. Public Health: Michael has been behind public health initiatives, including the Milken Institute Center for Public Health and FasterCures Center as well as the Milken Institute School of Public Health at George Washington University.

For the third time, I believed we had done everything in the proper manner, and I was again hopeful the President would favorably consider a pardon, though I did not expect him to address the issue until after the election in November 2020. Sitting in my office on the morning of February 18, 2020, I received a call at 8:30 a.m. It was Mike, who told me he had received a call from President Trump that morning informing him he had received a "full and unconditional presidential pardon." President Trump emphasized the fact that it was a true pardon since Michael had never done business with the president and had never supported the president when he ran for office.

I was overwhelmed with happiness and gratitude and could hear the relief and joy in Michael's voice. We'd had absolutely no warning the president was going to grant Michael a pardon or that he was going to grant it that day.

> It was Mike, who told me he had received a call from President Trump that morning informing him he had received a "full and unconditional presidential pardon."

When Mike arrived at the office that morning, I went to personally congratulate him. As I walked into his office, he jumped up from behind his desk, and we embraced. It was a moment of pure joy and pure emotion. It was that same emotion I witnessed in the fall of 1992 when Michael reached across that table with tears in his eyes and said, "Thank you."

It had been almost thirty-four years, and now it was over. Though Michael has certainly led a productive, blessed, and wonderful life, this ordeal had been so hurtful and so misunderstood that the pardon was very meaningful.

The White House issued a press release:

> Michael Milken, one of America's greatest financiers, pioneered the use of high yield bonds in corporate finance. His innovative work greatly expanded access to capital for emerging companies. By enabling smaller players to access the financing they needed to compete, Mr. Milken's efforts helped create entire industries, such as wireless communications and cable television, and transformed others, like Home Building. Mr. Milken's work also democratized corporate finance by providing women and minorities access to capital that would have been unavailable to them otherwise. In 1989, at the height of his finance career, Mr. Milken was charged in an indictment alleging that some of his innovative financing mechanisms were in fact criminal schemes. The charges filed against Mr. Milken were truly novel. In fact, one of the lead prosecutors later admitted that Mr. Milken had been charged with numerous technical offenses and regulatory violations that had never before been charged as crimes. Though he initially vowed to fight the charges, Mr. Milken ultimately pled guilty in exchange for prosecutors dropping criminal charges against his younger brother. As a result, Mr. Milken served two years in prison in the early 1990s. Since his release, Mr. Milken has dedicated his life to philanthropy, continuing charitable work that he began before his indictment. Over the years, Mr. Milken— either personally or through foundations he created— has provided hundreds of millions of dollars in critical funding to medical research, education, and disadvan-

taged children. Mr. Milken's philanthropy has been particularly influential in the fight against prostate cancer and has been credited with saving many lives. This pardon has widespread and long-standing support.

The pardon not only acknowledged a lifetime of creating opportunities for all Americans and addressing challenges but also the nature of prosecution and the technicality and uniqueness of the regulatory violations that certainly never would have been pursued had Michael not been so successful in disrupting the traditional way business was done on Wall Street.

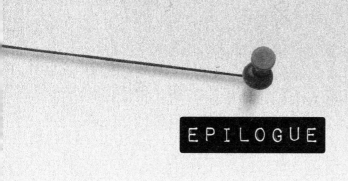

EPILOGUE

Looking back at this investigation and the past thirty-six years brings back so many thoughts and emotions. I went through a painful experience for which I had very little preparation. Fortunately, I learned early in my career that listening was more important than talking and that it was important to seek out knowledgeable and good and wise people to listen to. I was fortunate to have had wise people to listen to as I learned how to navigate uncharted waters.

Michael Milken and Lowell Milken both are talented and decent human beings. Michael believed he could work with anyone and do business with anyone without being adversely affected by the association. Lowell was always more discerning and had no interest in associating, in business or otherwise, with people he found objectionable.

Michael was investigated and eventually forced to plead guilty to six felonies for two reasons:

1. He was incredibly successful due to the genius of his ideas, his incredible work ethic, and his ability to both connect with people and execute upon his vision. His successes made him an attractive target.

2. He did business with people with personal flaws, and, because he was so nonconfrontational, he naively believed that whatever those flaws were, they would not touch him.

Lowell was investigated and indicted because he was Michael's brother and provided leverage for the US Attorney in his pursuit of an indictment and conviction of Michael.

Though Michael did plead guilty to six felonies, there was no chance he believed he was violating the law when he engaged in the five transactions that became the subject of the plea—especially since none of those activities caused any loss or damage to anyone. Nor had any of those activities previously been the subject of a criminal prosecution. Unlike others who pleaded and cooperated with the prosecutors, Michael never made or received illegal payments and always paid his taxes. As Attorney General Robert H. Jackson said, the law books are filled with a great assortment of crimes, and a prosecutor can choose his or her defendants and have a fair chance of finding a technical violation on the part of almost anyone. After three and a half years of constant attack and vilification in the media and by the government, Michael chose to end the ordeal, cut his losses, and try to move on with his life.

> If the criminal justice system could do what it did to Michael Milken, then one could only imagine what happens to the 99.9 percent of people who go through the criminal system without such resources and/or support.

This case also says much about the criminal justice system. Michael had the resources to try to defend himself. He had a loving and loyal family who knew who he was, loved him, and supported him throughout this ordeal. And he had so many colleagues, clients, and friends who stood by him. If the criminal justice system could do what it did to Michael Milken, then one could only imagine what happens to the 99.9 percent of people who go through the criminal system without such resources and/or support. The system was designed to put away bad people and protect the public, but like everything in life, the system depends on people to know how to use the immense power placed in the prosecutor's hands to see that justice is done. Unfortunately, when an ambitious and powerful prosecutor wants to use his office to advance a political career, he can abuse those powers and set an example for young prosecutors to use those powers to win at all costs.

I have now known John Carroll for almost thirty-four years. I have found him to be an honest, decent individual who was a very young and inexperienced yet talented lawyer when he entered the US Attorney's Office. He had no appreciation at the time that his actions affected the lives of people in dramatic ways. I believe he would do things differently today, but he has been clear with me that he still believes he was justified in pursuing the investigation. As a number of former prosecutors told me, young lawyers in a prosecutor's office often are trained to believe every file that comes across their desk represents someone who has violated the law. They have made up their minds before they even open the file and then use the process to obtain a conviction.

Many decisions made in the Milken case provide examples of abuse of the tremendous powers of prosecutors, such as the following:

1. Agreeing not to recommend a specific sentence and agreeing that Michael should not have consecutive sentences and then filing a sentencing memorandum that in effect asked for a far more severe sentence, giving examples of twenty-year sentences for totally unrelated conduct

2. Immunizing or intimidating witnesses, including after Michael had pleaded, so the witnesses would only testify for the government at the Fatico hearing in an attempt by prosecutors to convince the court to give Michael a more severe sentence

3. Refusing to cooperate with the court in computing the economic effect of the plea for the Parole Commission and then taking the very unusual action of filing the prosecutors' own form with the Parole Commission in an attempt to extend the time that Michael would be away from his family in prison

4. Leaking information to the media

5. Indicting Bruce Newberg twice and indicting Lisa Jones

6. Indicting Lowell Milken

7. Indicting Michael Milken

Every one of these actions was inappropriate and done, in my judgment, to justify a flawed investigation. There was little effort to seek truth or to see that justice was done. The reputation of the Southern District United States Attorney's Office and the enforcement division of the SEC were at stake, and that became more important than the rights of Michael Milken or anyone else. It was like the film *True Believer*. Life does imitate fiction imitating life.

There is no question Michael Milken made mistakes. As Lori said at the parole hearing, Michael was a person who hates confrontation, believes he can solve every problem, and too often gets caught up in the moment. He was a young man in his thirties creating and building a business/industry that forever changed finance. Unfortunately, none of us appreciated the political ramifications of what he was doing.

Michael could not disrupt Wall Street and corporate America without becoming a target, nor could he do business with certain individuals without their negative qualities affecting him or his business. Up to November 1986, a young Michael Milken had been able to build an industry, help people, and solve problems by using his intellect, people skills, and force of will. Fortunately, since 1993 a more mature and experienced Michael Milken has continued to do so even more effectively.

After this intensive investigation, the plea, and the trial to examine what else Michael Milken had done, the court found that Michael had violated rules in five instances and only five instances. Articles and books have been written accusing Michael of all kinds of wrongs that he never committed. Judge Wood gave the government the opportunity to prove that Michael committed wrongs in addition to what he'd pleaded to. It failed.

Notwithstanding all the pain Michael Milken went through from 1986 through 1998, he has spent the last twenty-four years using his gifted mind, big heart, and endless energy

> It was like the film *True Believer*. Life does imitate fiction imitating life.

to continue to pursue what Judge Wood called his "genuine commitment to spending substantial amounts of his own time and resources to improving society." Through the work of the Milken Institute and Prostate Cancer Foundation as well as the Milken Family Foundation and the Michael and Lori Milken Family Foundation, millions of people are leading meaningful and productive lives who might not otherwise have survived cancer and other illnesses or otherwise benefited from the good work of these foundations. The democratization of capital Michael created at Drexel beginning in 1972, when he was but twenty-six years old, has allowed small and medium-size businesses to access the financial markets and have access to the capital needed to realize the dreams of visionary entrepreneurs and create millions of jobs and better lives for tens of millions of people. He so exemplifies the qualities Rudyard Kipling describes in his poem "If":

> *If you can dream—and not make dreams your master;*
> *If you can think—and not make thoughts your aim;*
> *If you can meet with Triumph and Disaster*
> *And treat those two impostors just the same;*
> *If you can bear to hear the truth you've spoken*
> *Twisted by knaves to make a trap for fools,*
> *Or watch the things you gave your life to, broken,*
> *And stoop and build 'em up with worn-out tools:*

My lifelong friend Lowell, who was also instrumental in the growth of the Drexel Burnham Lambert High Yield Department, suffered his own pain and anxiety in being a target of a criminal investigation, notwithstanding the fact he had nothing to do with the subject matter of the investigation. Lowell was clearly a hostage, as confirmed by the fact that the prosecutors were willing to drop all charges against him by nolle prosequi (meaning literally "we shall no longer prosecute"). The Southern District of New York does not do that—especially in a

> **Michael Milken is a historical figure, whether he wants to be one or not, and history needs to know the truth about the Michael Milken case.**

high-profile matter. There was never any finding in any proceeding that Lowell had done anything wrong, because he had not. He, too, has moved on with his life in a productive and giving manner, also improving the world quietly through his own extensive philanthropic work through the Lowell Milken Family Foundation and the National Institute for Excellence in Teaching as well as the Milken Family Foundation.

Did Michael make the right decision by pleading? I believe so. It really does not matter now. What matters is that Michael Milken is a historical figure, whether he wants to be one or not, and history needs to know the truth about the Michael Milken case.

I still think about the four things that I discussed with Michael the night before he agreed to settle:

1. By pleading guilty, he would be labeled as a felon. Mike certainly knew this and accepted that fact, but he also committed himself to continuing a productive and meaningful life so that history would at least know who he really was, and as a result he received a presidential pardon.

2. He would be identified with the insider traders who pleaded, though Michael never was an insider trader. Over the last thirty years as Michael has remained so productive and so valuable in his contributions to society, this fact has become one of less importance, though he is often incorrectly so identified.

3. He would certainly face a prison sentence, which Michael also accepted, believing the amount of time he would spend in prison would be less than three years. The initial sentence was devastating for many reasons, but as it turned out, the time spent was two years, and

Mike was a model prisoner who comported himself admirably during those years.

4. He would have to accept some responsibility for allowing himself to be in a position where the government could come after him. This was certainly the most difficult of those four challenges, but everything I have discussed with and witnessed of Michael Milken over these past thirty years has convinced me that Michael learned a tremendous amount from this whole ordeal, as he has continued to be productive and have a positive effect on the world. I will forever admire how Michael continually would pick himself up, dust himself off, and make a positive difference in the world without bitterness.

Also, as I look back over the past thirty-four years, I never stop thinking about what I went through personally and asking myself, *Was it worth it?* After all, in 1986, when this started, I was thirty-eight years old; married to my college sweetheart, Ellen, for sixteen years; and had three incredible children: Scott, twelve years old; Tracy, eight years old; and Nicholas, who turned six years old on the day it all started. I literally put my life on hold. I was in New York or Washington almost weekly, having leased an apartment in New York and taken an office in the Paul, Weiss suite of offices. I missed school events and even a few birthdays. I still remember missing Tracy's eleventh birthday and her crying and asking Ellen if we could plan her future birthday in New York so I could be there. I made a pledge to myself that I would never miss another birthday or event, and I kept that promise. I was the person who lost the most from not being present and gained the most from being there.

On that day in Houston in February 1990 when I "lost it" with Steve Kaufman and Arthur Liman, it certainly was not caused by the issue about the global settlement we were discussing. It was all the result of being away from home and my family for over three years, worried and scared that my closest friends could actually be indicted by the United States government and then go to prison, and realizing that despite all my time and efforts I would not be able to stop it. Fortunately, I have an incredible wife who was able to hold everything together. My children always looked up to Michael and Lowell as family, understood what I was doing, and learned valuable lessons about people, loyalty, and meaningful relationships. They have each grown up as caring, loving, and passionate adults who make this world better, and I could not be more proud of each of them.

During the investigations, I certainly had my own grievances with everyone I thought was trying to hurt Michael or was not doing everything they could to help us. Those negative feelings started with the prosecutors and the SEC lawyers and included every government witness who gave testimony against Michael. I was even upset with every Drexel employee who did not volunteer to help. Over time, I gained perspective and began to understand that— the Drexel employees who did not step forward to help each had their

> I never stop thinking about what I went through personally and asking myself, *Was it worth it?*

own families, responsibilities, and concerns. I came to realize that by putting themselves at greater risk, they probably really would not have helped. It made me respect those who did step forward that much more. As for those who were government witnesses against Michael, none of them surprised me. They had their own problems and would do anything to protect themselves. I have mixed feelings about the prosecutors and SEC attorneys. They were trained to win at all costs and to assume Michael must be a bad guy. At the same time, I wish the system was better geared to learning the truth without being so zealous.

So, was it worth it? Yes, without a doubt. I believe we are all on this planet for a limited period of time and have a responsibility to help people and to leave the planet better than we found it. On November 14, 1986, circumstances placed me in the unique position of being able to "be there" for my dear friends. I believed in them, and they trusted and relied on me. We have always been there for each other, and I had a responsibility to do everything I could to try to help them through the horrible situation they were in. And I have no doubt they would have done the same for me. As a result of this ordeal, I understand people better; I understand the importance of relationships better; I understand better what my father meant when he taught me that no matter what the other person does, make sure you can look yourself in the mirror and know you acted properly and did the right thing. We really did go through hell during those years—the pressure, the uncertainty, the risks, and the effect on our families—but we were able to get through it and go on to lead productive and meaningful lives with a greater appreciation for our blessings and for each other.

ACKNOWLEDGMENTS

I owe thanks to many people who made it possible for me to write this book. First and foremost, I thank my wife, Ellen, who has provided me with total support and counsel throughout the years. Without her understanding and love, I could never have devoted the time and energy that I did during the years of the investigation. Ellen made sure our children knew they were loved and cherished by both of their parents during a very difficult period.

I thank my extraordinary children, Scott, Tracy, and Nicholas, who had to endure having their father traveling and distracted. They showed maturity beyond their years, having grown up with Michael and Lowell Milken and their children, and understanding the importance of loyalty and friendship. I also thank my son, Scott, for reading several drafts of this book.

I thank Professor David Mills of Stanford Law School, who made it possible for the two of us to teach a class twice on the subject of this book at Stanford Law School. And I thank John Carroll, the line prosecutor for the Milken case from the United States Attorney's Office in the Southern District of New York, who was a guest lecturer at those two classes. Likewise, I thank William McLucas, former Director of the Division of Enforcement at the Securities and Exchange Commision, who also was a guest lecturer at one of those classes. And I also thank all others who were guest lecturers which included attorneys Ted Wells and Daniel Bookin, Jay Reagan, who was a defendant in a related case, economist Glenn Yago, Larry Post, who worked in the High Yield and Convertible Bond Department at Drexel Burnham, our media consultant during the investigation, Ken Lerer, and media expert, Frank Luntz.

I thank Stephen E. Kaufman, who was part of our legal team and Donald McQuade, Professor of English at University of California, Berkeley, who reviewed early drafts of the manuscript.

I could not have completed this book without my former assistant, Jill Riseborough, who helped me start the project or my present assistant, Jackie Lyons, who typed the original manuscript and helped me with fact-checking and proofreading.

Finally I want to acknowledge Michael Milken, Lowell Milken, Lori Milken, Sandy Milken, and their children, Gregory, Lance, Bari, Jeremy, Ryan, and David, who paid the greatest price during this period, but who supported one another and me, allowing us all to continue to live productive and meaningful lives.